JAPANESE FANTASY
MANGA

ricorico

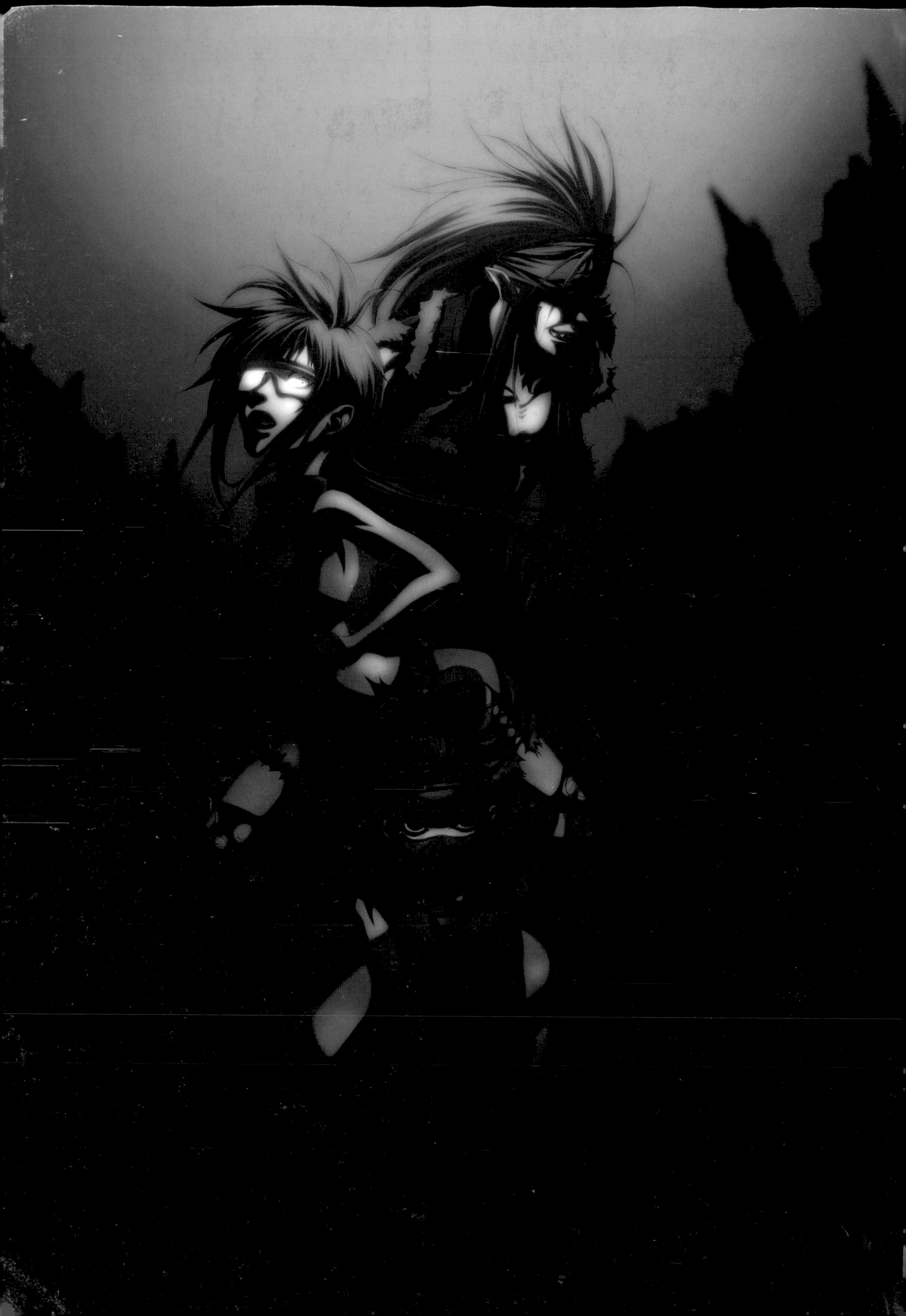

JAPANESE FANTASY
MANGA

ricorico

HARPER
DESIGN
An Imprint of HarperCollins Publishers

Japanese Fantasy Manga

HarperCollins books may be purchased for educational, business, or sales promotional use. For information, please write: Special Markets Department, HarperCollinsPublishers, 10 East 53rd Street, New York, NY 10022.

First published in 2011 by:

Harper Design
An Imprint of HarperCollins*Publishers*
10 East 53rd Street,
New York, NY 10022
Tel.: (212) 207-7000
Fax: (212) 207-7654
harperdesign@harpercollins.com
www.harpercollins.com

Distributed throughout the world by:
HarperCollins*Publishers*
10 East 53rd Street,
New York, NY 10022
Fax: (212) 207-7654

Front Cover Illustration: Chie Kazama
Book Design and Art Direction: Atsushi Takeda (SOUVENIR DESIGN)
Book Design: Naruaki Ishido(SOUVENIR DESIGN)
Illustrations: Eri Kamijo (digipop), Shinn Komamori, Chie Kazama,
Akiyoshi Sakemura, Jaclyn Huchel
Cooperation: Naonori Koya, Toyo Institute of Art & Design
Writer: Alma Reyes
Artist Coordination: Aki Ueda (ricorico)
Chief Editor and Production Manager: Aki Ueda (ricorico)

Library of Congress Control Number: 2010928177

ISBN: 978-0-06-200470-3

Printed in China
First Printing, 2010

Disclaimer

The information in this book is mostly made up of material reinterpreted from myths, legends, stories, games, and publications. References to people, events, establishments, organizations, or locales are intended only to provide a sense of authenticity and to familiarize readers with some aspects of Japanese fantasy manga. Neither the publisher nor the author can guarantee their accuracy.

Contents

Introduction

Adventuring through the world of Japanese fantasy manga can be heart-wrenching, jaw-dropping or terrifying, even deadly. It may require a keen intellect, trading skills, physical strength, weapons mastery or magical powers.

This book is structured like a role playing game (RPG), the fantasy hero games that spread like wildfire across Japan then throughout East Asia, and are now popular around the world. In a RPG, you must first choose your hero. You'll then assign your character a particular profession. Once its role in the world of Japanese fantasy manga is set, you should practice its superpower. If you are a skilled hero, you'll defeat your enemy and win the game.

In the following pages, we guide you through the world of Japanese fantasy manga, so you can create your own authentic world and masterfully manipulate RPG games. We'll provide you with the names of Japanese fantasy manga characters, both heroes and enemies. We'll give you visual illustrations of what they look like, along with quick tips for identifying them or creating them yourself. You'll get a visual snapshot of them with their defining physical traits and notable features highlighted, as well as an action shot of them from an established Japanese fantasy manga illustrator. You'll also get all the background information you need to know on them in a section devoted to providing you with an outline and origin of who they are.

This book is broken down by RPG themes: Yuusha, choosing a hero, Tenshoku, developing a character, Gikou, practicing your superpower, and Mamono, fighting the enemy. Each chapter also includes special bonus information connected to its subject. Through the wide array of fabulous illustrations and the wealth of information found in this book, illustrators, RPG players, and manga enthusiasts will learn about the world of Japanese fantasy manga—to conquer it or create it themselves.

How to Read
This Book

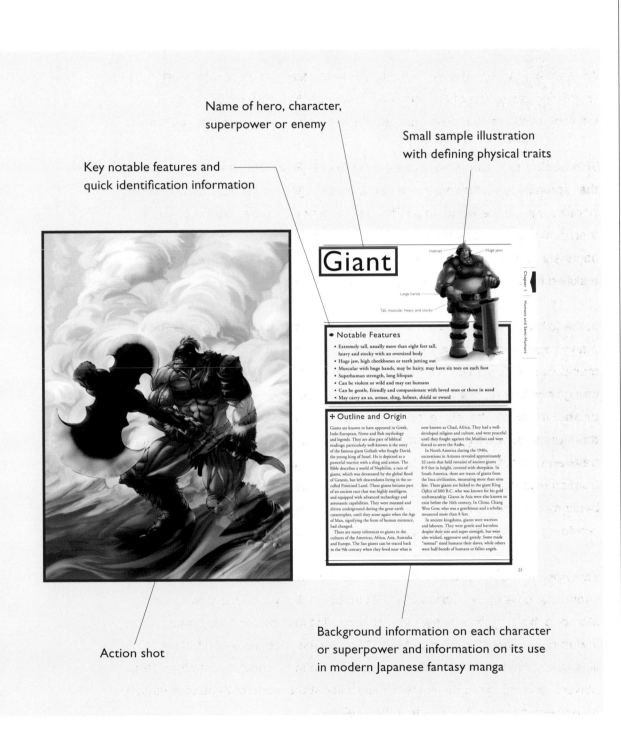

Name of hero, character, superpower or enemy

Small sample illustration with defining physical traits

Key notable features and quick identification information

Giant

Helmet — Huge jaws

Large hands

Tall, muscular, heavy and stocky

Chapter 1 | Humans and Semi-Humans

➡ Notable Features

- Extremely tall, usually more than eight feet tall, heavy and stocky with an oversized body
- Huge jaw, high cheekbones or teeth jutting out
- Muscular with huge hands, may be hairy, may have six toes on each foot
- Superhuman strength, long lifespan
- Can be violent or wild and may eat humans
- Can be gentle, friendly and compassionate with loved ones or those in need
- May carry an ax, armor, sling, helmet, shield or sword

✛ Outline and Origin

Giants are known to have appeared in Greek, Indo-European, Norse and Balt mythology and legends. They are also part of biblical readings; particularly well-known is the story of the famous giant Goliath who fought David, the young king of Israel. He is depicted as a powerful warrior with a sling and armor. The Bible describes a world of Nephilim, a race of giants, which was devastated by the global flood of Genesis, but left descendants living in the so-called Promised Land. These giants became part of an ancient race that was highly intelligent, and equipped with advanced technology and aeronautic capabilities. They were mutated and driven underground during the great earth catastrophes, until they arose again when the Age of Man, signifying the form of human existence, had changed.

There are many references to giants in the cultures of the Americas, Africa, Asia, Australia and Europe. The Sao giants can be traced back to the 9th century when they lived near what is now known as Chad, Africa. They had a well-developed religion and culture, and were peaceful until they fought against the Muslims and were forced to serve the Arabs.

In North America during the 1940s, excavations in Arizona revealed approximately 32 caves that held remains of ancient giants 8-9 feet in height, covered with sheepskin. In South America, there are traces of giants from the Inca civilization, measuring more than nine feet. These giants are linked to the giant King Ojihir of 600 B.C. who was known for his gold craftsmanship. Giants in Asia were also known to exist before the 16th century. In China, Chang Woo Gow, who was a gentleman and a scholar, measured more than 8 feet.

In ancient kingdoms, giants were warriors and laborers. They were gentle and harmless despite their size and super strength, but were also wicked, aggressive and greedy. Some made "normal" sized humans their slaves, while others were half-breeds of humans or fallen angels.

23

Background information on each character or superpower and information on its use in modern Japanese fantasy manga

Action shot

Bonus manga included!

This book includes an original manga on pages 202-205, which summarizes each chapter of this book. The heroine in the story is conceptualized from the characters in Chapter 1; the monster in the story is taken from one of the characters in Chapter 4; and the climax of the story depicts themes in Chapters 2 and 3. This traditional Japanese manga also covers other various fantasy characters illustrated in this volume, and will guide you to enjoy the world of fantasy manga.

*The bonus manga is a work of fiction. Any resemblance to real persons, living or dead, and historical fact is purely coincidental.

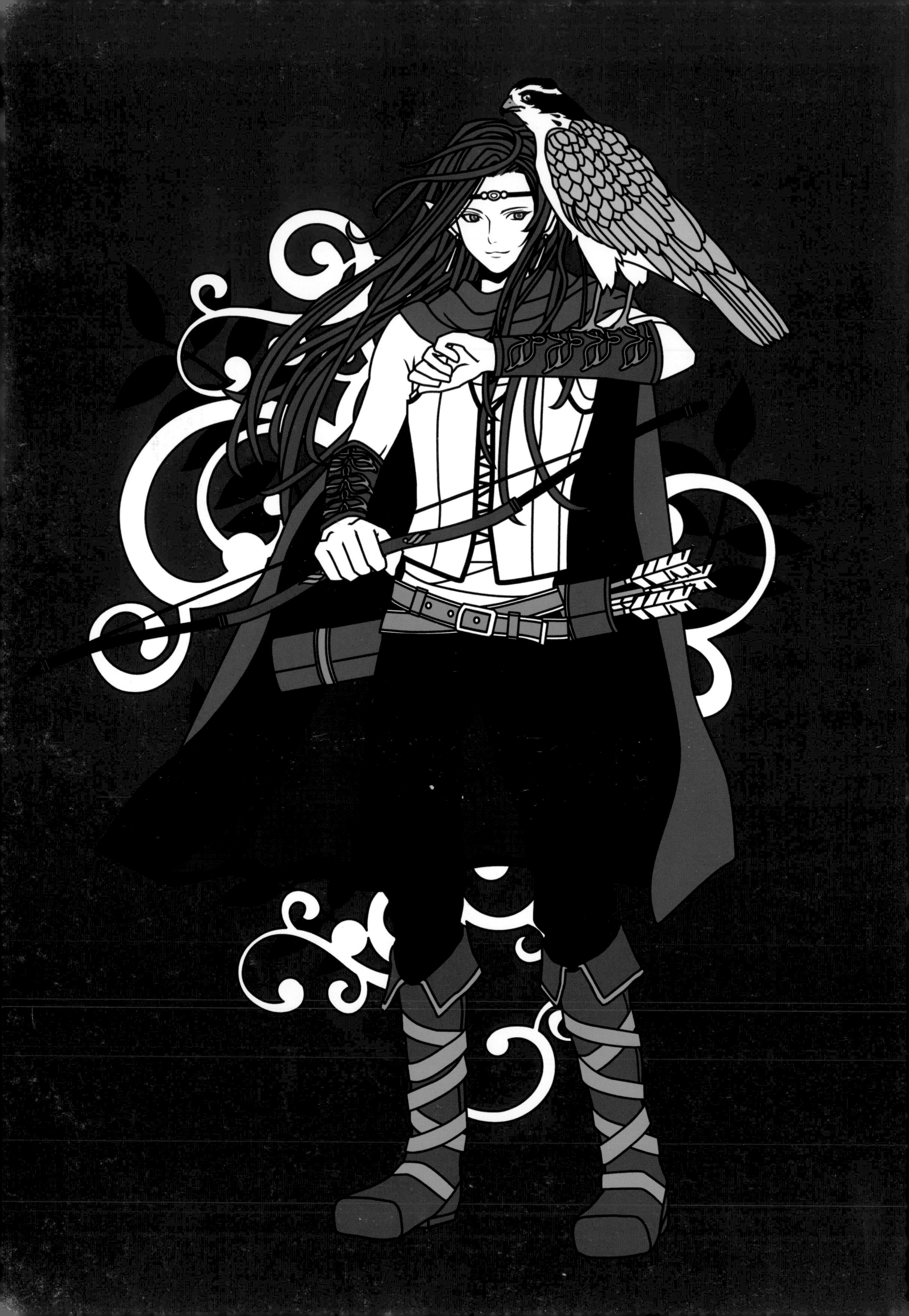

Chapter **I**

YUUSHA

Choosing a Hero

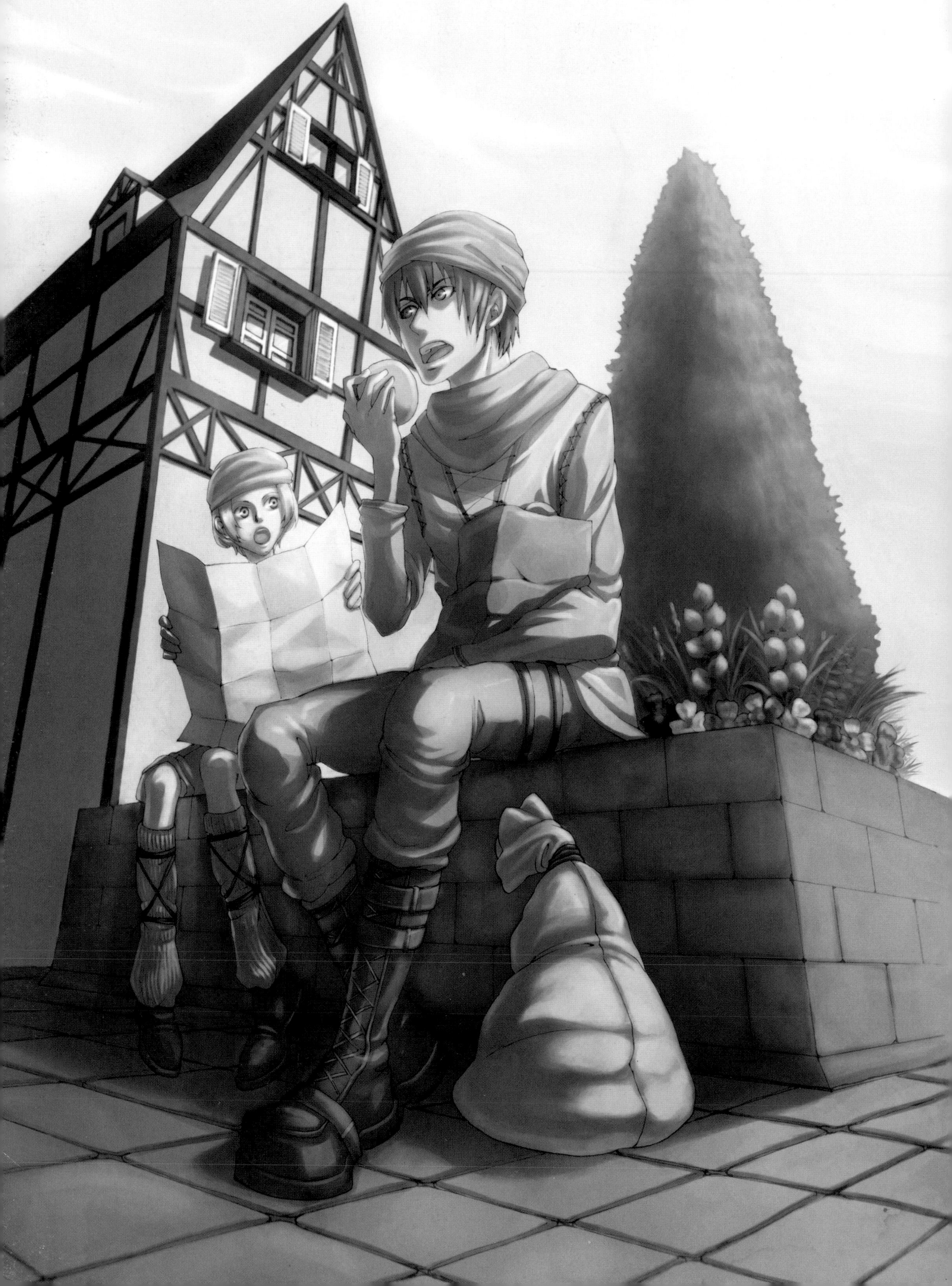

Human

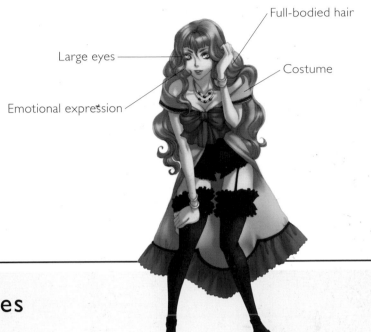

Full-bodied hair

Large eyes

Costume

Emotional expression

➤ Notable Features

- Large eyes, full-bodied hair, exaggerated facial expressions
- Typical human body proportions
- Capable of expressing emotions and intellect
- Mortal, capable of being killed or injured
- Portrayed either as heroes or villains, good or evil
- Appearance is often European or Western
- Wardrobe consists of various costumes
- May possess skills in labor, defense, or warfare

✛ Outline and Origin

One of the most widely used characters in manga, humans depict cultural traits from Oriental, African, Norfolk, English, Anglo-Saxon, and other racial groups. This diversity is created in their light or dark skin tones, facial features, such as slanting or exaggeratedly huge eyes, short or long limbs, and light or black hair. Most human characters are stereotyped by race or geographical origin. A human character of African descent may have pronounced lips, kinky hair, and dark skin. A European character may appear with a sharp nose, jutting jaw, light hair, long limbs and long fingers.

Male humans typically have more pronounced muscles and bones than female humans, and often embody a particular skill in work or battle by carrying a specific weapon, such as a dagger or pistol. Female humans are typically more gentle than males, and have more slender bodies and softer skin tones. They are either depicted as passive and emotional with no particular skills or as bold heroines with as refined skills as those of their male counterparts.

Humans, as opposed to supernatural creatures or semi-humans, are mortal, and therefore, exhibit traits of weakness and vulnerability. They are also highly emotional, and their distinct human traits, such as anger, selfishness, strength, compassion or forgiveness, can be manipulated by their opponents in conflict or battle.

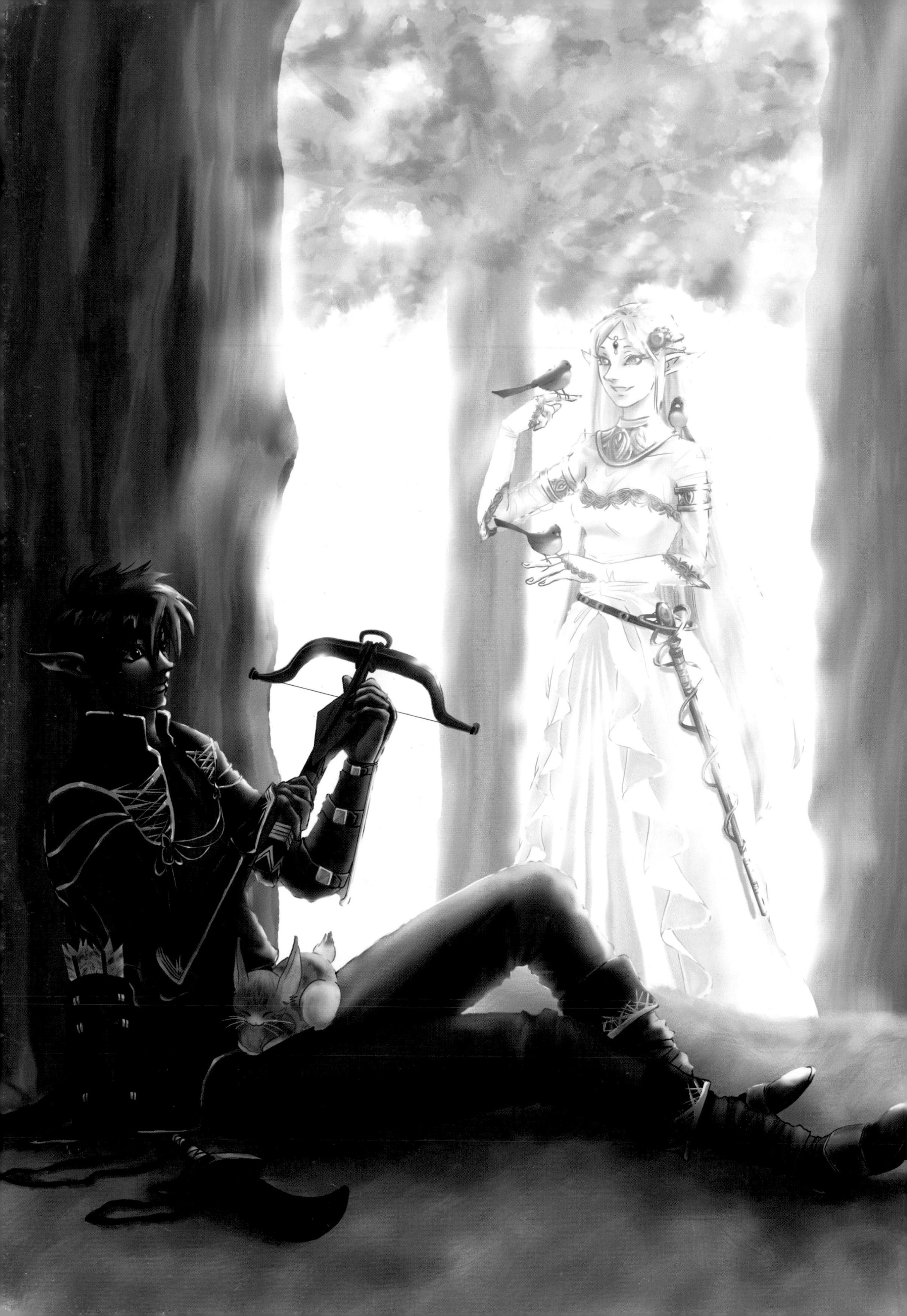

Light Elf, Dark Elf

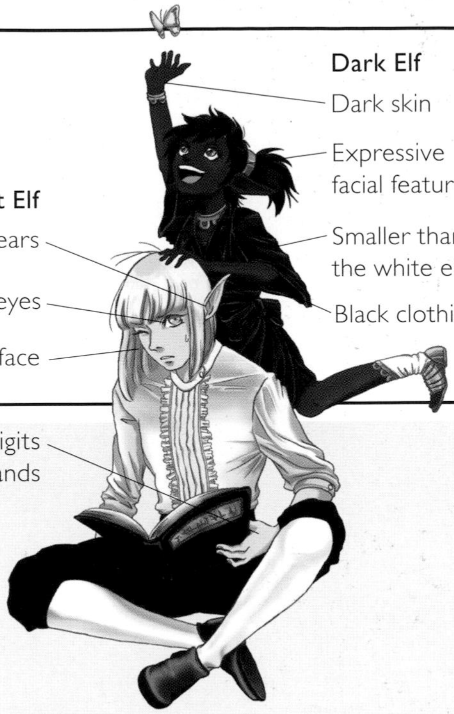
Dark Elf
Dark skin
Expressive facial features
Smaller than the white elf
Black clothing
Light Elf
Pointy ears
Large eyes
Youthful face
Four digits on the hands

Notable Features

Light Elf

- Pointy ears and long, narrow nose
- Youthful looking with beautiful facial features
- Fair skin and silky, golden hair
- Large blue or green eyes with slanted eyelids and high, sharp cheekbones
- Shorter or taller than humans, usually thinner
- Wears clean and light-colored clothes, may wear stockings or a cap
- Immortal and uses powers, such as healing, flying or giving a paralyzing stare
- Gifted, mentally stronger than humans, peaceful, and has a zest for life

Dark Elf

- Expressive facial features and misshaped body
- Dark-skinned with coal black hair and red, shining eyes
- Smaller than the light elf, and associated with the dwarf
- Sometimes greedy and troublesome for humans
- Deadly and evil
- Friendly with animals, uses astral projection and fire control through magic
- Dresses in loose and flowing garments in black, white and grey
- Uses a dagger, steel whip, tiger claw, tiger hook sword or crossbow for fighting

Outline and Origin

The light elf originates from German mythology, and is associated with Norse elves, fairies of Romance folklore, and elves in Scandinavian, Icelandic and English folklore. Light elves come from a race of divine beings possessed with magical powers who lived in underground caves or in mountains, wells and springs.

In the Norse belief, it was possible to crossbreed light elves and humans. The crossbred creatures assumed semi-divine features linked with fertility and ancestor worship. They were thought of like spirits who pass through walls and doors. In English folklore, light elves were usually lighthearted beings, yet they could be annoyed at humans who offended them.

Dark elves are obsessed with power and are portrayed as "evil," as they lead a very rigid lifestyle. In contrast to light elves, dark elves typically have dark skin, and possess a higher degree of magical power. They are as immortal as the light elves and do not die from old age or sickness, but only from violence or a lost desire to live. Many dark elves inflict sickness on humans as they, themselves, are immune to disease.

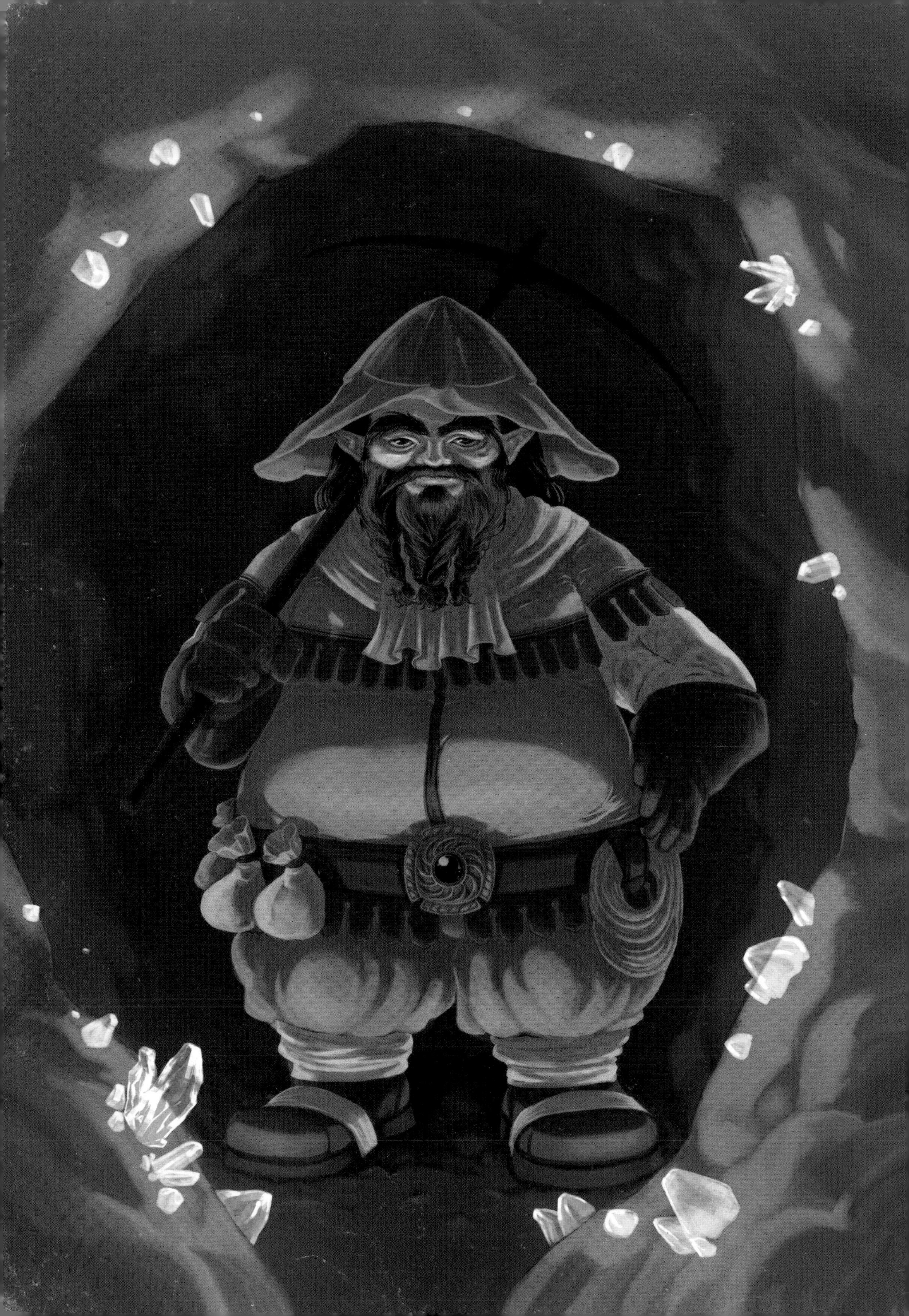

Dwarf

Dark hair

Pale skin

Gloves and boots

Hammer for fighting

➡ Notable Features

- Short and stout, pale skin and dark hair
- Male dwarf is always bearded, female dwarf is sometimes bearded
- Large head and large belly
- Mortal, but has a long lifespan
- Hardworking, skilled, gifted in warfare
- Lives underground and loves mining, but also enjoys the outdoors
- Happy and cheerful
- Possesses magical talents related to metallurgy
- Has a hearty appetite, loves feasts and alcohol

✚ Outline and Origin

Dwarves are midget beings from German mythology and fantasy fiction. They are the source of fairy tales in English, German and Dutch folklore. They are similar to elves, especially the dark elves that have animistic beliefs, such as the belief that a human spirit may reside in a physical object after its body is dead. The Norse dwarves are highly skilled and especially devoted to metal crafting. Despite their deformations and stunted growth, they work hard, have exceptional craftsmanship and have come to be known as comical and free-spirited.

In modern fantasy fiction, dwarves are short, long-bearded and skilled in mining and metallurgy. Although they are considered as a sub-race of elves, they are known to dislike elves and distrust other races. They are, however, wealthy and active in weapon trading. Many modern dwarves carry Scottish or Scandinavian accents.

Dwarves can live about 250 years. Although they are not as fertile as humans and there are very few women among them, dwarves adore their children and will defend them from known enemies.

In battle, dwarves are tough and anxious to fight. They are proud of their adeptness in using axes and war hammers, and firing canons strapped to their backs. They leap into the air, use heavy blows on their enemies, and spin fire. They are also known for their savage hits, kicks, and head-butts.

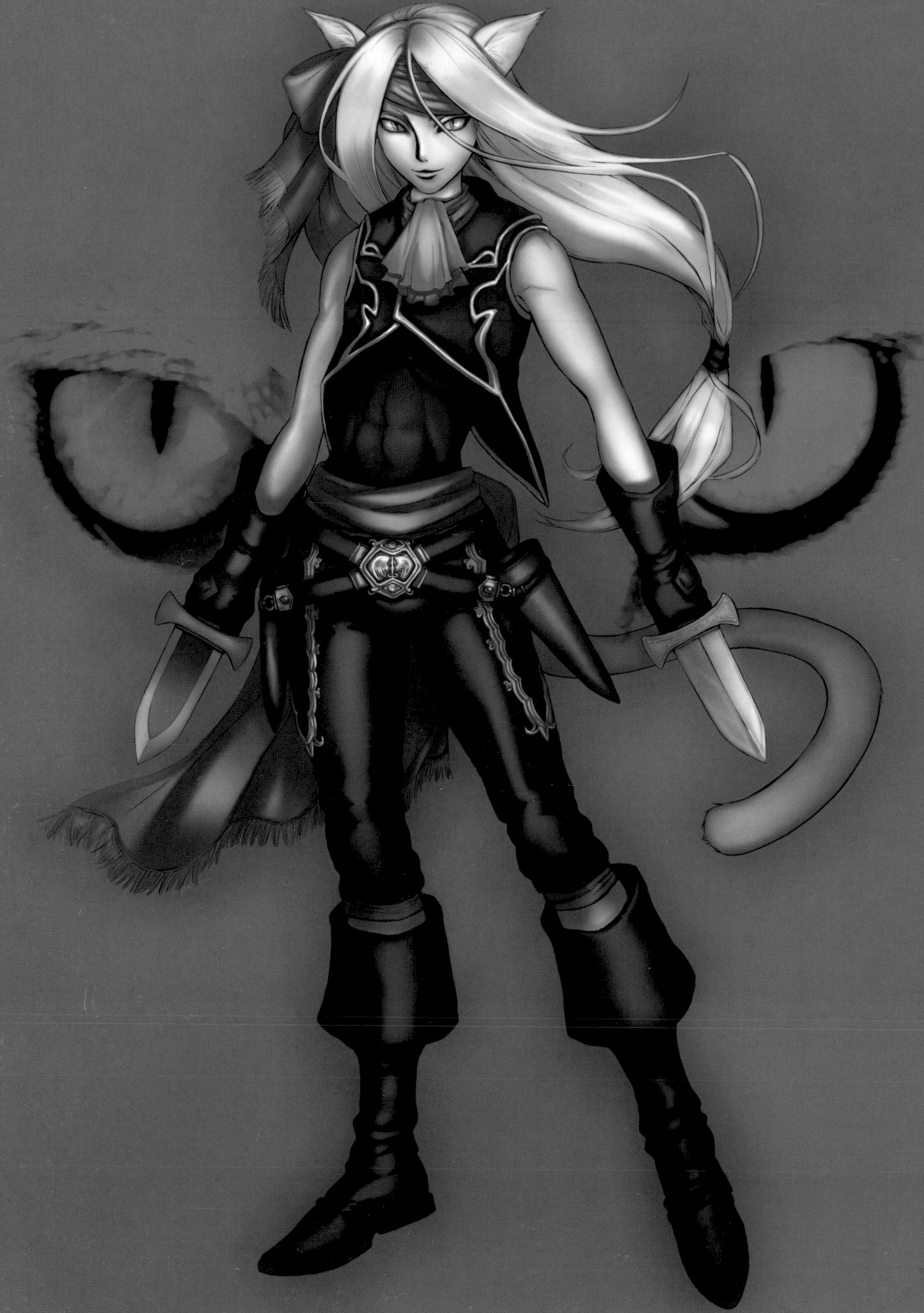

Cat-Man, Cat-Woman

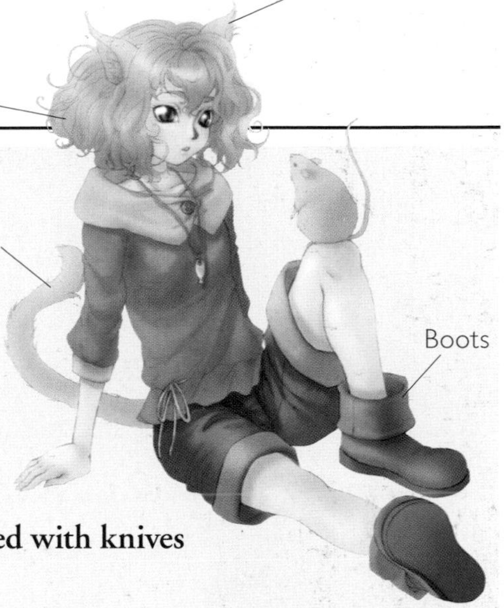
Cat's ears
Young, attractive and gentle looking
Cat's tail
Boots

Notable Features

Cat-Man

- Human body with a cat's head, ears and tail
- Tough-looking and athletic
- Noble and heroic
- A skillful warrior and a fine hunter
- May wear razor-tipped gauntlets or gloves equipped with knives

Cat-Woman

- Young and attractive, independent and modern
- Gentle protector of cats, yet fierce and powerful
- Possesses gymnastic and martial arts skills
- May wear gloves and boots with metal claws on the fingertips and toes
- Japanese cat-girl is portrayed as overtly feminine and cute, and has long hair

Outline and Origin

An early description of a cat-man can be traced to an aboriginal myth about two ancestral brothers, the Bagadjimbiri, who rose from the ground as dingos, made water-holes, then became gigantic men. They had an argument with a cat-man known as Ngariman who was upset with the brothers for their annoying laughter. Ngariman killed the brothers, and was consequently drowned into the underground by milk from the brothers' mother, Dilga, the earth goddess.

This story reveals the cat-man's fighting instincts, although he is looked down upon by his enemies for easily losing battles. In West Norfolk mythology, the cat-man is a character that saves people from burning buildings or being killed on the roads, and rescues kittens from trees. In modern days, the cat-man is seen as a character that becomes a criminal thief because he has grown tired of hunting. His favorite weapon is a pair of steel claw-tipped gloves and a razor-edged cat boomerang.

In Egyptian mythology, the cat-woman can be traced to the cat goddess, Bastet, who was known to be the daughter of Ra, the Egyptian sun god. Bastet was a protector of domestic cats and awarded joy and pleasure to those who favored cats. She is portrayed as a woman with a cat's head, and carries a sacred rattle, box, or basket. Her likeness, when portrayed as a modern cat-woman, is known as a cunning thief like the modern cat-man. Both the cat-man and the cat-woman fight excellently with a whip, and use a pistol, plastic ties for tying hands and feet, and duct tape.

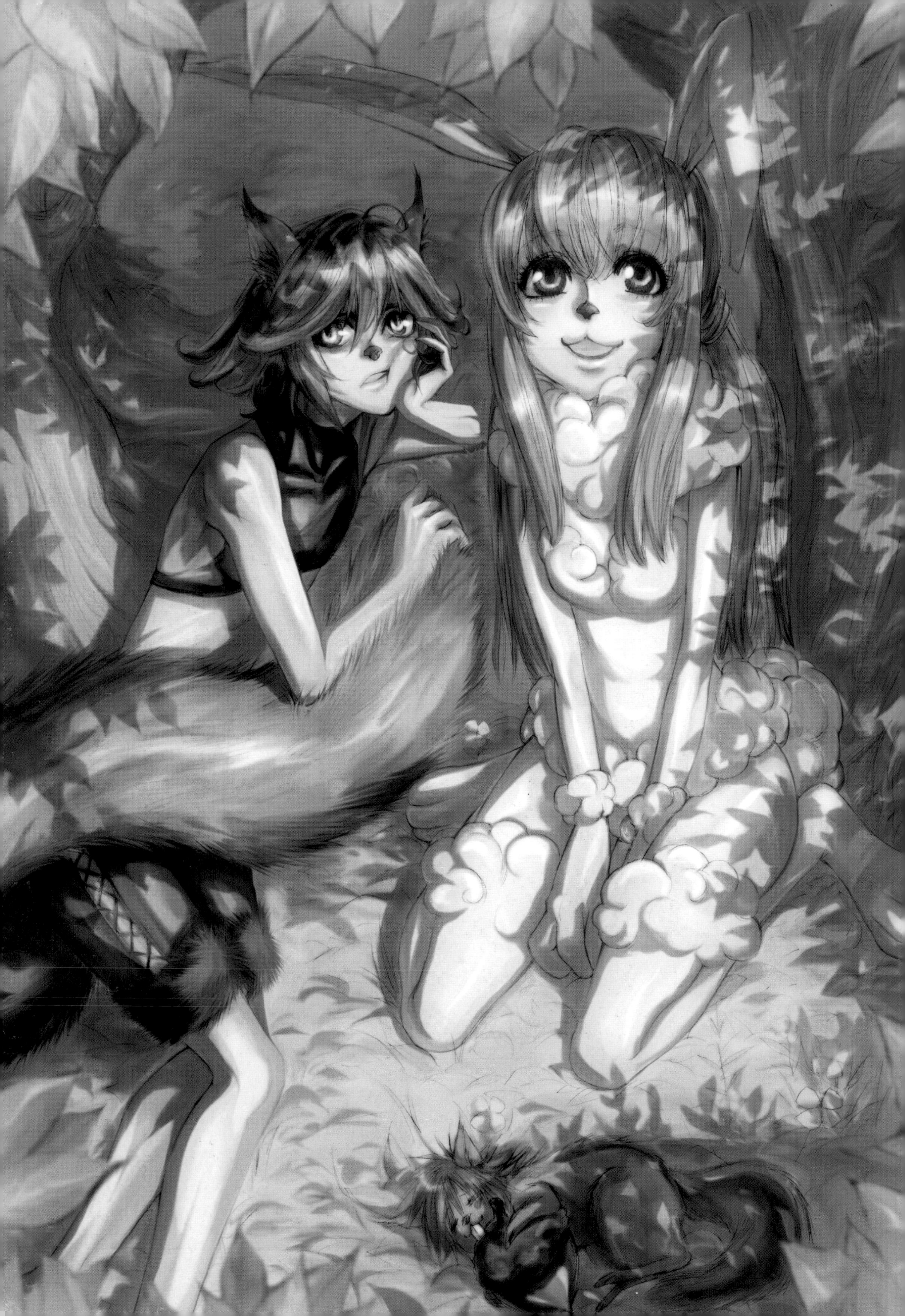

Beast-Man, Beast-Woman

Ram's horns

Furry hair

Whip for fighting

Combination of animal and human body

➡ Notable Features

Beast-Man

- Physical and mental fusion of man and beast
- Possesses barbarian strength
- Furry legs, horns of goat or ram on head, sharp teeth
- May be combination of cow, bulldog, wolf or others
- Cannibal, evil, and lives a short life
- May carry weapons, shield, whip or sword

Beast-Woman

- Half-female human and half-beast, such as a dragon, chimera or changeling
- Hairy and muscular body with thick or scaly skin
- May have a tail or horns
- Carnivorous or herbivorous, fierce, fearless, and aggressive
- Skilled in acrobatics and melee attack
- May carry armor, sling, bow or flint dagger

✚ Outline and Origin

The legend of the beast-man comes from barbaric beast-like humans. At a time when lands were dominated by chaos, destruction, and savagery, monsters inhabited the dark forests and became creatures with human and beast-like features in mind, body, and spirit. In an English story, the beast-man is depicted as a leader of a tribe of beast people from the jungle. The European beast-man has especially long, brown fur with no tribal face paint and wears Oriental-style chest armor.

Beast-men are proud and fight for dominance among their breed. They may use magic and have gifted intellect like humans. Some beast-men adopt physical attributes of various animals to prove their devotion to certain gods. Their sizes and the number of horns on their heads determine the quality of their strength. They are considered nomads, moving from place to place in the wilderness.

The beast-woman can be a dragonewt (humanoid reptile), dragon maid (female humanoid dragon), melusine (serpent woman), or a beast-girl similar to a changeling. Like the beast-man, she possesses powerful strength and can use healing magic.

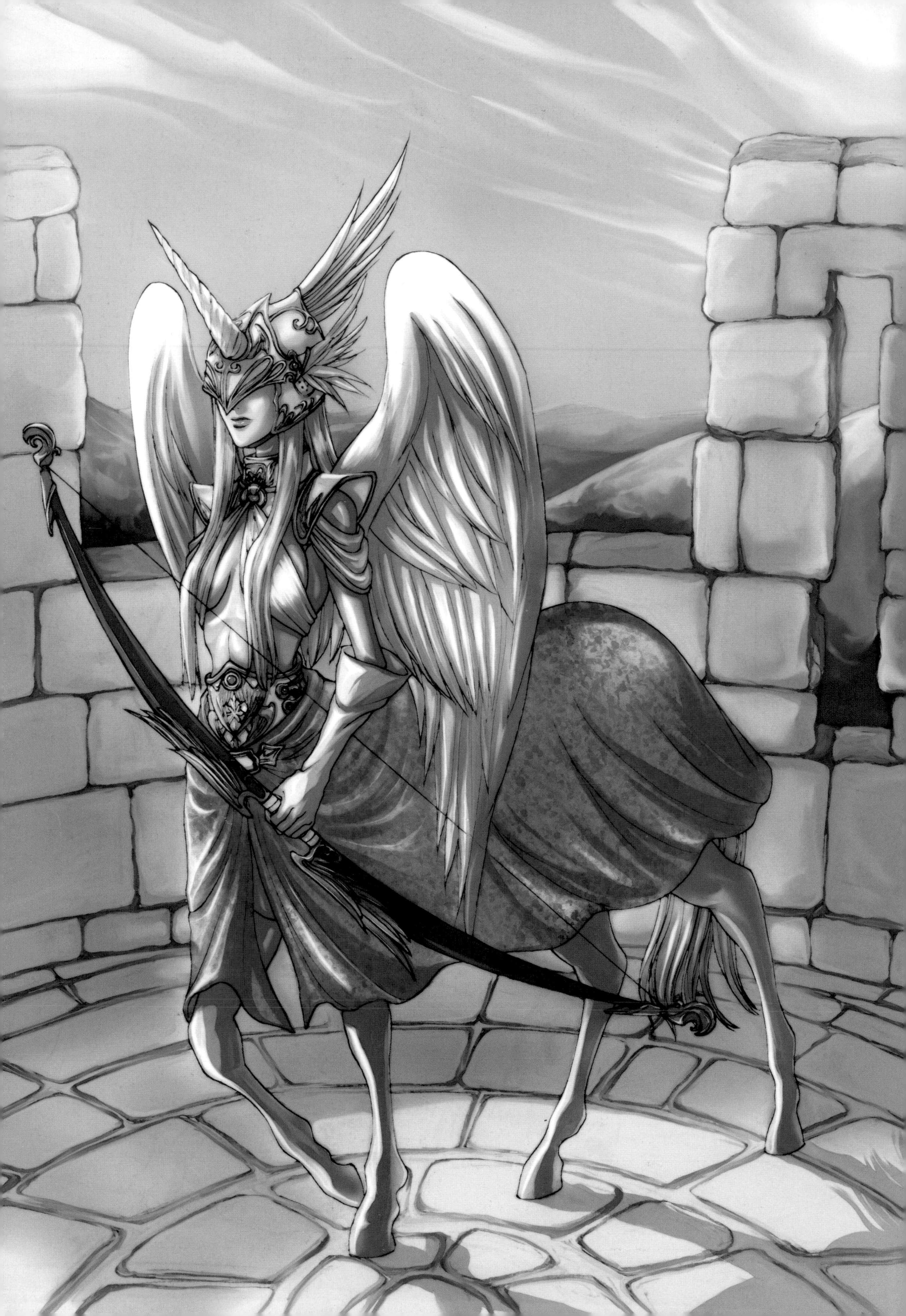

Centaur

Muscular build
Amulet
Spear for warfare
Lower body of a horse and upper body of a human

➡ Notable Features

- **Horse creature with human head, arms, and chest**
- **Wild fighter, skilled at warfare and archery**
- **May have wings and horns**
- **A symbol of chaos and passion**
- **Wise, noble and gifted in astrology, prophecy and healing**
- **Nomad that roams around hills and valleys**
- **May carry a spear and wear an amulet, brooch or cloak**

+ Outline and Origin

Illustrations of centaurs can be traced back as far as 2000 B.C. in Assyria and 3000 B.C. in India. In Greek mythology, the centaur was known to be either the child of Ixion or a descendant of Apollo. It had the head, arms, and chest of a man, but the legs and lower torso of a horse. Centaurs appeared in myths circulating in ancient Greece, as well as in Roman mythology. There are also references to such half-men, half-animal creatures among the Aztecs and Eurasians.

The centaurs were known to fight against the Lapiths, ancient Greeks from Thessaly. Once, when they were invited to their stepbrother's wedding, the centaurs got drunk, harmed the women and stirred a fight with the Lapithae. As a result, they became symbols of the dark and undisciplined forces of nature.

Chiron, a famous centaur, was the son of Titan Kronos, and was accidentally wounded by Heracles with a poisoned arrow while Heracles fought other centaurs. To relieve himself of his wounds, Chiron gave his immortality to the Titan Prometheus. Another story of Chiron relates that he summoned Zeus to transform him into the constellation Sagittarius, which may explain the Sagittarian symbol of a half-human and half-horse archer.

Centaurs were known to live in herds in Thessaly, Greece, and were feared by humans. They ate raw flesh, destroyed crops and assaulted women. Being driven away from their land made them intellectually ignorant. They symbolize lust, adultery, brutality, revenge and sometimes the devil, however, the human part in them may cause them to struggle between good and evil, passion and discipline, belief and disbelief in gods.

Some female centaurs also existed in Greek literature and art. They were known in reference to the males in their lives, their husbands and brothers, and were described as having white horse legs instead of the dark legs of the male centaurs.

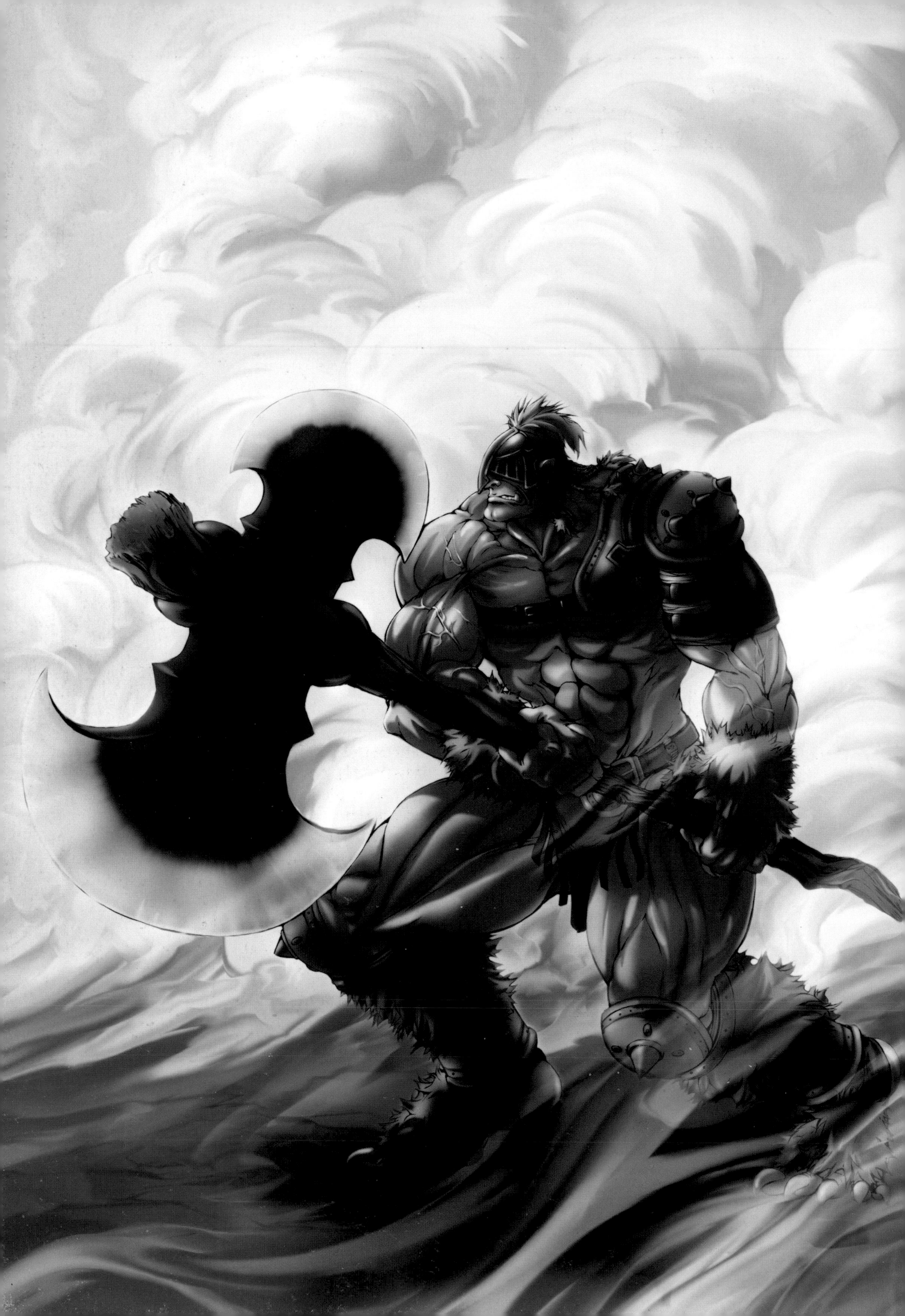

Giant

Helmet

Huge jaws

Large hands

Tall, muscular, heavy and stocky

➡ Notable Features

- Extremely tall, usually more than eight feet tall, heavy and stocky with an oversized body
- Huge jaw, high cheekbones or teeth jutting out
- Muscular with huge hands, may be hairy, may have six toes on each foot
- Superhuman strength, long lifespan
- Can be violent or wild and may eat humans
- Can be gentle, friendly and compassionate with loved ones or those in need
- May carry an ax, armor, sling, helmet, shield or sword

✛ Outline and Origin

Giants are known to have appeared in Greek, Indo-European, Norse and Balt mythology and legends. They are also part of biblical readings; particularly well-known is the story of the famous giant Goliath who fought David, the young king of Israel. He is depicted as a powerful warrior with a sling and armor. The Bible describes a world of Nephilim, a race of giants, which was devastated by the global flood of Genesis, but left descendants living in the so-called Promised Land. These giants became part of an ancient race that was highly intelligent, and equipped with advanced technology and aeronautic capabilities. They were mutated and driven underground during the great earth catastrophes, until they arose again when the Age of Man, signifying the form of human existence, had changed.

There are many references to giants in the cultures of the Americas, Africa, Asia, Australia and Europe. The Sao giants can be traced back to the 9th century when they lived near what is now known as Chad, Africa, They had a well-developed religion and culture, and were peaceful until they fought against the Muslims and were forced to serve the Arabs.

In North America during the 1940s, excavations in Arizona revealed approximately 32 caves that held remains of ancient giants 8-9 feet in height, covered with sheepskin. In South America, there are traces of giants from the Inca civilization, measuring more than nine feet. These giants are linked to the giant King Ophir of 600 B.C. who was known for his gold craftsmanship. Giants in Asia were also known to exist before the 16th century. In China, Chang Woo Gow, who was a gentleman and a scholar, measured more than 8 feet.

In ancient kingdoms, giants were warriors and laborers. They were gentle and harmless despite their size and super strength, but were also wicked, aggressive and greedy. Some made "normal" sized humans their slaves, while others were half-breeds of humans or fallen angels.

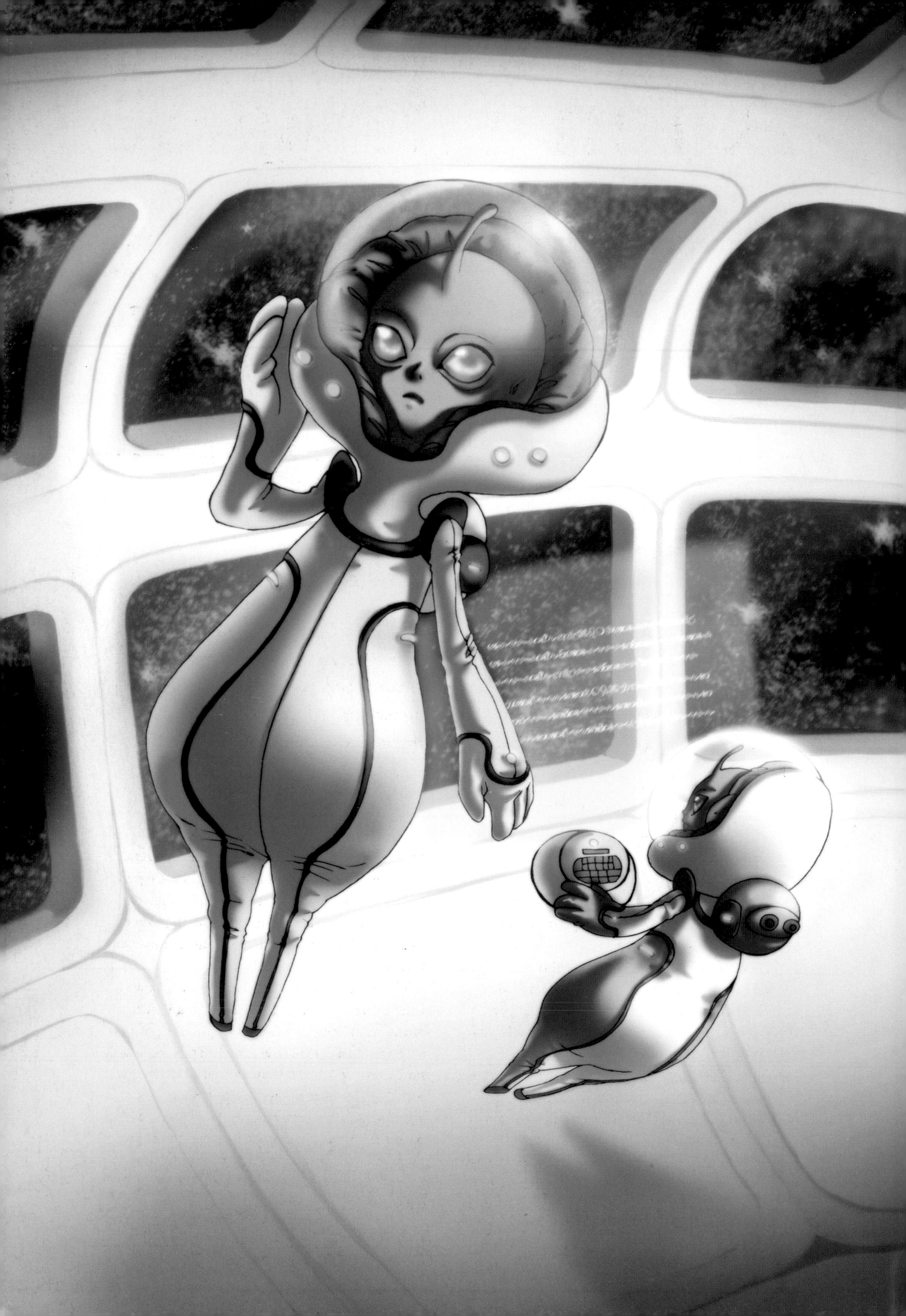

Alien

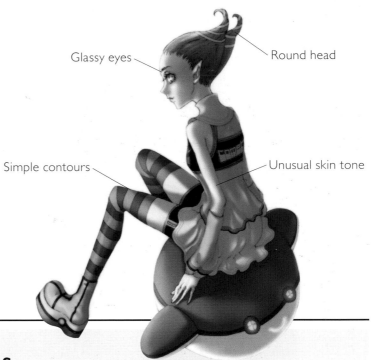

Glassy eyes

Round head

Simple contours

Unusual skin tone

➥ Notable Features

- Distorted human-like features, skeletal structure
- May appear in body colors of black, blue, green, grey, bronze or be colorless
- Simple body contours and round head
- Physically agile and strong, can move or crawl on ceilings and walls
- May wear bodysuit, may have antennae on the head, may have beak or wings
- Superlative intelligence, mentally stronger than humans
- Hard-working and functions well in group settings
- Travels in spaceships, discs, spheres or other geometrically-shaped spacecrafts

✚ Outline and Origin

There are many mythological references linked to extraterrestrials or aliens—some that refer to them as creators of the human race, ancient gods, or intelligent travelers that came from the stars and descended on Earth.

One theory about aliens existed in the ancient Egyptian mythological age, Zep Tepi—the Genesis or "First Time," a period when gods and humans lived together. The story tells that the god of Atlantis left Atlantis in a pyramid-shaped spaceship as an alien creature, to create the human race. In the classic Mayan theory of Guatemala, intelligent alien beings originate from the stars and studied the Earth.

Some ancient figurines were found to possess the features of aliens: simple lined bodies, rounded heads and a double oval at the head's

center. They became associated with Martians (coming from Mars). Primitive cave drawings also exist all over the world, across America, Africa and Europe, depicting strangely-looking forms, wearing suits with gears and having antennae on their heads.

There are some theories that consider these creatures, not to be foreign beings, but humans of the future who travel through time to prevent a world chemical crisis, and make appearances on Earth to warn us about the dangers of chemical technology—that it can cause physical mutations.

They are, therefore, not generally viewed as harmful, unlike portrayals in many films about them, but as curious intelligent beings that come to our planet to study the progress of our technological advancement.

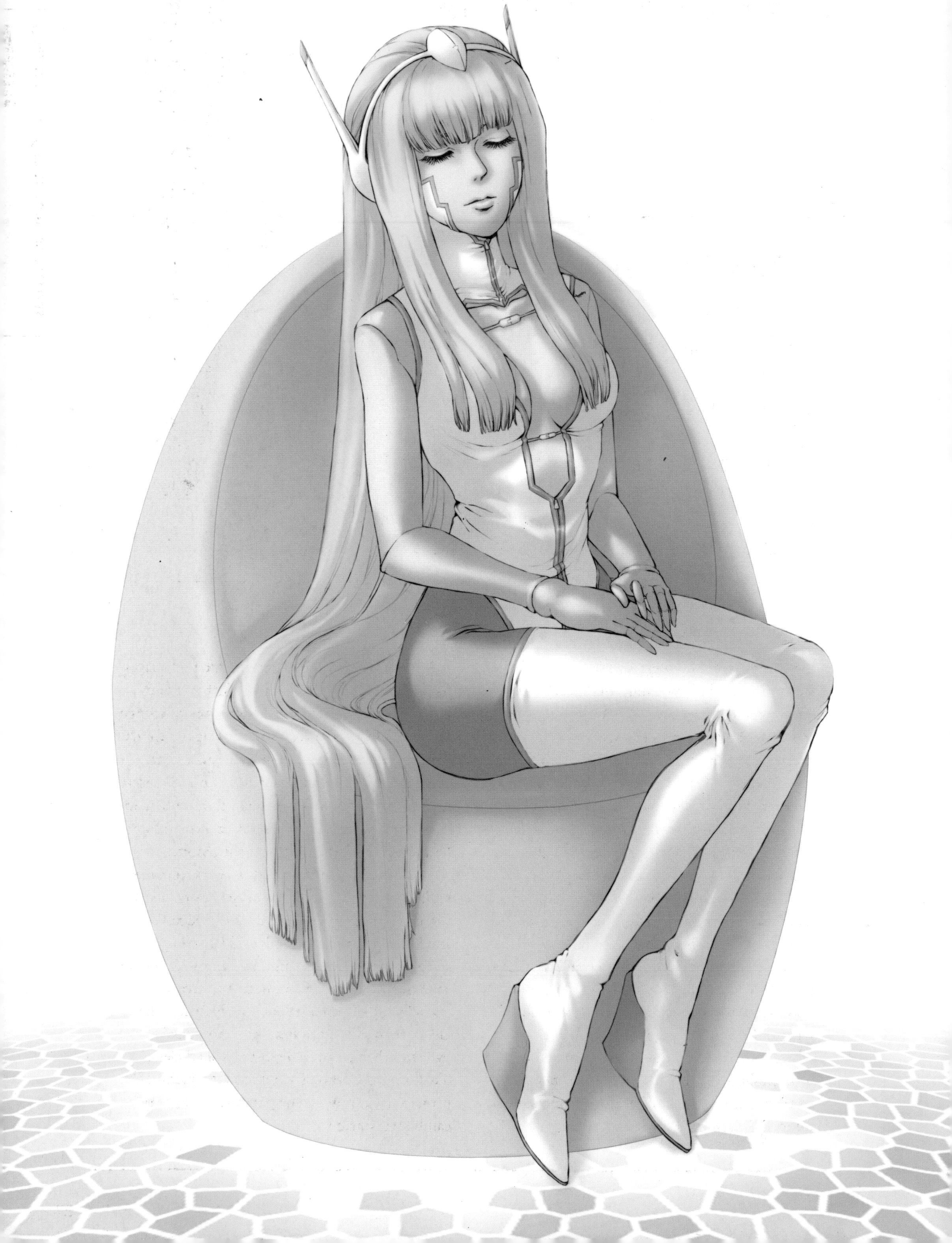

Android

Human-like face

Twistable hands

Mechanical body made of metal or silicon

Long limbs

➡ Notable Features

- Synthetic mechanism that looks and acts like a human
- Can change facial expression and move and twist hands, legs and body
- May have skin or hair resembling human skin and/or human hair
- Can adopt human voice and express emotion
- Body is made of mechanical equipment or highly advanced synthetic jelly silicon
- Physically and mentally equal or superior to humans
- Can malfunction if equipment is damaged

✛ Outline and Origin

The term "android" originates from the Greek word "androeidēs" meaning "manlike," and the suffix "oeidēs" translated as "oid" and meaning "species." The term was first used in 1270, then appeared in U.S. patents in 1863 and was popularized in France in 1886. Unlike robots, androids have bodies made of metal or silicon that are made to look like humans on the outside, while having robot systems on the inside. The creation of a machine emulating humans may stem from man's instinct to own a slave or companion who is selflessly interested in him.

As far back as the 4th century B.C., a Greek mathematician was said to have conceptualized a mechanical, steam-operated bird. There is also a Greek myth, which tells of Pygmalion, King of Cyprus, falling in love with a statue of the goddess Aphrodite. Out of frustration, he brought it to life, making her the "perfect" woman, with a beautiful form, and an obedient mind and personality.

Around 1635, the philosopher René Descartes was known to have built for himself a female machine that he took with him on his sea voyage. In 1070, Heron of Alexandria, an ancient Greek mathematician, made automated devices that could sing, dance and drink. Many other robotic inventions also took place in the 11th century in Al-Jazira, Mesopotamia. And later, Leonardo da Vinci created plans for humanoid robots.

The essential part of an android is its computer brain. This sophisticated circuitry of mechanical synthesis can be programmed to operate tasks and to express human emotions, such as anger, disappointment and surprise, or to engage in human actions, such as giving kindness or forgiveness.

Androids are also equipped with sensors that allow them to react to heat, pressure or pain by using the five human senses. Nonetheless, like humans, androids are mortal. By technical computer malfunction or physical abuse, they can be terminated.

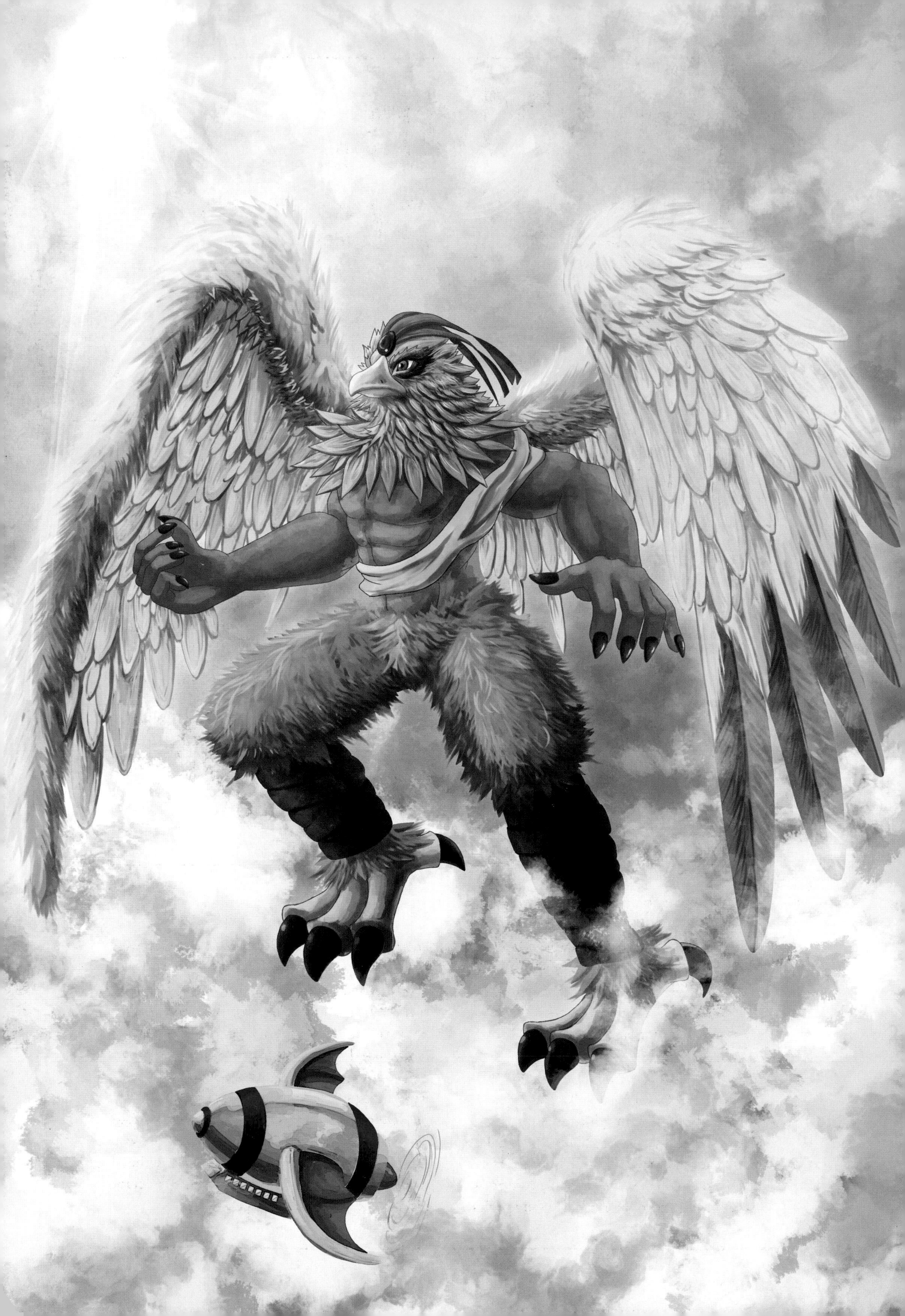

Bird-Man, Bird-Woman

Bird's head with gems

Large wings with golden feathers

Gigantic body

Bird tallons

➨ Notable Features

Bird-Man

- Human body with wings and the head of a bird
- Bird may be falcon, eagle, hawk, ibis or other type
- Huge wings can block the sun
- May have golden feathers or gems on the head
- Fierce and brave, a symbol of majesty and power

Bird-Woman

- Bird with a woman's head, bird's legs and feathers
- May be a female night elf or hunting bird, swan, dove, crane or other type
- May or may not have wings
- Has a beautiful voice or plays a musical instrument
- Attacks with beak and claws

✦ Outline and Origin

In Egyptian mythology, there are bird-headed gods that represent rebirth and resurrection.

Horus, who had the head of a falcon, was Egypt's national patron god. Thoth had the head of an ibis or baboon, and sometimes wore a headdress.

Karura, which is also the Japanese transliteration of the Sanskrit "Garuda," is a mythical bird-man from Hindu folklore. He had a human body and wore gold clothing, but had the wings, face and beak of an eagle. He was known in Tibetan and Japanese culture as a fire-breathing eagle-man. He was semi-divine and fought dragons and serpents. He symbolizes force, speed and martial strength.

Bird-women are goddesses in Greek mythology, such as the sirens and the harpies. Sirens were portrayed as dangerous and seductive. They often played musical instruments to accompany their singing, and may or may not have had wings. Harpies, conversely, were ugly winged bird-women who stole food. Other forms of bird-women are the swan maidens, the swanmays who can shapeshift from swans to humans, and the crane wife from a Japanese folktale who is a crane disguised as a human.

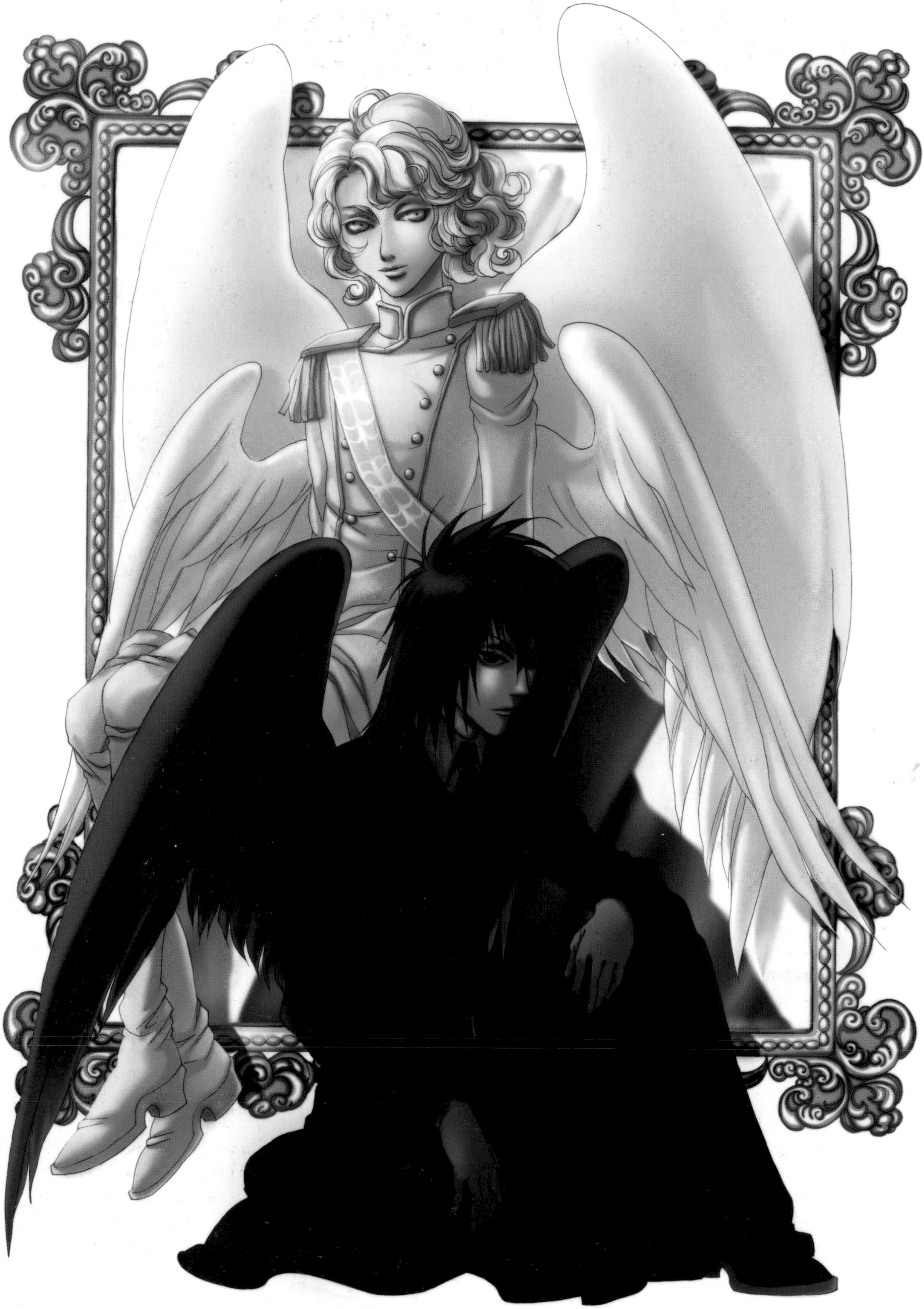

Holy Angel, Fallen Angel

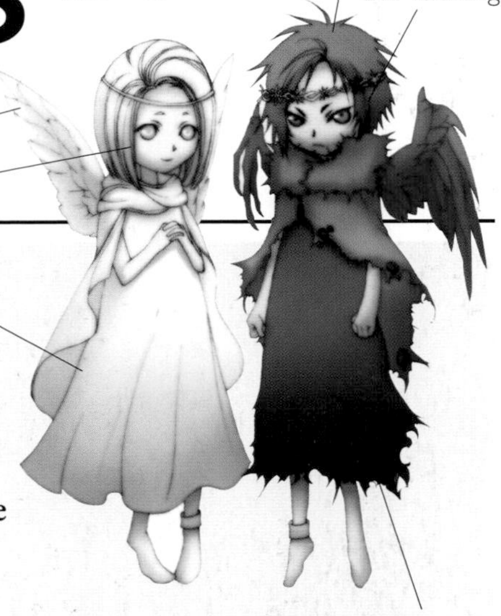
Fallen Angel
Miserable appearance
Evil-looking
Holy Angel
Light-colored wings
Pure and gentle facial appearance
White tunic
Dark clothing

➡ Notable Features

Holy Angel

- **God's messenger with an immortal spirit**
- **Has beautiful facial features, and is pure and gentle**
- **Usually male with four to six wings**
- **Intelligent, strong and holy**
- **May wear military attire with body armor or long robe**

Fallen Angel

- **Dark angel without light, and has one to twelve wings**
- **Evil, miserable, lonely, tricky and envious of God's power**
- **Not as intelligent as the holy angel**
- **May cause harm to or be a bad influence on humans**
- **May dress in dark, thin or torn clothing**

✛ Outline and Origin

Holy angels are supernatural beings depicted with wings and originate from Jewish, Christian and Islamic religions, as well as early Babylonian, Persian, Egyptian and Greek writings. In Judaism, angels are messengers of justice and power who heal, protect, or perform kindness on behalf of God. Angels in Islamic faith are followers of God, servants whose responsibility is to obey Him. In Christianity, angels are spiritual beings and act as direct messengers of God, promoting goodness and love; they are popularly called "beings of light."

Humans look up to angels for mercy, help or guidance, especially during times of crisis. An angel with a gift of strength or power may be seen in a warrior uniform and holding a spear. An angel that brings comfort to a dying person may be clothed in a white robe, and have a halo over his head. Angels are immortal, emotional, may be invisible and are able to move rapidly from one place to another.

Fallen angels belong to the same kingdom as holy angels, but have turned against God, and are now closely associated with the devil. They are afflicted by greed, deceit, jealousy and other evil characteristics that lead humans away from righteousness. Lucifer is the widely known fallen angel who is believed to have created the war in heaven that separated the good angels from the bad ones.

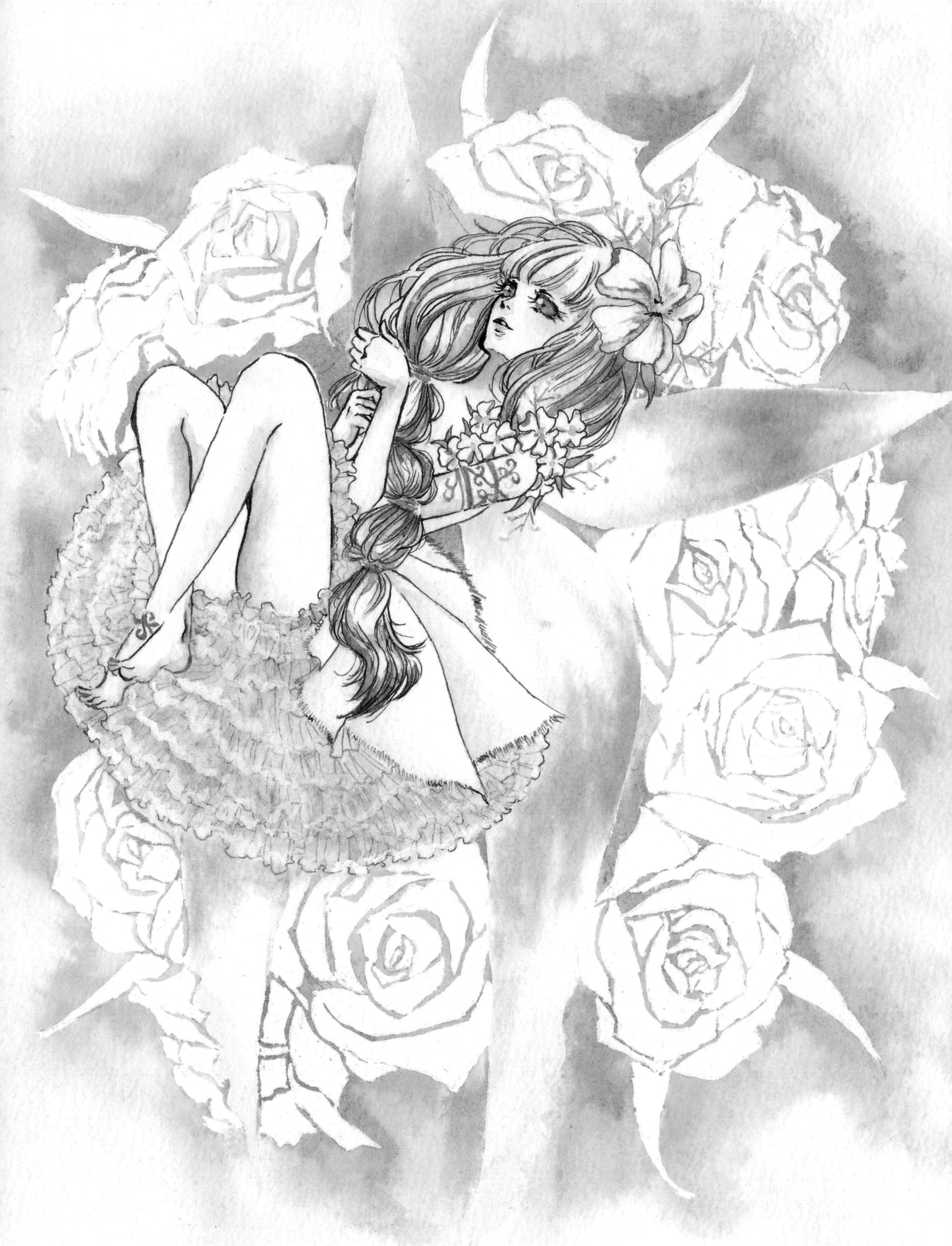

Fairy

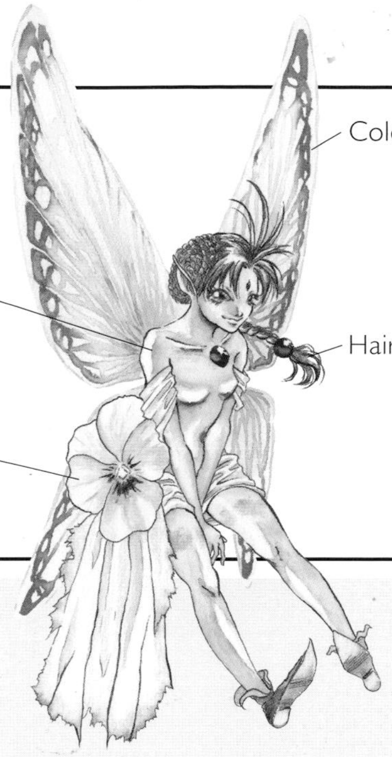
Colorful wings
Pastel-colored body
Hair ornament
Clothing with flowers

Notable Features

- Supernatural being in form of a spirit
- Has human features, but possesses magical powers that can be used to disguise its appearance
- Ancient fairies were tall, radiant and sometimes wingless, modern fairies are small, young and always have wings
- Highly intelligent and skilled in all kinds of arts and crafts, has the ability to fly, to cast spells and foresee the future
- May appear in different mythological forms, or as an animals or insect
- Can be gentle and angelic or powerful, naughty and deceiving
- May wear green attire and cap with flowers

Outline and Origin

Legends, folklore and the myths of various cultures have different theories as to the origin of fairies. Small-statured races were known to occupy parts of Europe during the Bronze and Neolithic Ages. They lived in the underground of hills and later relocated to the forests. In Scandinavian, Scottish and Irish folklore, fairies were thought of as fallen angels who were cast out from heaven by God for their arrogance and fell into the forests where they became fairies of nature.

An Irish belief claims them to be spirits of the dead, neither good enough to remain in heaven, nor bad enough to be cast into the fires of hell.

In West European stories, fairies were thought to originate from Italy where they were known as "fatae," then to have traveled to France where they were known as "fees" and later to have gone to Britain where they were known as "fays," until the country folk changed their name to "fairies."

There are two known classifications of fairies: the blessed and unblessed. In Scottish folklore, blessed fairies, also known as holy fairies, are helpful and kind, and often seen during twilight. They seek help from humans and return kindness with gifts and favors. They like to dance, feast and hunt. Unblessed fairies are wicked and malicious and harass humans. They may also cause sickness and death among animals.

A common feature among fairies is their use of magic to disguise appearances, to move objects, people and animals, to make them fly or to change them into other forms. They can also make themselves invisible through the use of charms or potions. Some fairies are known to carry arrows, spades or magical stones. And being spirits of nature, they are known to have power over plants and animals. They can speak the language of animals, which obey them and help them with tasks. Although they have long lives, they are not described as being immortal.

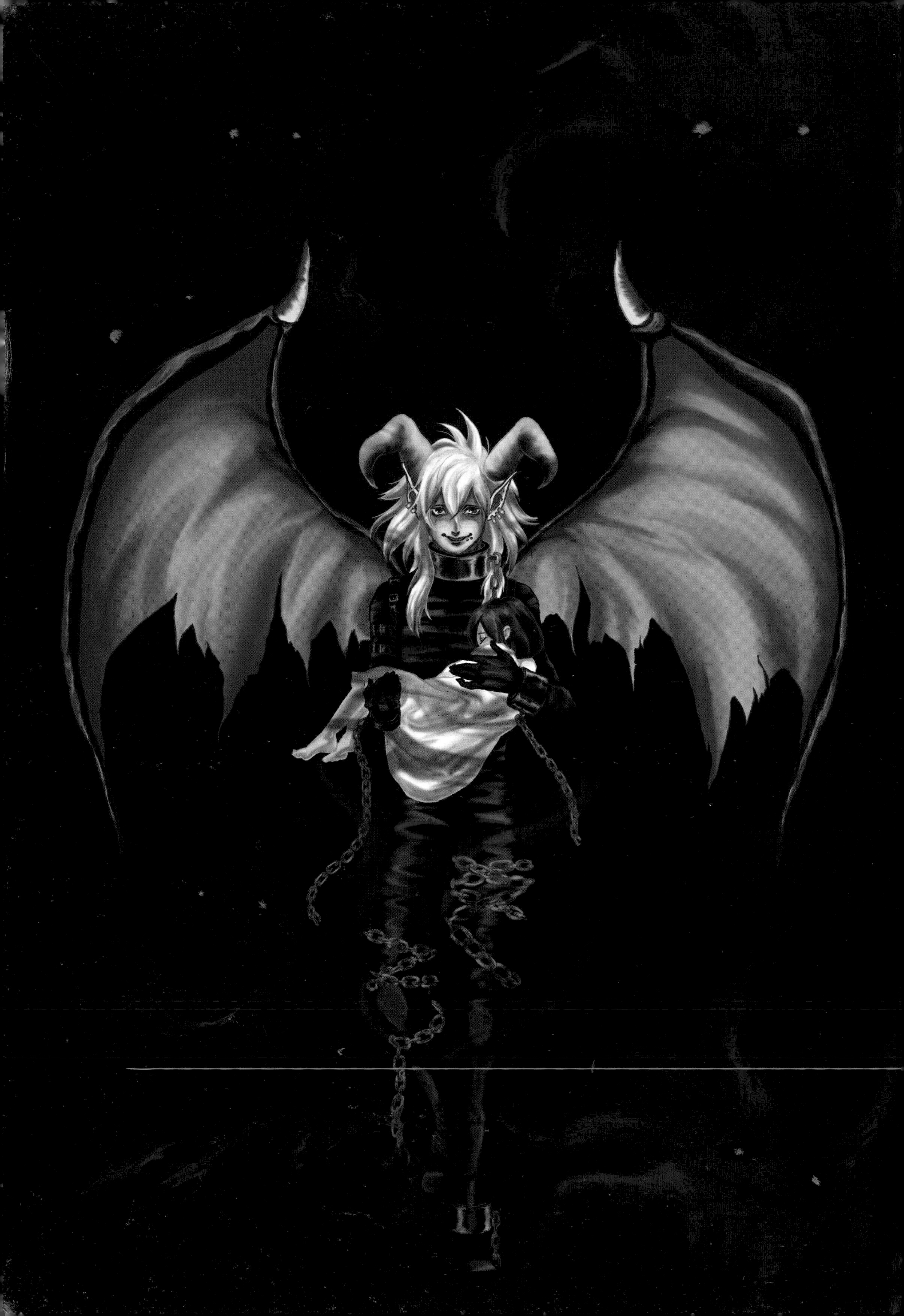

Devil, Demon

Horns

Sinister appearance

Pitchfork

Boots and gloves

➧ Notable Features

- Supernatural being that depicts evil
- Frightening, aggressive and dark with a wretched or deformed appearance
- Possesses magical powers, can transform into other forms and can cause death
- May have horns on the head, hoofed feet or a long tail, may carry a pitchfork
- May be invisible or disguised as a serpent or dragon
- Devil is immortal but demon is not
- Devil controls and leads the demon
- Demon is evil spirit that can dwell inside a human

✝ Outline and Origin

There are many references to the devil's existence in Judaism, Christianity, Islam, neo-paganism, Hinduism, Buddhism and other religions and world folklores in ancient Egypt, Ireland, Italy, and the United Kingdom. In the Bible's Old Testament, he is known as Satan. The Old Testament tells how Satan formed himself into the shape of a serpent to tempt Eve to eat God's forbidden fruit, and therefore depicted evil and treachery. As Satan, the devil is believed to have been the highest of all angels in God's kingdom, but he turned against God in an attempt to rule heaven. He enlisted other evil spirits to support him in this. These spirits, referred to as demons, are thought of as followers of the devil and considered to be strictly under the devil's control. The devil and his demons are powerful and have the ability to inject evil thoughts into the human mind, although the devil is known to be far more superior in this than demons.

The Islamic devil is known as a creature God created from fire, who later rebelled against him. In neo-paganism, he was referred to as a horned god who later became the deity of worship for witchcraft. A devil-like figure exists in Buddhism and is known as a tempter of negative spirits. In ancient Babylon, traces of evil gods were worshipped who had wings and looked like hooded bulls with human heads.

Ancient Eastern religions, Abrahamic traditions and medieval Christianity considered demons as unclean spirits that needed to be closely pursued by exorcists. They were thought of as carriers of disease who inflicted sickness on humans. Demons vary in their levels of power, wickedness and intellect. Like devils, they can travel and influence human events, possess human bodies and minds, and deceive humans to draw them away from the truth. Devils and demons have the mission to kill and destroy all forms of human life.

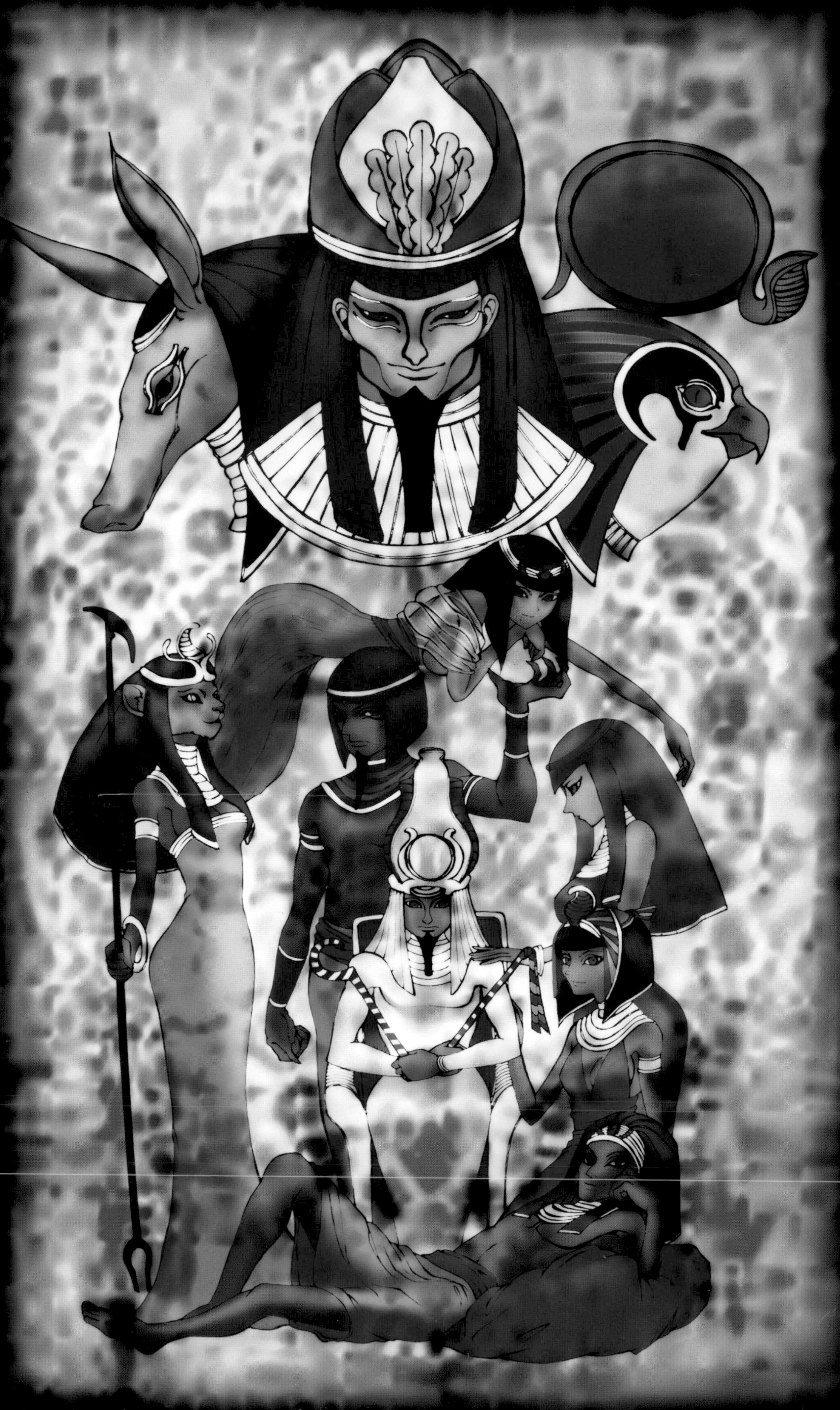

Gods
from Egyptian Mythology

Headgear

Human; may have an animal's head

Gold jewelry

Slim physique

Loincloth around the waist

➥ Notable Features

- Human bodies with heads of animals, plants or objects
- Mixed African, Middle Eastern, Asian or Greek facial features
- Slim with muscular physique
- Wear a white tunic and short loincloth wrapped around the waist
- Wear a crown with horn, snake, sun disc, or flower decoration
- Wear jewelry with animal or plant motifs
- May hold a shield, axe, spear or other war weapon
- Supremely strong and may control storms, floods or rain

✚ Outline and Origin

Ancient Egyptian religion taught the understanding of the celestial bodies and the existence of life after death. The ancient Egyptians' gods and goddesses represented the solar system and the movements of the sun, moon, stars and planets. They also worshipped animals and other objects. It is, therefore, not unusual to find many Egyptian gods with heads of animals, each representing a certain mythological belief.

The creation of the gods and goddesses is described in a myth of Ra, the sun god, who supposedly rose from the ancient sea of chaos and gave birth to Shu, the god of air who had an ostrich's feather on his head, and Tefnut, the goddess of dew and rain who had a lion's head. These two children then gave birth to Geb, the god of the Earth, and Nut, goddess of the heavens, who was a woman sometimes depicted as a cow. These gods then created all the physical elements of the universe.

The most significant aspect of Egyptian mythology is its belief in life after death. It says that after death, a person's soul is manifested in the form of a spirit and integrated with nature. The highest level of the gods was that of the great gods, like Amun, god of the hidden who was depicted with a ram's head; Atum, the original sun god of Heliopolis; and Ra who was depicted with a sun disc on her head. The middle or cosmic level consists of the primary gods and goddesses, like Isis, goddess of motherhood who is depicted with a throne on her head; or Osiris, god of the underworld or afterlife who is depicted holding a flail. The lower level or terrestrial level is home to the secondary gods and goddesses, like Ptah, god of craftsmen who is depicted holding a scepter or staff; or Anubis, god of judgment who is depicted with a jackal's head.

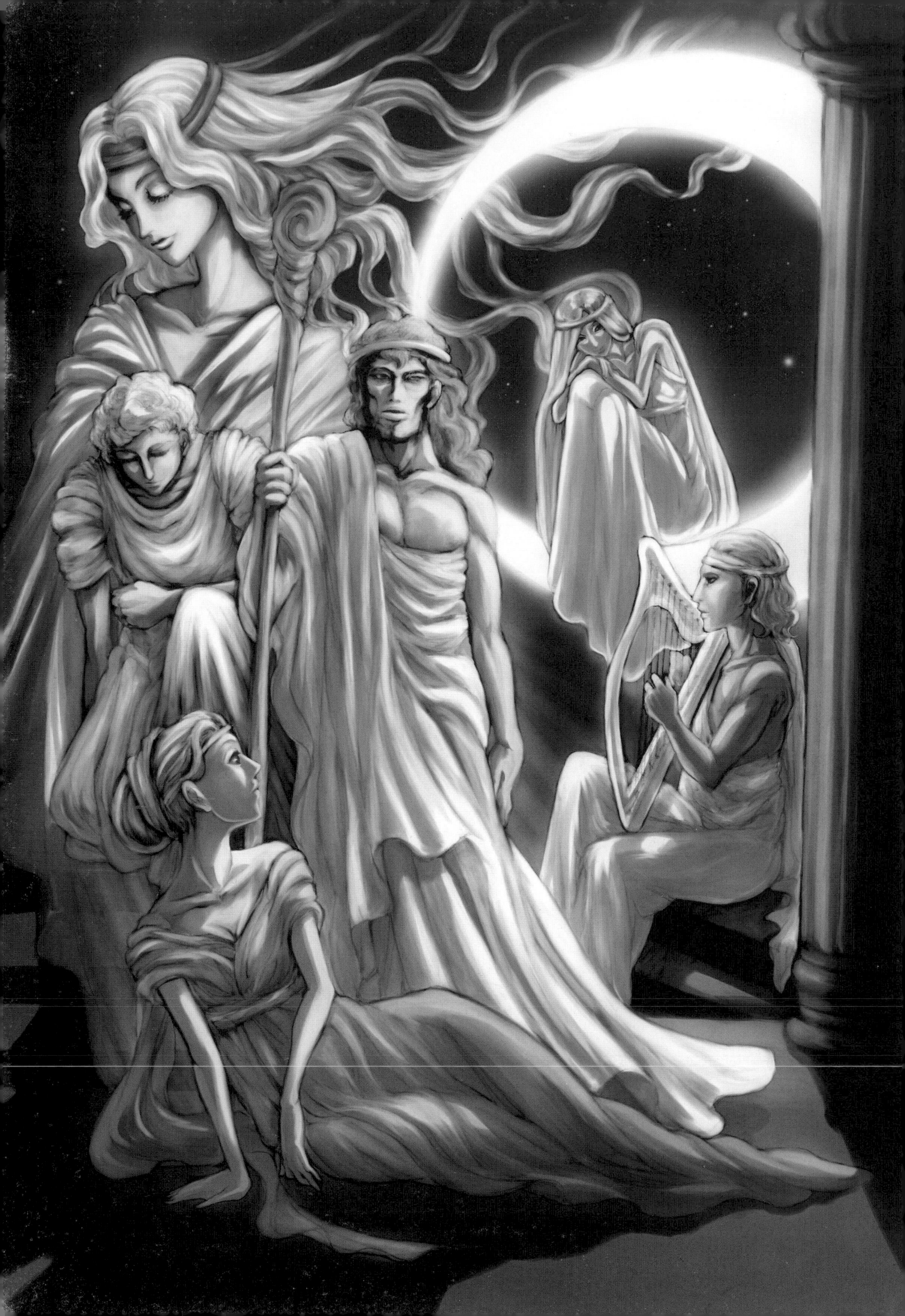

Gods
from Greek
Mythology

Female God
- Blue eyes
- Wings
- Light skin

Male God
- Golden hair
- Bearded face
- Broad shoulders
- Scepter and shield

➡ Notable Features

- Light or dark skin; bright golden, curly hair; blue, grey, brown or blue-green eyes
- Tall with broad shoulders and chest, athletic, may be bearded
- Indo-German, Asia-Minor and Hither-Asiatic facial features
- May have wings, tail or animal head
- Wears short tunic or robe
- May wear a helmet, crown with leaves, breastplate, jewelry and sandals
- May hold shrubs, fruit, scepter, arrows, agricultural tools or scales
- May ride on a horse or chariot

✠ Outline and Origin

An ancient belief depicts Greek gods as originally having been humans who were made into gods by their ancestors and were given divine powers from Egyptians and Phoenicians. Another belief traces them to the early tribes who invaded the inhabitants of the Balkan Peninsula and brought with them their own temple, a pantheon, of gods who symbolized their victory and heroism in battles. The older gods fused with these powerful "new" gods, which made a lineage of gods that defines Greek mythology.

In the beginning, Chaos, the void, filled the world until Gaia, the earth, emerged with Tartaros, the underground depth, and Eros, love. Chaos created night and day. Chaos and Gaia united, and Gaia gave birth to Ouranos signifying the sky, and Pontos, the sea. Gaia then sleeps with Ouranos and they produced twelve gods known as the Titans. Among these gods were the god of the ocean, goddess of the moon and Kronos, who became a deceiver. Kronos killed his father Ouranos and threw his genitals into the sea, which formed white foam that became Aphrodite, the goddess of love. Kronos and his sister Rhea married and produced six major Greek gods that were to be known as the Olympians. Kronos, however, disliked his children and swallowed them except the last-born Zeus, who then became the king of the gods.

Greek gods symbolize various aspects of life. Dionysus was the god of wine and feasts; Hades, god of the underworld and wealth; Hypnos, god of sleep; Caerus, god of luck; Hermes, god of commerce and travel. They are unaffected by disease or wounds, and can maintain eternal youth.

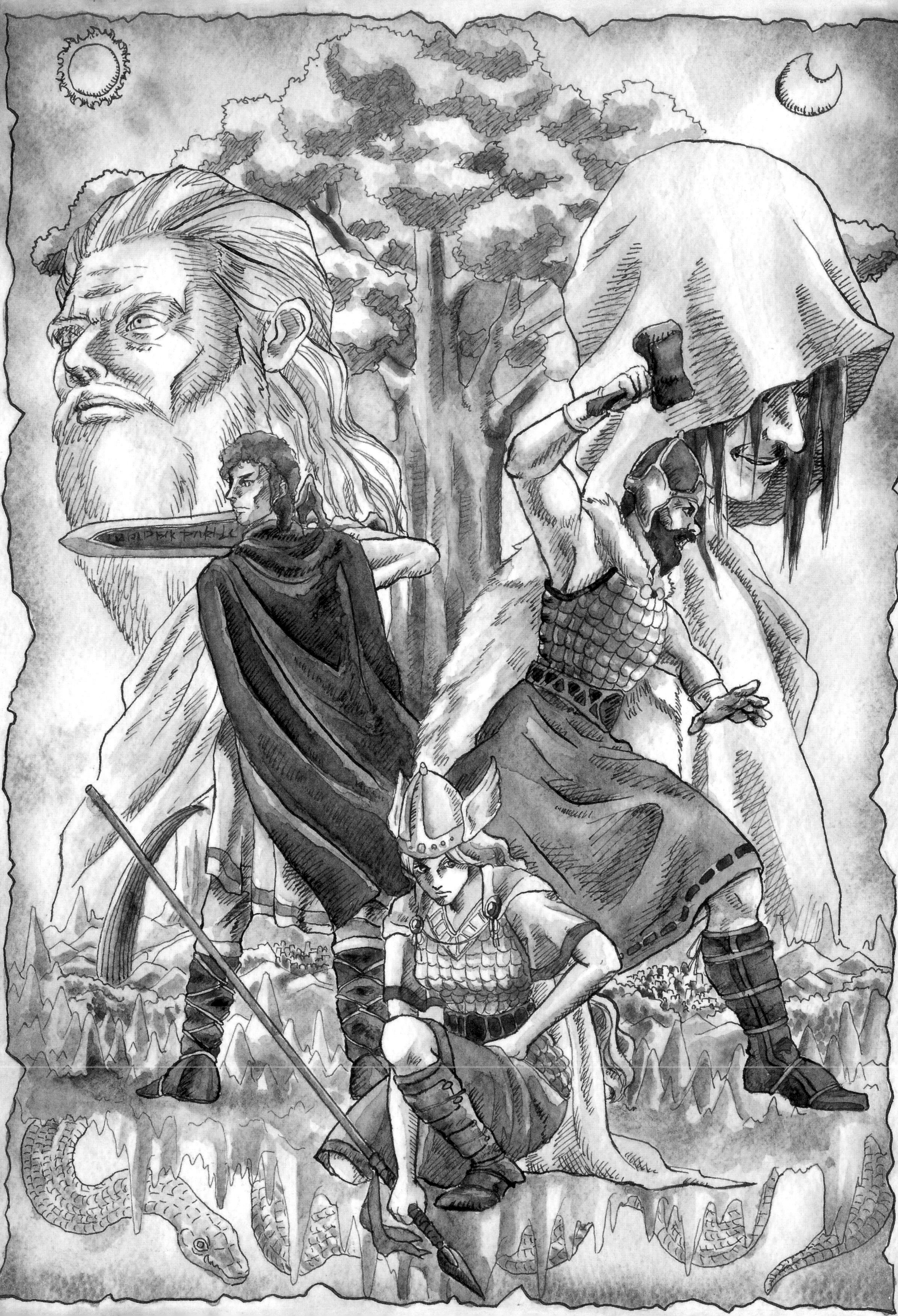

Gods
from Scandinavian Mythology

Fair skin

Leather belt

Tall and slim

Long cloak

➤ Notable Features

- Long-living with supernatural abilities; may also take forms of animals
- Light-skinned, muscular
- Wise, strong and highly skilled
- Can run and move faster than humans
- May wear a cloak, short tunic, breastplate and strapped shoes
- May wear a helmet with horns, hat or crown with jewels
- May carry a hammer, sword, spear, arrow, raven or other animal
- May ride a boar or chariot

✚ Outline and Origin

In Norse mythology, life began with the fusion of fire (Muspelheim) and cold mist (Niflheim) that created Ymir, the founder of a race of frost giants, and Audhumla, the ice cow. Extreme heat made Ymir sweat and lead to the creation of the sun. By drinking Audhumla's milk and Audhumla licking a salt stone, Búri the first Norse god was born. His son Borr, married a giantess, Bestia, and they had three sons: Odin who became the chief god in Norse mythology and gave soul and life to the world, Vili who gave intelligence and the sense of touch, and Vé who gave appearance and facial expression, speech, hearing and sight.

These gods later killed Ymir whose blood flooded the world. Then, they created seven more worlds with Ymir's flesh. They used his blood to create oceans, rivers and lakes, his bones for rocks, his brains for clouds, his skull for the heavens and the light that from this became stars. The gods formed humans from tree trunks and Odin and his brothers gave them life, creating the first humans, Ask and Embla.

Other major Scandinavian gods include Loki, the tricky and malicious god; Thor, the thunder god; Magni, the god of strength; Fenrir, the wolf god; Týr, the god of war; Freyr, the god of fertility, sun and rain.

Odin, the chief god, ruled the world of Asgard, home of the gods. These gods possessed superhuman abilities and can endure injury. They have long lives, but are not immortal. They can control cosmic energy, which can change their shapes and appearances. They are also skilled in agriculture, battle, fertility, and controlling the power of the moon, stars, thunder, and rain.

GREEK GODS FAMILY TREE

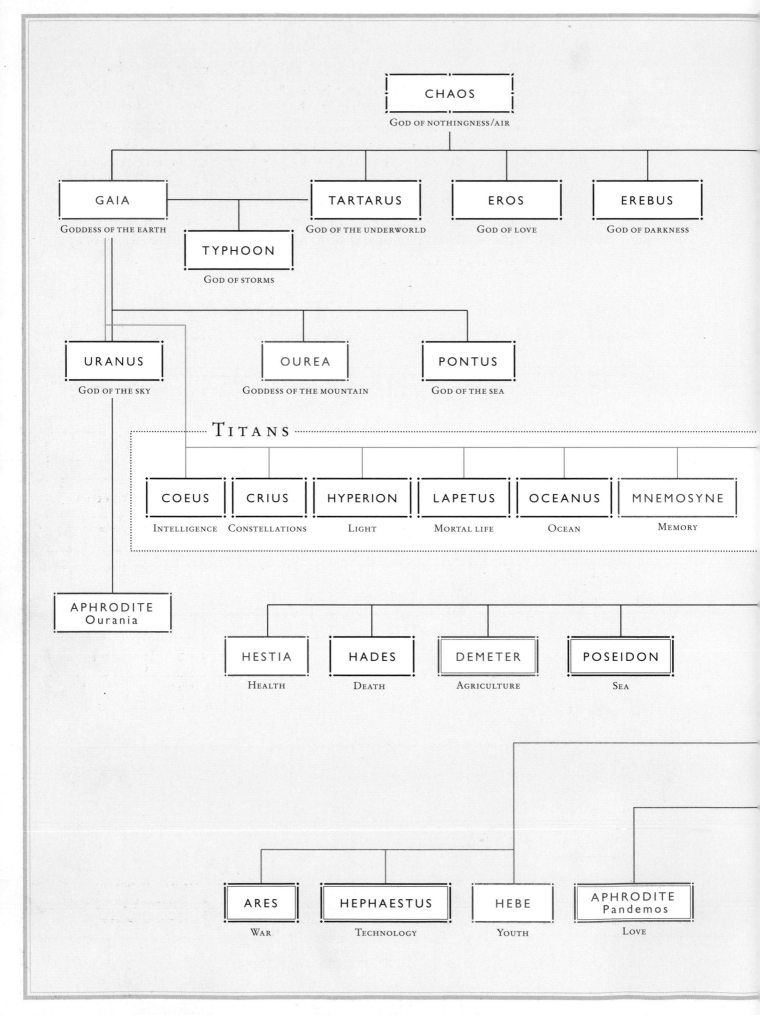

CHAOS
God of nothingness/air

GAIA
Goddess of the earth

TARTARUS
God of the underworld

EROS
God of love

EREBUS
God of darkness

TYPHOON
God of storms

URANUS
God of the sky

OUREA
Goddess of the mountain

PONTUS
God of the sea

TITANS

COEUS
Intelligence

CRIUS
Constellations

HYPERION
Light

LAPETUS
Mortal life

OCEANUS
Ocean

MNEMOSYNE
Memory

APHRODITE
Ourania

HESTIA
Health

HADES
Death

DEMETER
Agriculture

POSEIDON
Sea

ARES
War

HEPHAESTUS
Technology

HEBE
Youth

APHRODITE
Pandemos
Love

The Olympian gods were the mighty gods of the Greek Pantheon in Mount Olympus. Zeus (Jupiter) was the king of the gods and controlled the universe. He was the youngest offspring of Cronus and Rhea, who also bore Hestia (Vestia), Hades (Pluto), Hera (Juno), Poseidon (Neptune) and Demeter (Ceres). Zeus had many wives. Zeus and his sister Hera bore Ares (Mars), Hephaestus (Vulcan) and Hebe (Juventas). But he pursued nymphs, which made Hera very jealous. With Semele, Dionysus (Bacchus) was born; with Leto, Apollo and Artemis (Diana); with Metis, Athena (Minerva); and with Maia, Hermes (Mercury). Aphrodite (Venus) was the daughter of Uranus, but was also said to be borne from Zeus and Dione. Hades was Zeus' brother who lived in the underworld and became the god of darkness and death. Hestia, Zeus' sister, is regarded as one of the Olympian goddesses, and was known as the virgin goddess of the home and hearth.

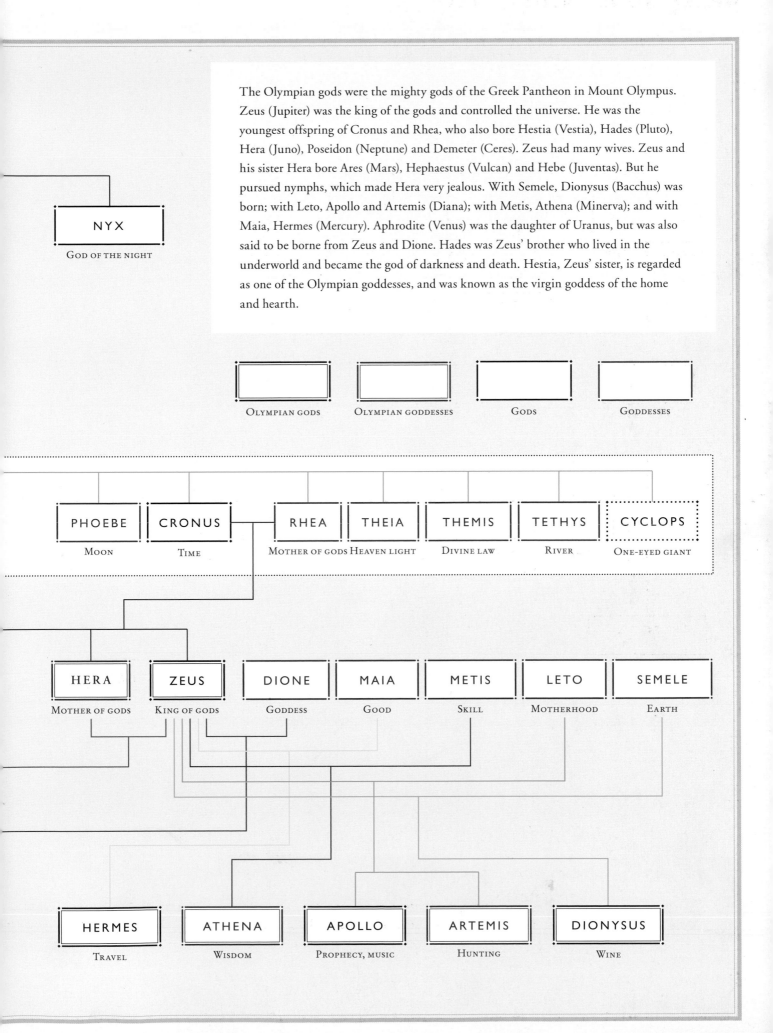

NYX
GOD OF THE NIGHT

OLYMPIAN GODS   OLYMPIAN GODDESSES   GODS   GODDESSES

PHOEBE	CRONUS	RHEA	THEIA	THEMIS	TETHYS	CYCLOPS
MOON	TIME	MOTHER OF GODS	HEAVEN LIGHT	DIVINE LAW	RIVER	ONE-EYED GIANT

HERA	ZEUS	DIONE	MAIA	METIS	LETO	SEMELE
MOTHER OF GODS	KING OF GODS	GODDESS	GOOD	SKILL	MOTHERHOOD	EARTH

HERMES	ATHENA	APOLLO	ARTEMIS	DIONYSUS
TRAVEL	WISDOM	PROPHECY, MUSIC	HUNTING	WINE

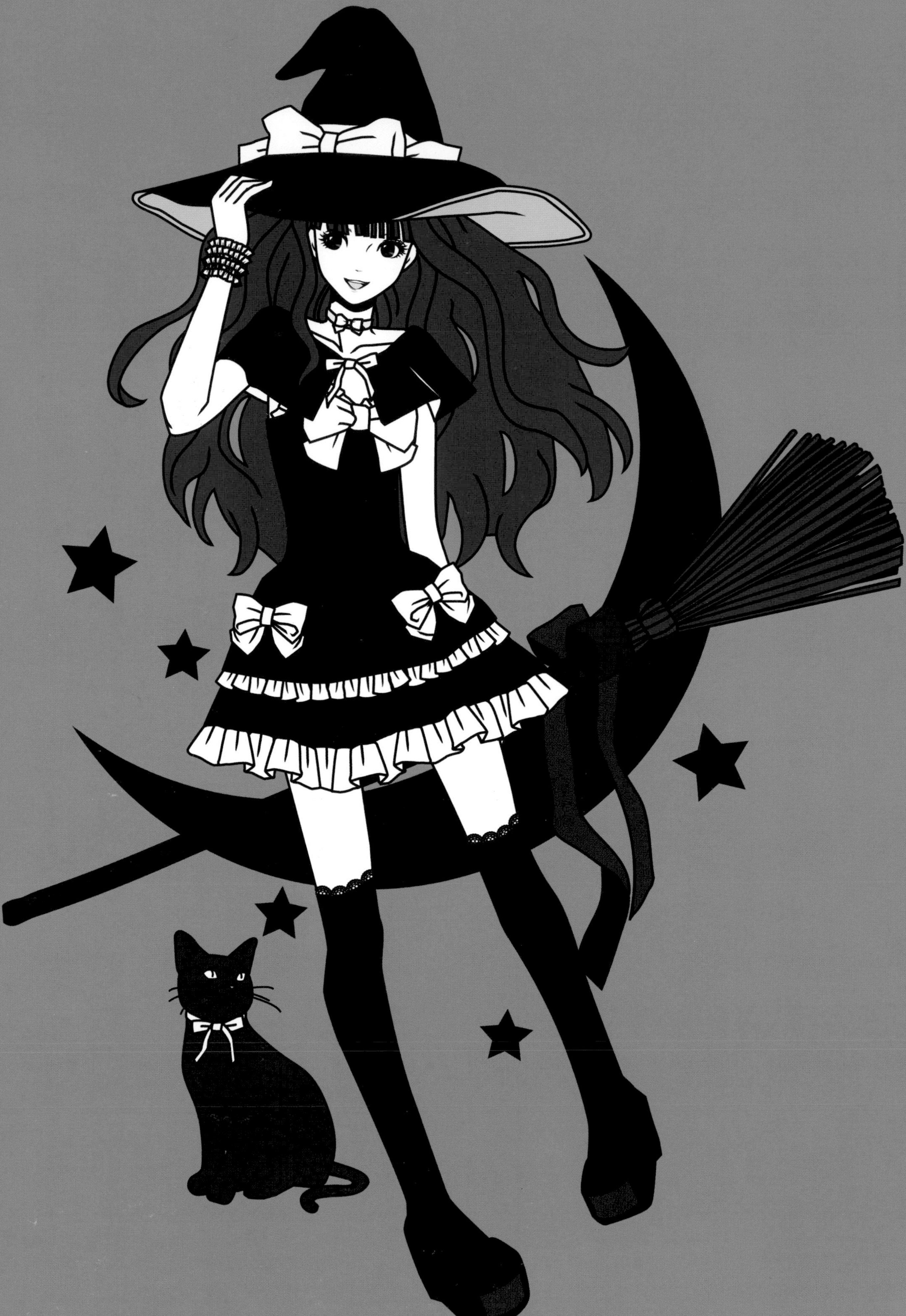

Chapter

2

TENSHOKU

Developing a Character

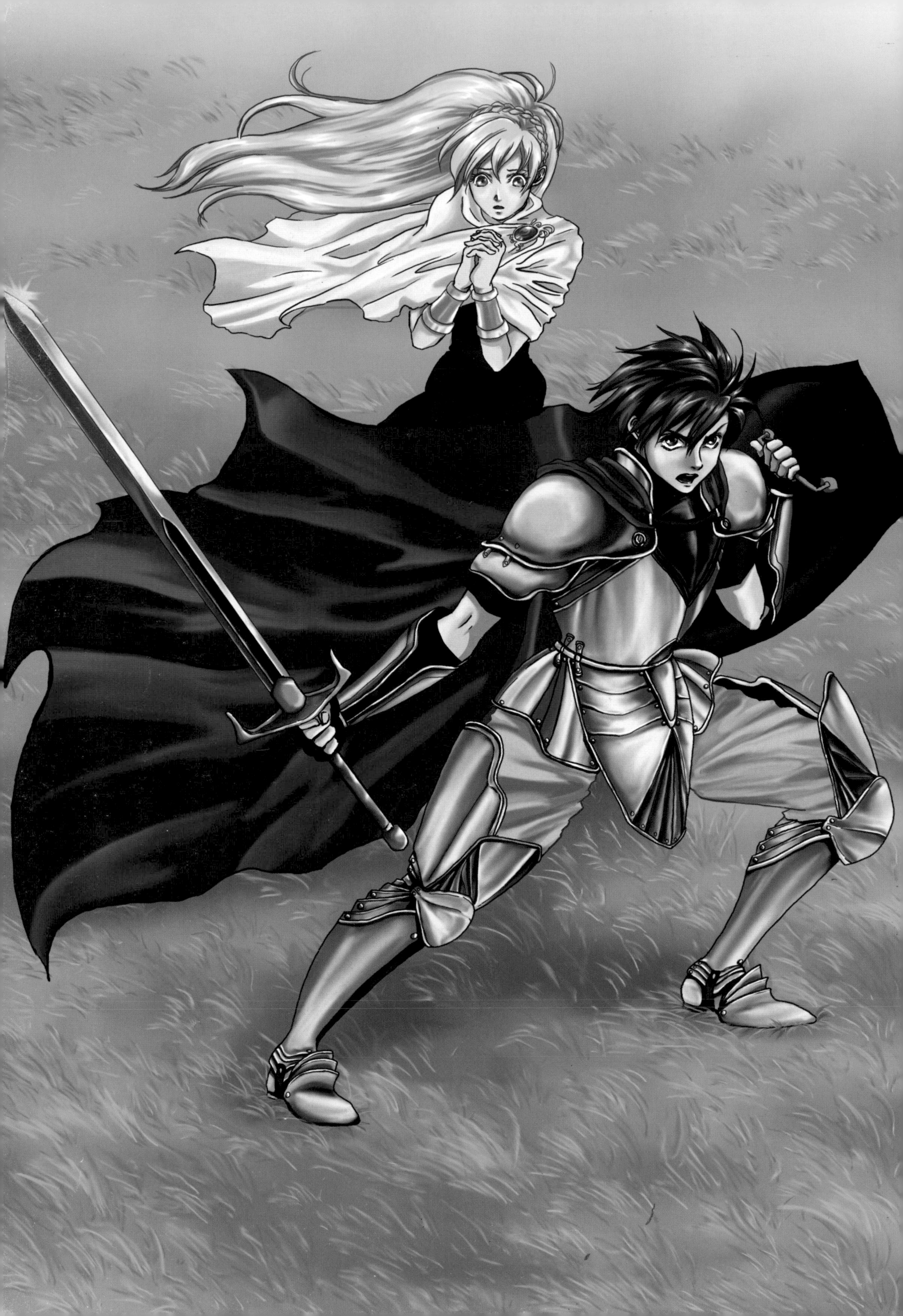

Knight

Rides a horse

European features

Body armor and breastplate

Sword

➡ Notable Features

- May be human, dwarf, elf or gnome
- European features
- Wears linen undershirt and underpants, wool stockings, quilted coat, robe with belt over body armor, breastplate and a headdress or helmet
- Costume shows coat of arms symbol or insignia
- Highly proficient and skilled in use of martial weapons, shield, armor, sword, spear, bow, battle-ax and war hammer
- Usually rides a horse

✛ Outline and Origin

Knights are best known as noble soldiers of the Middle Ages' warrior class in Europe. They arose during the reign of Charlemagne, emperor of the Roman Empire and king of the Frankish empire in the 8th century. They crossed battlefields in large infantry armies, fighting on horseback. There were also traces of cavalries among the Germanic tribes of the 3rd century, and among Arab armies in the year 580. Knights Templar of the First Crusade was a military order of intellectual fighters who wore long tunics with the red cross emblem, and carried swords and bows.

The duty of the knight is to defend the people and protect the law. He abides strictly by justice and righteousness and makes war against those that cause threat to his land. Usually, he pledges his service to a lord or a noble king who might summon him to fight against a group of bandits or disloyal citizens. Knights who do not have a lord, adventure on their own—some to gather wealth and power, others to fight evil. The most distinctive characteristic of a knight, compared to other fighters, is his allegiance to a chivalric code of honor that varies by race and region. Thus, a knight is expected to be loyal, obedient to the law, brave, courteous with others, and sound in mind and spirit.

Human knights are usually mounted on horses, and use longswords and greatswords while elf and dwarf knights can be seen battling on foot and favoring the simple sword and bow. A knight is ranked by his various classes and is awarded a piece of battle equipment when he completes a combat mission. A knight who violates his code of honor may not be allowed to advance to a higher level of knighthood. If this happens, he will be considered a fallen knight or a black knight.

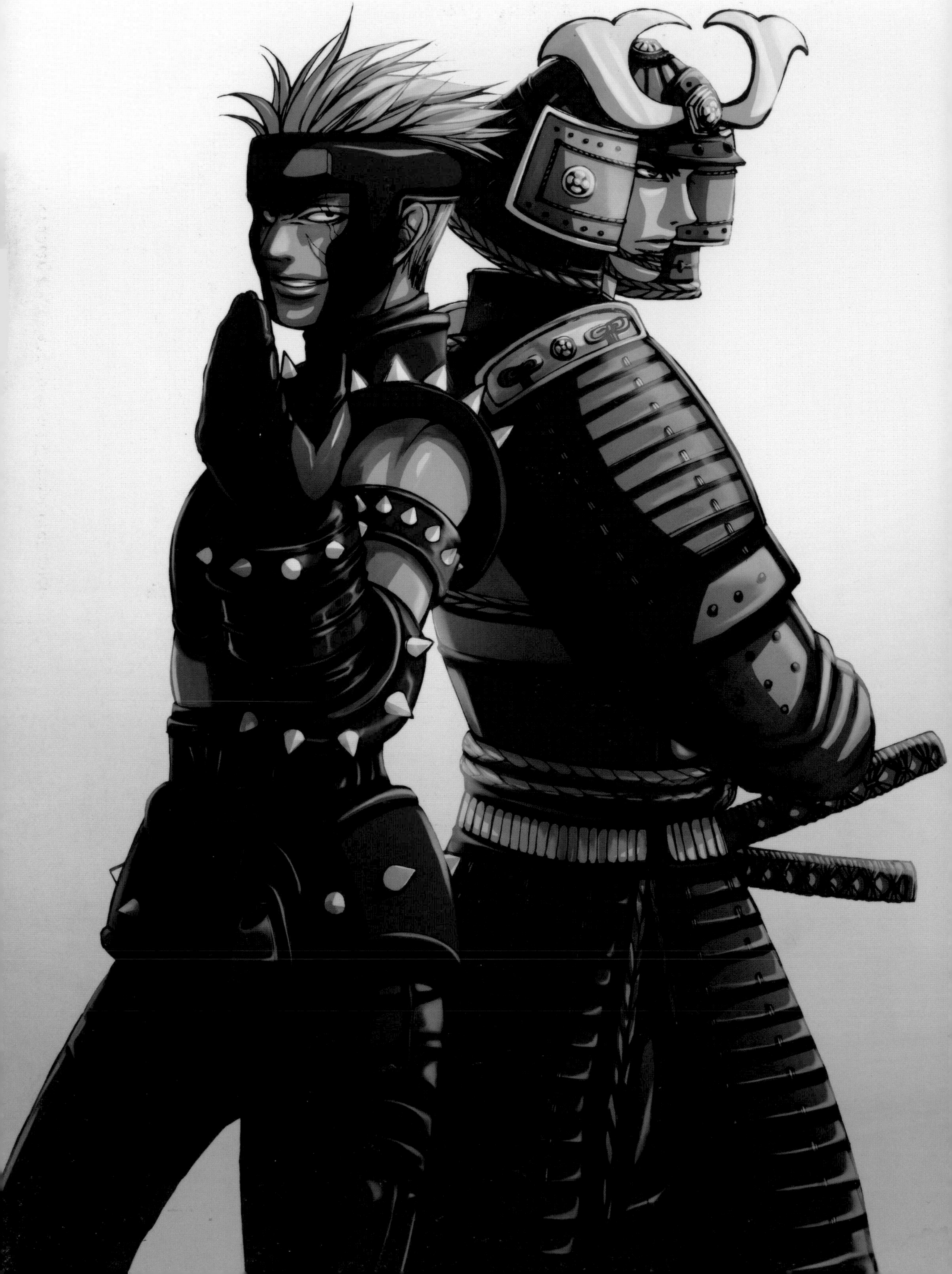

Warrior, Samurai

Headdress

Katana

Sword

Breastplate

Alert posture

Hakama and haori

➡ Notable Features

Warrior

- Usually European
- Physically fit, strong, aggressive, fearless, agile, flexible, confident
- Has physical and mental balance, and a strong desire to win
- May wear breastplate, arm guard, helmet and boots
- Armed with a weapon, such as sword, spear or knife

Samurai

- Japanese
- Loyal, honorable, quick, alert, intelligent, disciplined, possesses military skills
- Has no fear of death
- Dresses in a hakama (divided skirt) and haori (coat), or with an armor
- Fights with a katana (sword), spear and bow, or while mounted on a horse

✛ Outline and Origin

Warriors were the face of heroism in mythological stories—frequently used by kings and queens to conquer enemies. Well-known warriors were Hector, the Trojan prince and greatest fighter of Troy; Athena, the armed warrior goddess of Greek mythology; and the Einherjar, the Norse warriors who died in battle.

The strong and powerful soldiers of the Roman army of the 1st centuries B.C. and A.D. dressed in heavy armor, wore iron helmets, and carried spears, shields and bows. The Spartans of ancient Greece were one of the most feared and respected warrior groups in history. In the East, the Mongols were soldiers trained from youth to be expert horsemen and archers. The kingdom of Nubia (now Sudan) in the heart of African civilization was the center of military power from

3100 B.C. The Egyptians were known as the greatest bowmen warriors. Other well known warriors were the Amazons who fought with bows, spears and battle axes; the Scythians who fought as mercenaries for the Greeks; the Persians, Celtic warriors, and the Ch'in warriors of China.

The Samurai is the military noble class of pre-industrial Japan. They did not become military men until the mid-Heian period, when they were taught the way of the Bushido, learned calligraphy, poetry and music, and adopted aristocratic traits. They were driven by Buddhist teachings and had immense self-control, discipline, loyalty and a strong sense of duty. The samurai is protected by his Japanese combat clothing, katana, his soul; he fights with a bow and arrow or a knife.

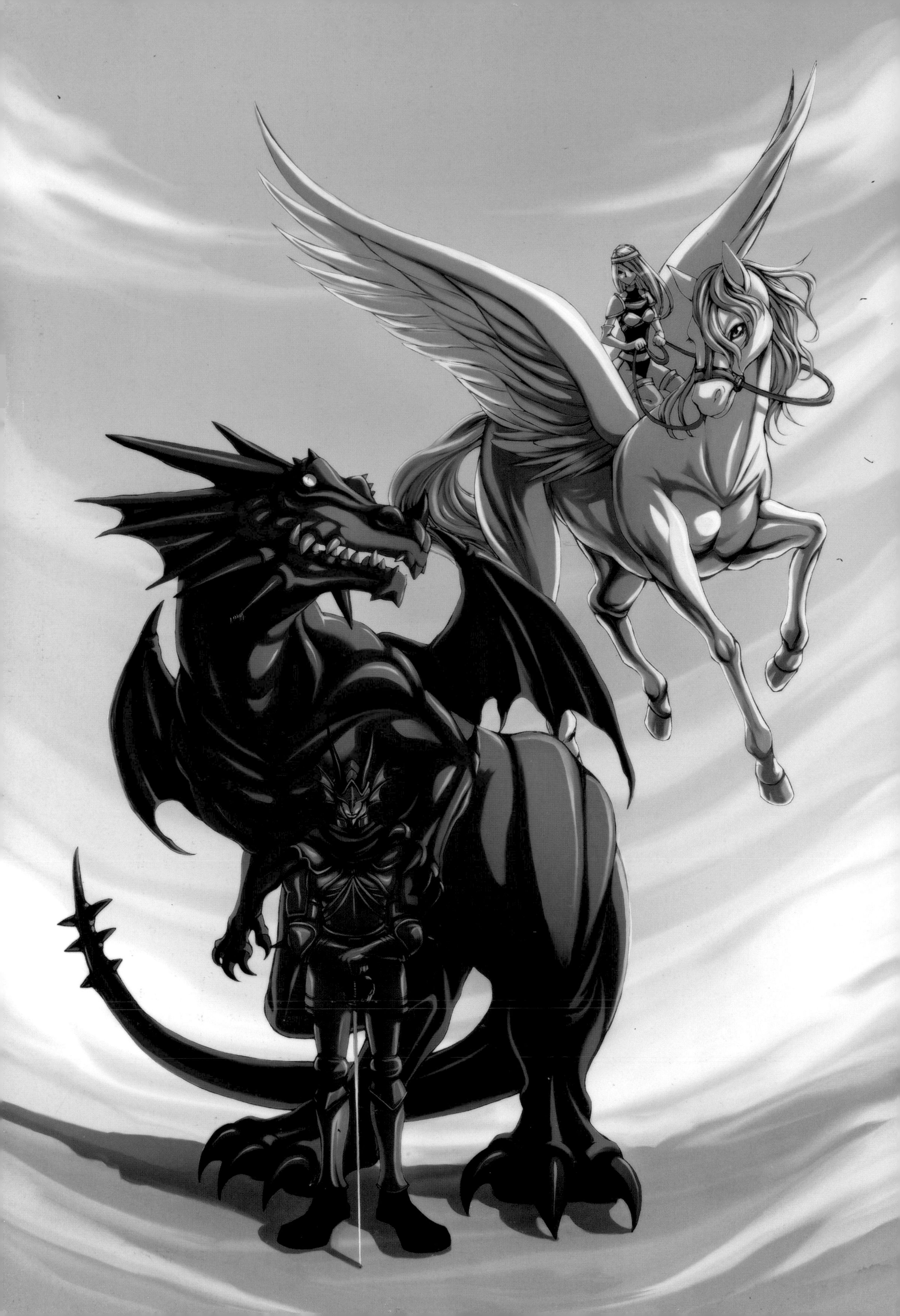

Dragon Knight, Pegasus Knight

➡ Notable Features

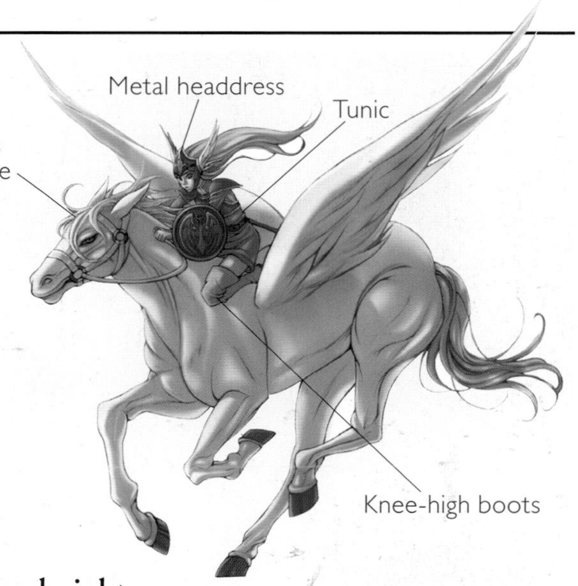
Metal headdress
Tunic
Horse
Knee-high boots

Dragon Knight

- Strong, muscular and fast
- Wears long robe or shawl, breastplate, arm guard, metal boots and headdress
- Uses a spear or sword and a shield
- Rides a horse and slays dragons or rides a dragon and fights enemies

Pegasus Knight

- Courageous, hefty and fast like the dragon knight
- Wears a breastplate, shoulder guards, a long tunic and knee-high boots
- Uses a sword or spear
- Flies and fights on the Pegasus, a flying winged horse
- Can fly on the Pegasus over long distances without fear

+ Outline and Origin

In medieval Europe, many fascinating tales and legends existed about fierce, evil and dangerous fire-breathing dragons that could fly and cause chaos to villagers.

The Knights of the Round Table were well known in the time of King Arthur of England as dragon knights, and slayed dragons to receive the crown of achievement. Other noted dragon knights were: the Norse hero Siegfried who after slaying a dragon, bathed in the dragon's blood thereby making him immune to injury; Beowulf, the North Germanic hero who fought a dragon, but was killed by it; Tristan, the Celtic hero who slayed a dragon for his lover Isolde; and Lancelot who, like Tristan, killed a dragon for his lover, Elaine. There was also the early Christian legendary dragon fighter, St. George, who fought a dragon around the 11th century to save a princess, and St. Sampson who led a dragon from its cave to die in the sea. There are also dragon knights who regularly mount dragons to fight their enemies.

Like dragon knights, pegasus knights also use dragons to fight their enemies. Pegasus, the winged horse from Greek mythology, was the son of Poseidon, who is best remembered as the god of the sea and of earthquakes, but was also the horse god. Because of his form, he became the horse of Bellerophon, the son of the king of Ephyra, and together they fought against the Chimera, a fire-breathing monster.

Like other knights, the dragon knight and pegasus knight dress in noble attire with armor, a spear or sword, and a shield. Both knights are quick in action, and while lacking in defense skills, their creatures allow them to excel in high speed.

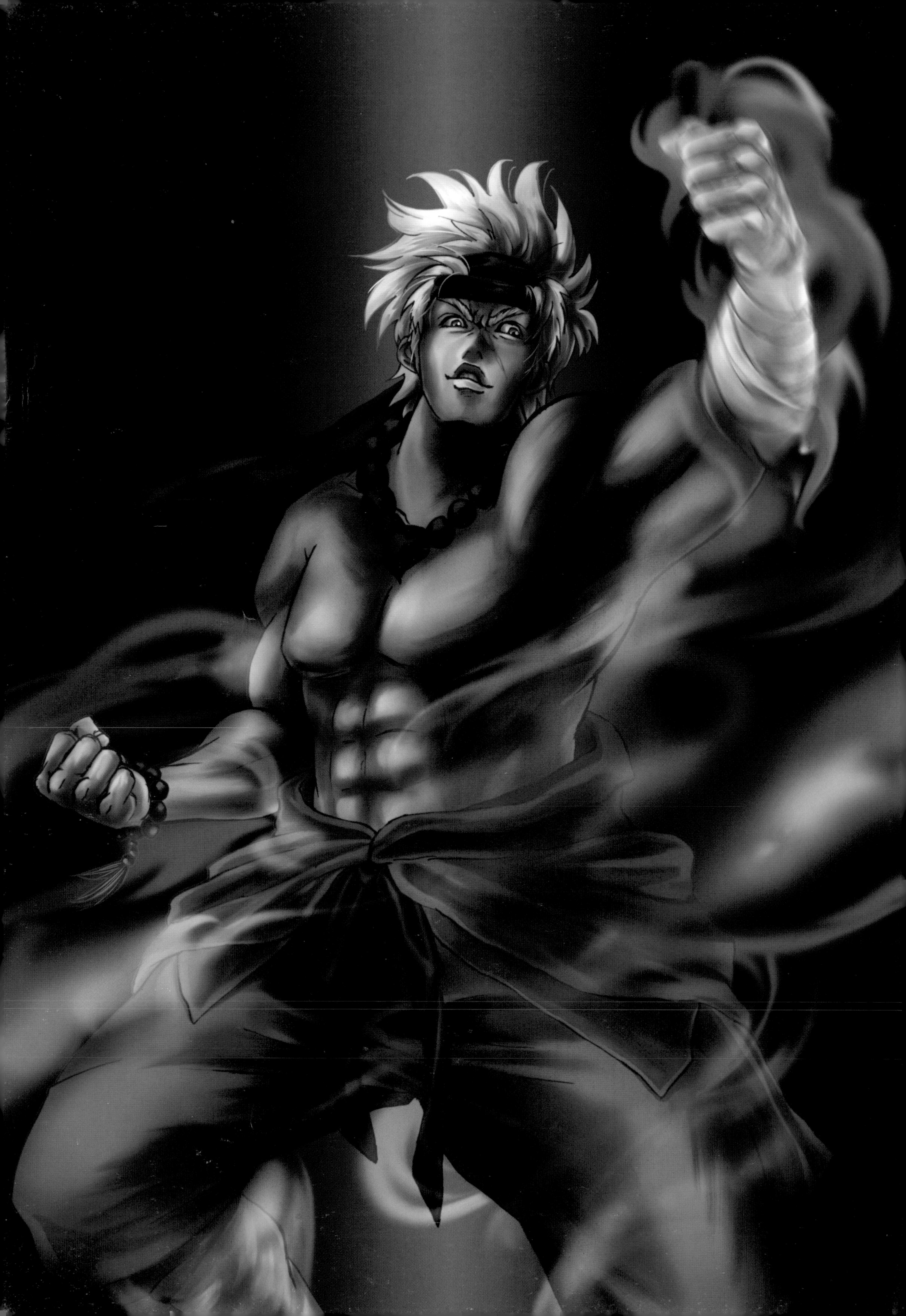

Warrior Monk

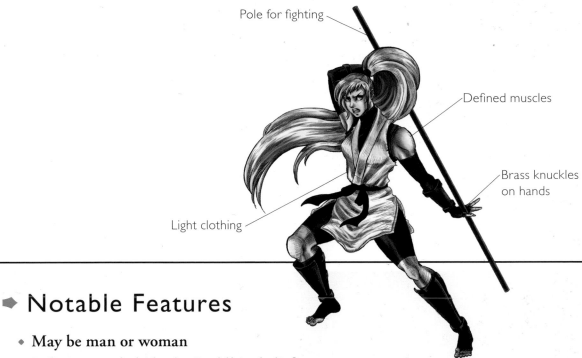

Pole for fighting

Defined muscles

Brass knuckles on hands

Light clothing

➡ Notable Features

- May be man or woman
- Religious and abides by Buddhist beliefs
- May wear light clothing, like a robe and hat, a kimono with a white under-kimono, loose trousers, tabi socks, straw sandals or wooden clogs
- May wear helmet or cloth headdress wrapped around the forehead
- Skilled in martial arts: bare-hand combat, jumps, spins, fistfights and kicks
- May use claws, brass knuckles strapped on hands, bayonet rifle, flamethrower, bow, sword, dagger or pole as weapon, or use hands for fist-fighting

✛ Outline and Origin

Around the 10th century in Japan, warrior monks appeared during political conflicts among various temples and sects of Buddhism. The feuds usually concerned appointing imperial positions in the top temples. They operated in brotherhood groups under a monastic order, and centered mostly in temples around Nara and Kyoto. They were highly skilled in warfare, like the samurai, rode horses, and fought with bows, swords and daggers. Sometimes, they used religious symbols or prayers to intimidate their enemies. The ancient warrior monk dressed in a kimono-like robe, with long wide sleeves that reached down to the knee, loose trousers that were tied below the knee or to the base of the

calf, and straw sandals or wooden clogs.

In the modern age of fantasy, depictions of warrior monks show them as fighters of bare-hand combat who use minimal weapons. The absence of weapons increases their combat ability, so that a very violent punch or fistfight could easily cause body damage or death to their enemies. Some warrior monks are seen with claws or brass knuckles strapped to their hands, which are used for extremely harsh spin fist battles. These warrior monks are able to jump very high and extend their legs in the air. There are also warrior monks in the fantasy world who use flamethrowers; they are often seen clad in heavy armor and helmets.

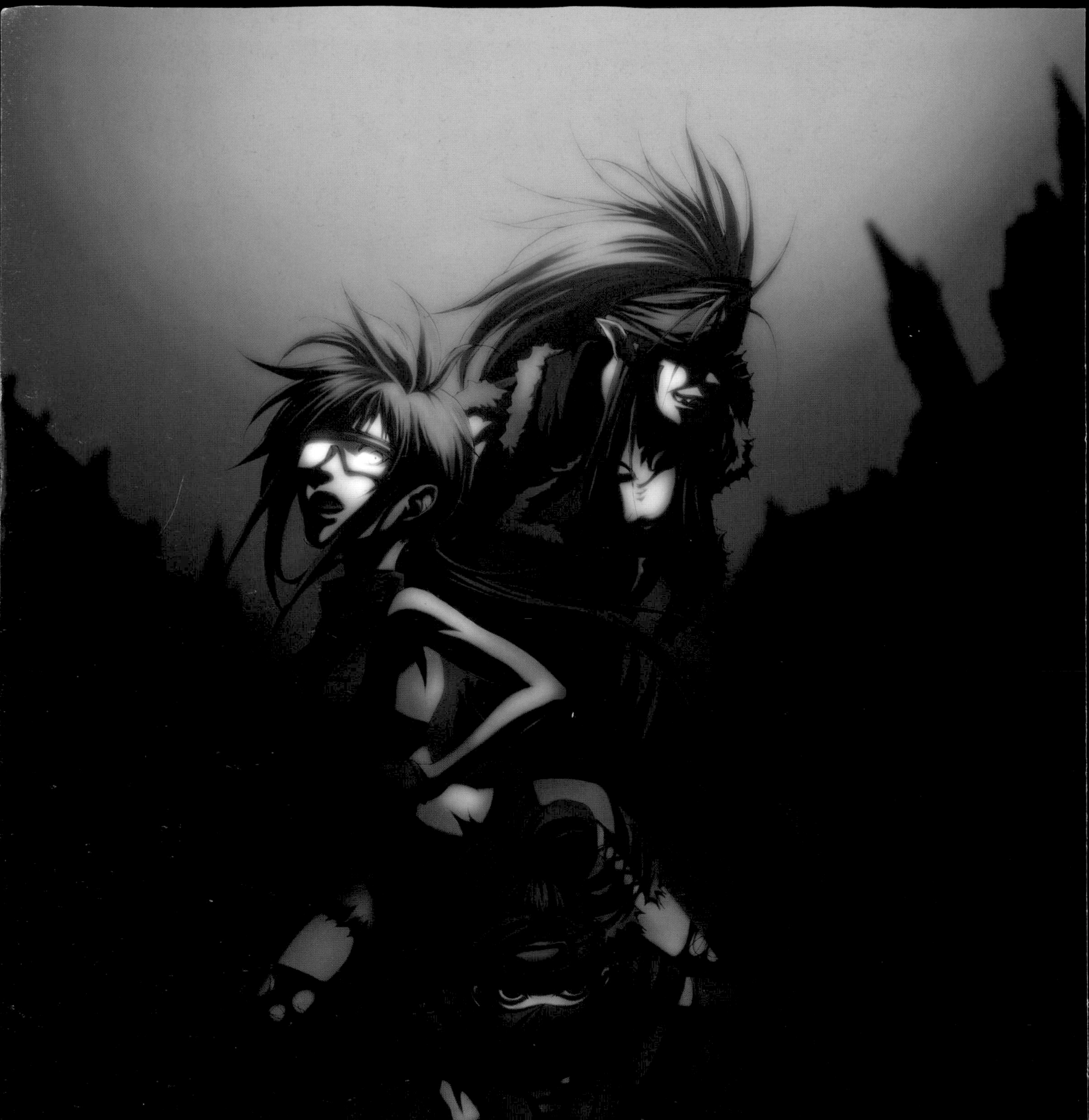

Thief, Assassin, Ninja

Mask

Covering for face

Gloves

Disguise or black robe

Stolen goods

Lean figure

➡ Notable Features

Thief, Assassin

- Highly alert, moves quickly, fights using martial arts
- Fights like the ninja, but uses more modern devices, and dresses more modern
- Wears black top and pants or body suit, black gloves and dark glasses; may wear a disguise or a mask
- Carries a rope, computer or electronic device, tear gas, and knives or guns
- Thief is trained to steal; assassin is trained to murder.

Ninja

- May be both a thief and an assassin
- Wears a breastplate and arm guards, disguise, black robe or a red robe to hide bloodstains
- Wears loose leggings or tucked trousers tightened with a belt
- Uses tenugui, a cloth towel, as covering for face, as a belt, or to aid in climbing
- May carry climbing equipment, spear, rope, hooks, chisel, hammer, trowel, darts or star-shaped discs (shuriken) for stabbing enemies

✚ Outline and Origin

Thieves have long been recorded in history. Robin Hood, the English folklore hero, was said to be a thief during the 12th and 13th centuries. Thieves may steal art, rob banks and counterfeit money or commit computer crimes, fraud or identity theft. They are greedy and are eager to possess material wealth, like writer Maurice Leblanc's famous French fictional character Arsène Lupin and real-life New York mob leader Al Capone (1899-1947).

Assassins are considered more dangerous than thieves, as their main objective is to kill. Two of the most infamous crimes committed by assassins were Julius Caesar's assassination in 44 B.C. in Pompeii and the French King Henry III's assassination in 1589 in Hauts-de-Seine, France. Assassins are well trained in handling special weapons, martial arts and combat. They'll use any means necessary to kill their victims.

The ninja is both an assassin and a thief. From the early 15th to 17th centuries in Japan, mercenaries and spies existed during the Sengoku period. In the 4th century, Prince Yamato Takeru disguised himself as a maiden and assassinated chiefs of Kumaso tribes from Kyushu. Ninjas came from the lower classes and were recruited as spies. They were highly skilled soldiers and trained in psychological warfare, long distance running, fast climbing and martial arts.

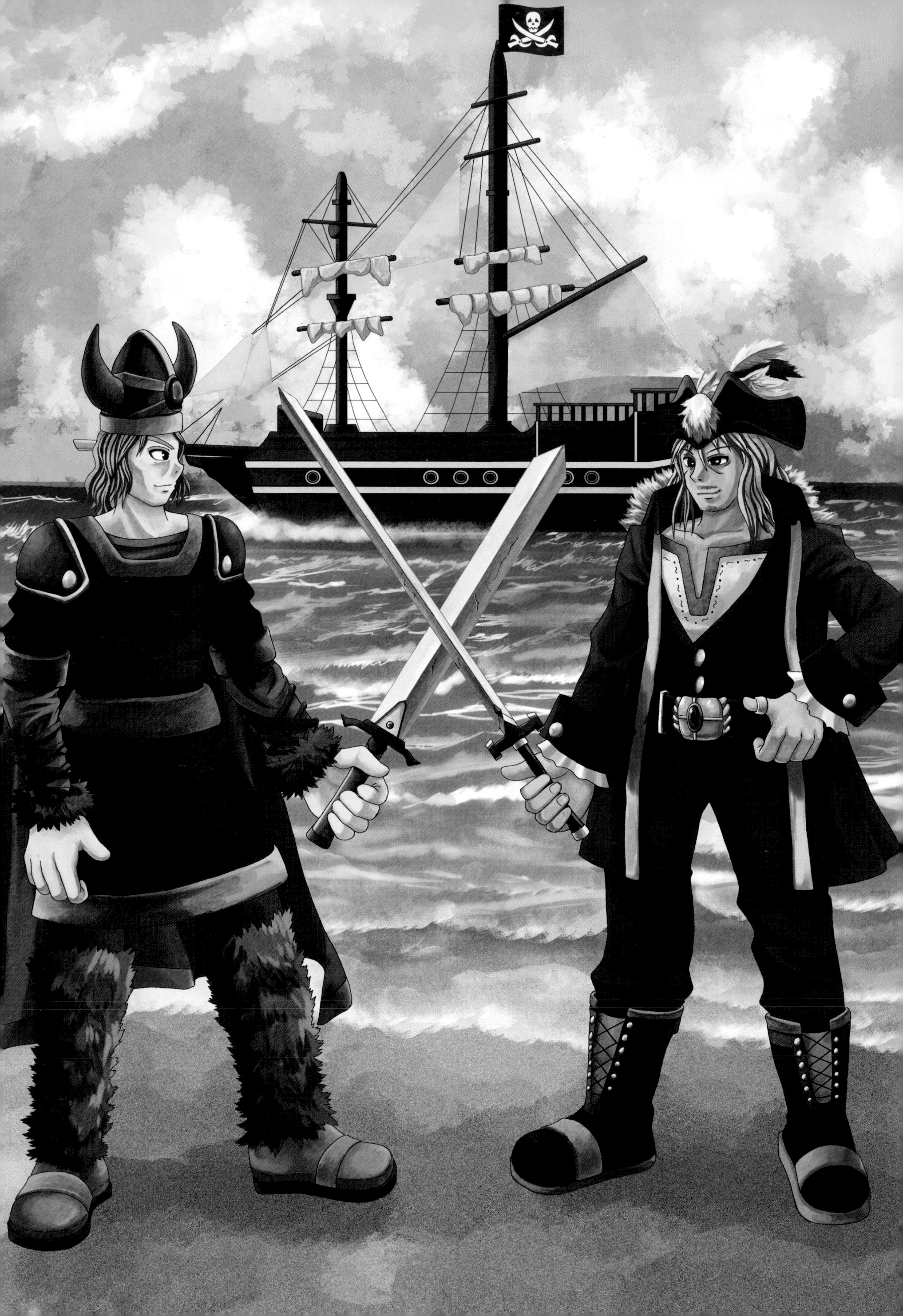

Pirate, Viking

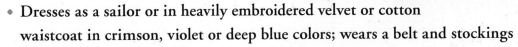

Long hair and beard —

Muscular —

— Waistcoat with belt

Headdress —

➡ Notable Features

Pirate

- **Not limited to one race**
- Usually tall, muscular with rugged features, has long hair and beard or moustache
- Dresses as a sailor or in heavily embroidered velvet or cotton waistcoat in crimson, violet or deep blue colors; wears a belt and stockings
- May wear jewelry like ring, bracelet, chains or earrings
- Wears a tri-cornered feathered hat, and carries a sword or dagger

Viking

- Indo-European, Scandinavian or English
- Muscular, highly athletic
- Skilled in crafts, agriculture, cattle breeding, fishing and hunting
- Wears wool and leather tunic, long cloth trousers held by a sash or drawstring, three-quarter coat with belt and long leather boots
- During battle: wears an iron helmet, heavily protected vests and armor, and carries shield and sword, spear, axe, dagger or bows

✛ Outline and Origin

The earliest pirates were known as the "Sea People" who raided the Aegean and Mediterranean in the 13th century B.C. There were also Greek, Roman and Phoenician pirates who kidnapped children to sell them as slaves.

Pirates are rebellious, clever, and fierce. They travel on vessels and raid land borders, stealing treasures, or fighting other armies. Historically, they have traveled with foot soldiers and slaves who relied on theft and crime for income. The popular tale of the Pirates of the Caribbean is based on the seizure of two Spanish treasure ships in 1523, and extends until the peak of piracy in the mid-1720s.

Vikings are often Nordic pirates who hail from medieval Europe during the middle ages to the 19th century. They were warriors, explorers, merchants and looters who became active from 783 to 1066 along the coasts and rivers of Western Europe. They were said to originate in the ancient Nordic homelands between the Black and Caspian Seas. They made their livings through agriculture and trade and retained their Indo-European religion, culture, language and military skills longer than any other tribe. They pursued robbery, trading, warfare and drinking, but had a visible sense of family unity, brotherhood, and loyalty. They also engaged in hunting, fishing and other skilled crafts. They often wore horned or winged helmets and chain mail shirts, and carried a shield, sword, spear, axe or bow during battles.

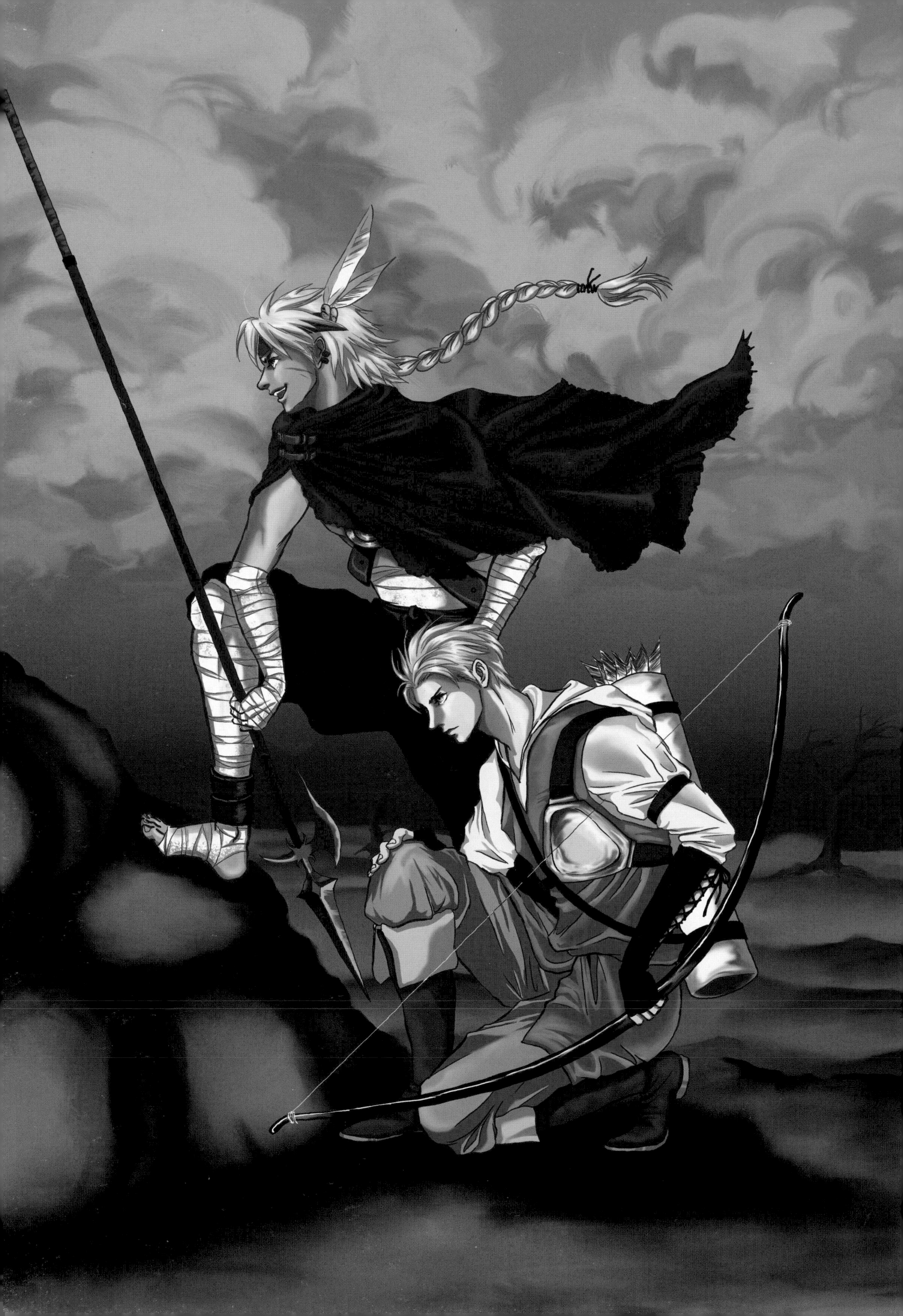

Archer, Hunter

Leather clothing

Spear

Bow and arrow

Gloves

➡ Notable Features

Archer

- Expert in fighting with a bow and arrow
- Has strong, muscular features
- Medieval archer wore long hooded gown or long jacket and hat, layered shirts or vests, loose trousers fitted at the knees and tucked in high-laced boots
- Wears a bracer or arm guard and a chest guard, glove or thumb ring
- May ride a horse

Hunter

- Expert in pursuing live animals or birds
- Physically fit, well-trained and has a good sense of focus and speed
- May wear leather or cloth armor and a helmet
- Uses spear, sling, rock, axe, atlatl or bow and arrow
- May ride a horse, but usually hunts on foot

✛ Outline and Origin

The bow used for archery was invented during the Paleolithic or early Mesolithic period. Archery existed in north Hamburg in Germany as early as 9000-8000 B.C., and across Africa, stone points that were used as arrowheads were made about 60,000 years ago. In ancient Egypt and during the classical civilizations in Persia, India, Korea, China and Japan, armies consisted of trained archers.

In Greek mythology, Apollo was the god of archery, Artemis was the goddess of the wild and hunting, and Odysseus was often seen with a bow. Roman armies depended highly on archers who were mounted on horses. To be an archer, one had to fulfill basic training in the use of the bow and arrow, and to have discipline, concentration and dedication to the nobles, kings, and armies who used them for battle.

Hunting existed well before archery, and its use as a means of gathering food has been traced back to the Paleolithic age. The early man used a spear and stone tools to hunt animals. In ancient Mesopotamia, kings rode on war chariots to hunt lions and tested their men with hunting missions to determine the degree of their bravery. Skulls of reindeers, antlers, deer and other animals were kept as trophies and symbols of victory.

The archer and the hunter are popular characters in the fantasy world and can be human, elf, half-elf, dwarf or humanoid. They possess strength, intelligence, wisdom and charisma, and may use armor or shields. They fight with a bow, dagger, axe, spear, javelin or darts, and some of them may have magical powers. The wild hunter has pets that he can train and tame to assist him in battles. He is a marksman and a skilled fighter.

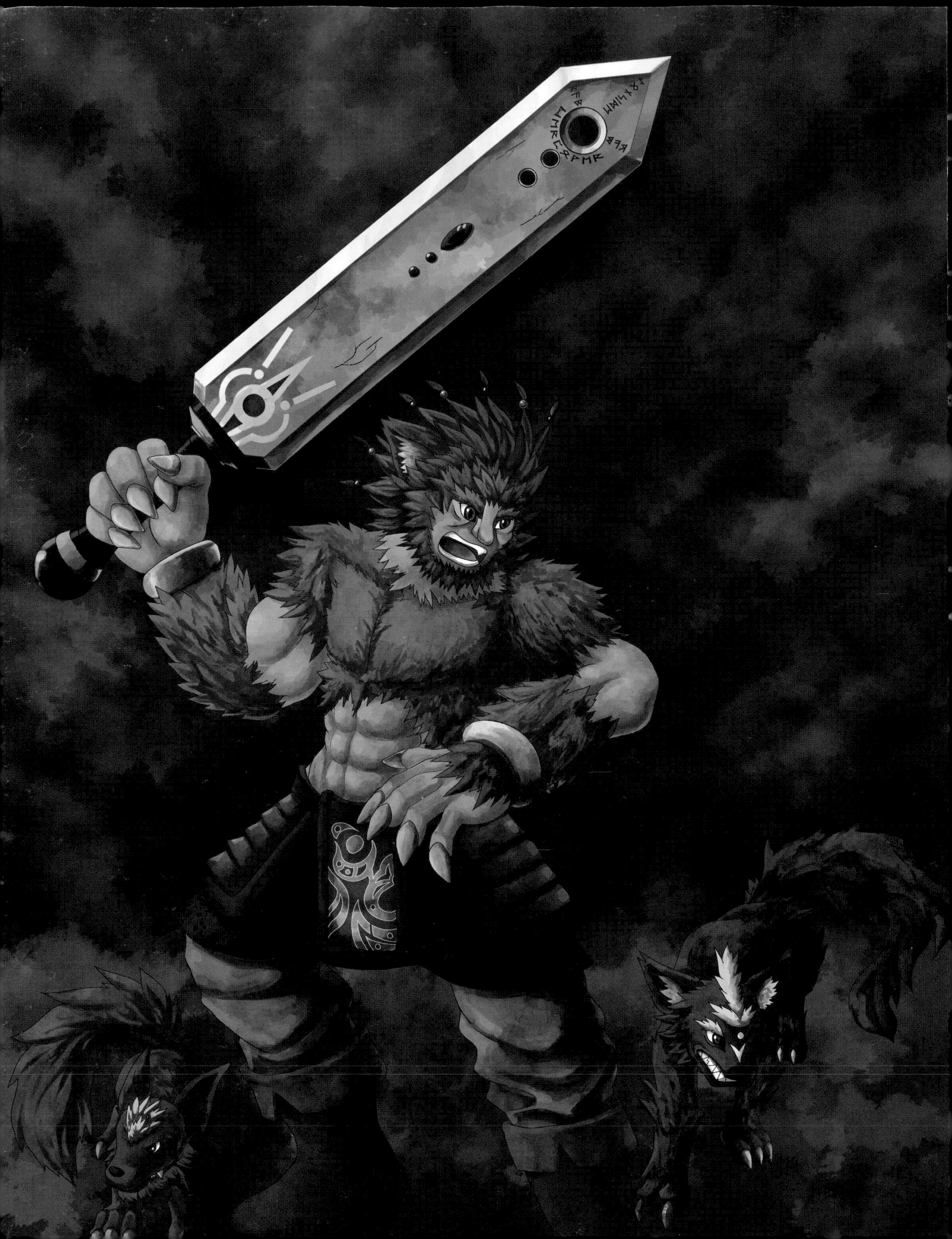

Beast Master

Beard and hairy muscular body

Half-orc or multi-formed creature

Lives with other animals

Clawed fingers

➡ Notable Features

- Commands wild animals to fight and attack
- Huge half-orc or multi-form creature with claws, fangs or horns
- May have long beard and hairy, muscular body
- Strong, agile, and has powerful ability to crush or kill other creatures by quickly attacking them from a distance
- May wear headdress, robe or body armor
- May carry weapons, such as sword, axe, dagger or club

✛ Outline and Origin

Greek myths and legends speak of a wide variety of beasts, generally created to serve and protect the gods and goddesses they were associated with. Beasts were multi-formed and came in various shapes and sizes, mostly combining the forms of two or more animals with a human form.

The beast master refers to a fictional character in the fantasy world that is usually a half-orc. Orcs originate from Old English literature, primarily J. R. R. Tolkien's fantasy stories about a warlike humanoid creature that is brutal, sadistic, and enjoys destroying and hurting other creatures.

In the fantasy world, the beast master is a warrior hero who commands animal creatures to obey and serve him. It lives in the wilderness with other animals and birds, like hawks, bears or giant lizards, and communicates with them to join him in combat against other wild species.

The beast master may use its charm and intelligence to outwit another creature, or may use weapons, such as swords, clubs, daggers or axes to force their compliance. There are many types of beast masters, such as the night elf beast master or the orc beast master—each one with its own unique abilities and powers.

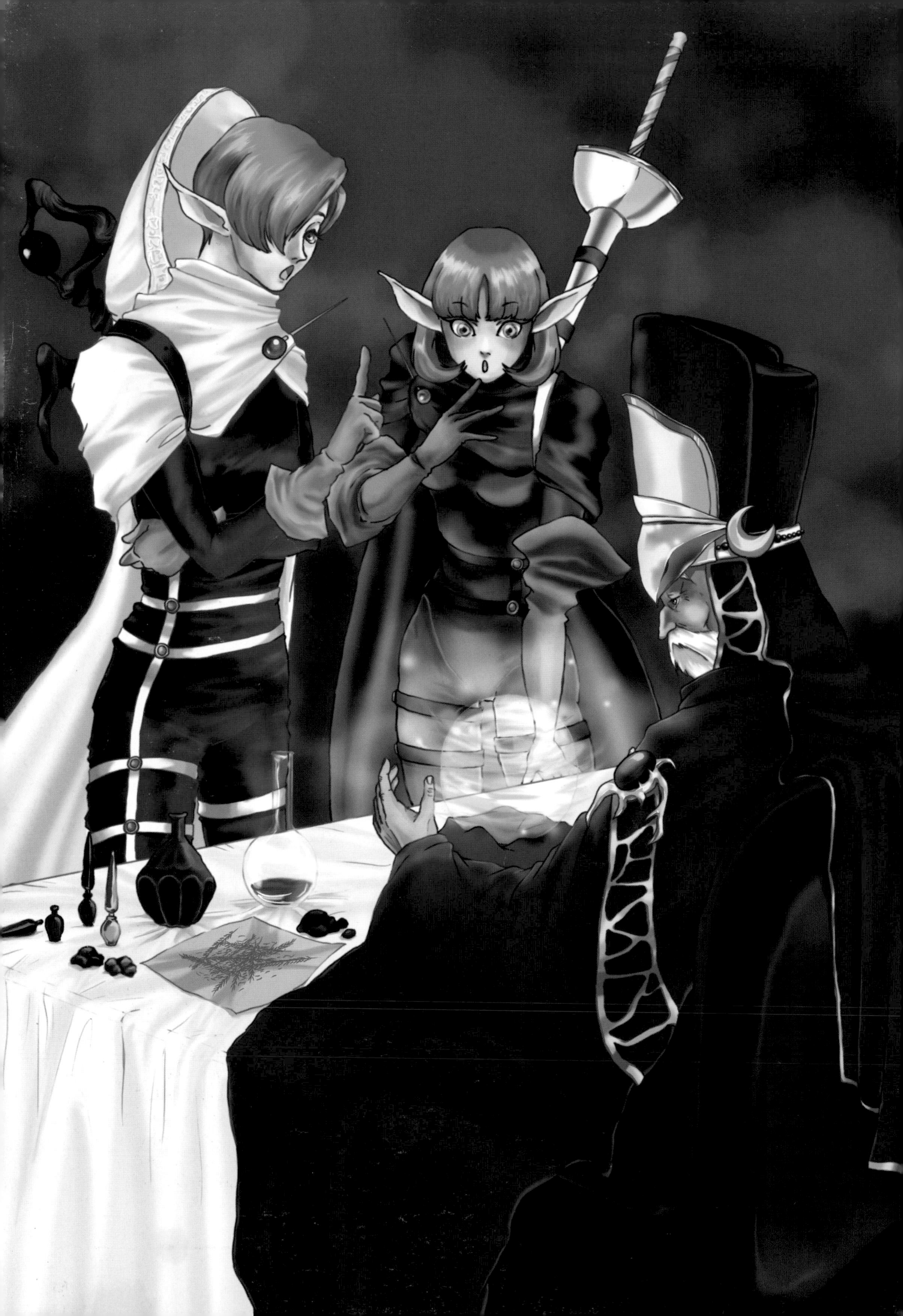

Wizard, Sorcerer, Sorceress

Pointed hat

Old and white-haired

Loose robe

Stick or wand

➡ Notable Features

Wizard

- Usually old with white hair and a long, white beard
- Extremely intelligent, curious, and experimental
- May wear a loose robe and a wide, pointed hat with a star, moon or other astrological motif
- Carries a long stick and a crystal ball, wand, book, potion, scroll or bell
- May attack without being physically present or visible

Sorcerer, Sorceress

- May be human or half-human, half-animal or spirit
- Has long hair, powerful eyes and long nails
- Undisciplined, barbaric and violent
- May dress like the wizard and have black or white demon-like wings
- Fights using spells or weapons, such as spears or short spears

✚ Outline and Origin

Stories of wizards can be traced back to 1400. They appear in many Shakespearean, Welsh and English fairy tales and legends. Some stories tell how their magical powers are acquired by spying on a god while he performs spells. During the Renaissance period, the Achaean region in Greece bred scholars who studied magic. These wizards summoned demons and devils to acquire superior knowledge and power, but also tricked people to take advantage of them. When confronting their enemies, wizards use their magic spells as self-defense. They can create fire and frost or use the power of transformation.

Like wizards, sorcerers and sorceresses use spells against enemies, but sorcerers and sorceresses are usually evil and specialize in black magic.

Wizards learn their powers through advanced study, but sorcerers and sorceresses believe their power is inherent, and this leads them to more violent and barbaric than the wizards.

Sorcerers and sorceresses are frequently thought to be descendants of dragons, which explains their ferocious characters. They can cause sickness and plagues. They can use daggers or long sticks for attacking their enemies, or they can use their greatest power, their charisma and psychological influence.

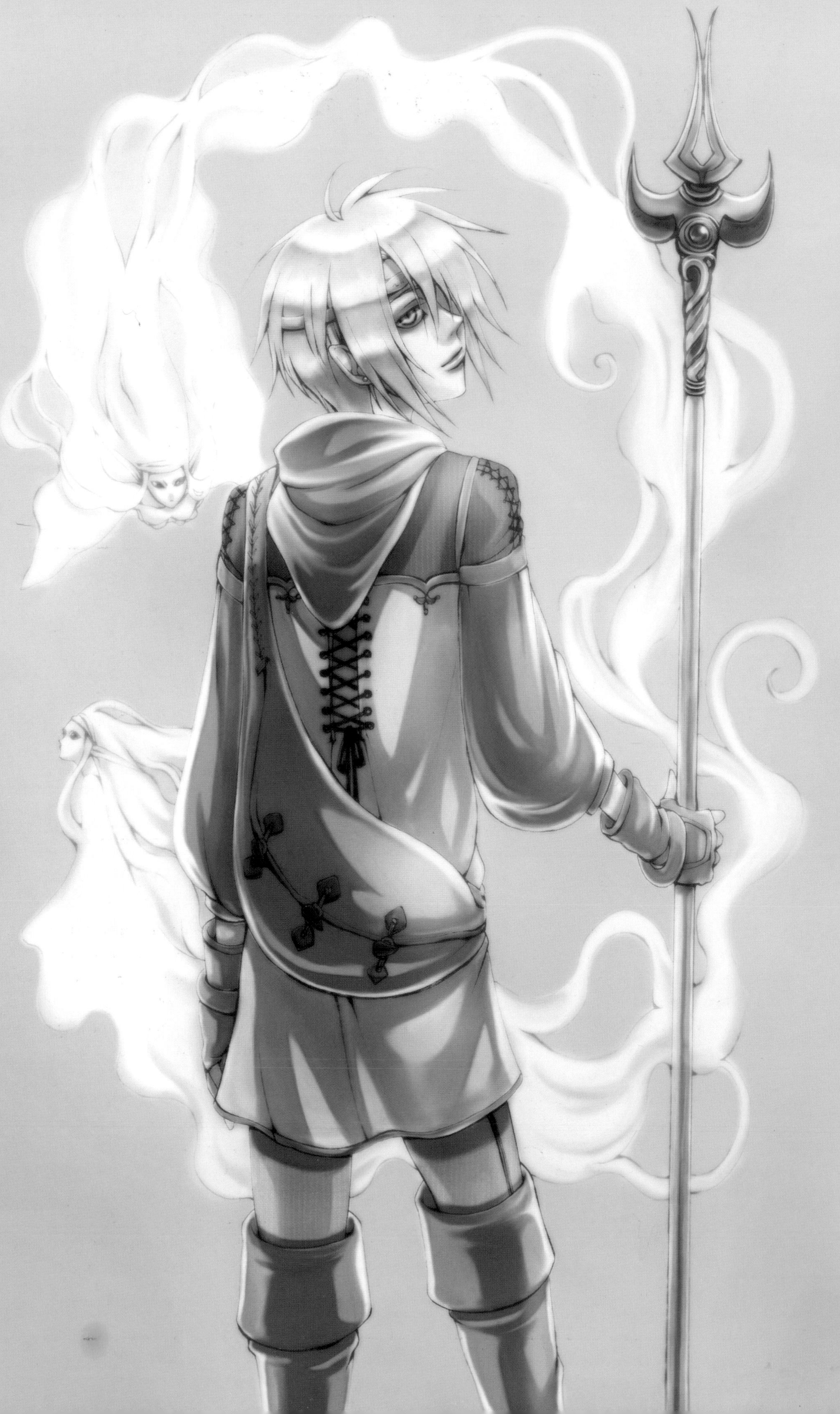

Summoner

Young human

Physically fit

Spear

Long robe or dress

➡ Notable Features

- **Young human with astral abilities and ability to communicate with spirits**
- **Physically strong, agile and possesses skills for fighting**
- **May be dressed casually in a tunic and high boots, wear arm braces and carry a sword or spear**
- **May wear a long robe with a headdress or armor and helmet**
- **Can perform magic or cast spells**

✚ Outline and Origin

The act of summoning demons can be traced back to the Middle Ages when black magic was frequently used. It was an ancient belief that diseases were born from evil gods, and so people sometimes summoned demons to banish sickness. Other times, people summoned evil spirits or demons to cause harm, to request favors from the demons, or be taken under their spell. A summoner must be familiar with demonic rituals and the unique qualities of the demon he or she summons. The summoner should understand what sacrifices must be offered to summon a particular demon, what incense and gifts are needed to appease the demon and the ways to control it.

Many demon summoners are excellent warriors who can summon monsters and use their magic for healing and creating fire, but some have trouble controlling the demons or their own powers.

In the fantasy adventure novel *The Summoner* by Gail Martin, the hero is a prince who avenges the cruelty of his brother, and seeks supernatural help by using his special ability to communicate with and control spirits. The spirits help him create a balance between the living and the dead. A similar plot is seen in the fantasy game Summoner, which tells the story of a young man who summons a demon to save his village from attack, but instead causes its destruction because he is unable to control the overwhelming power of the demon and his enormous powers a summoner.

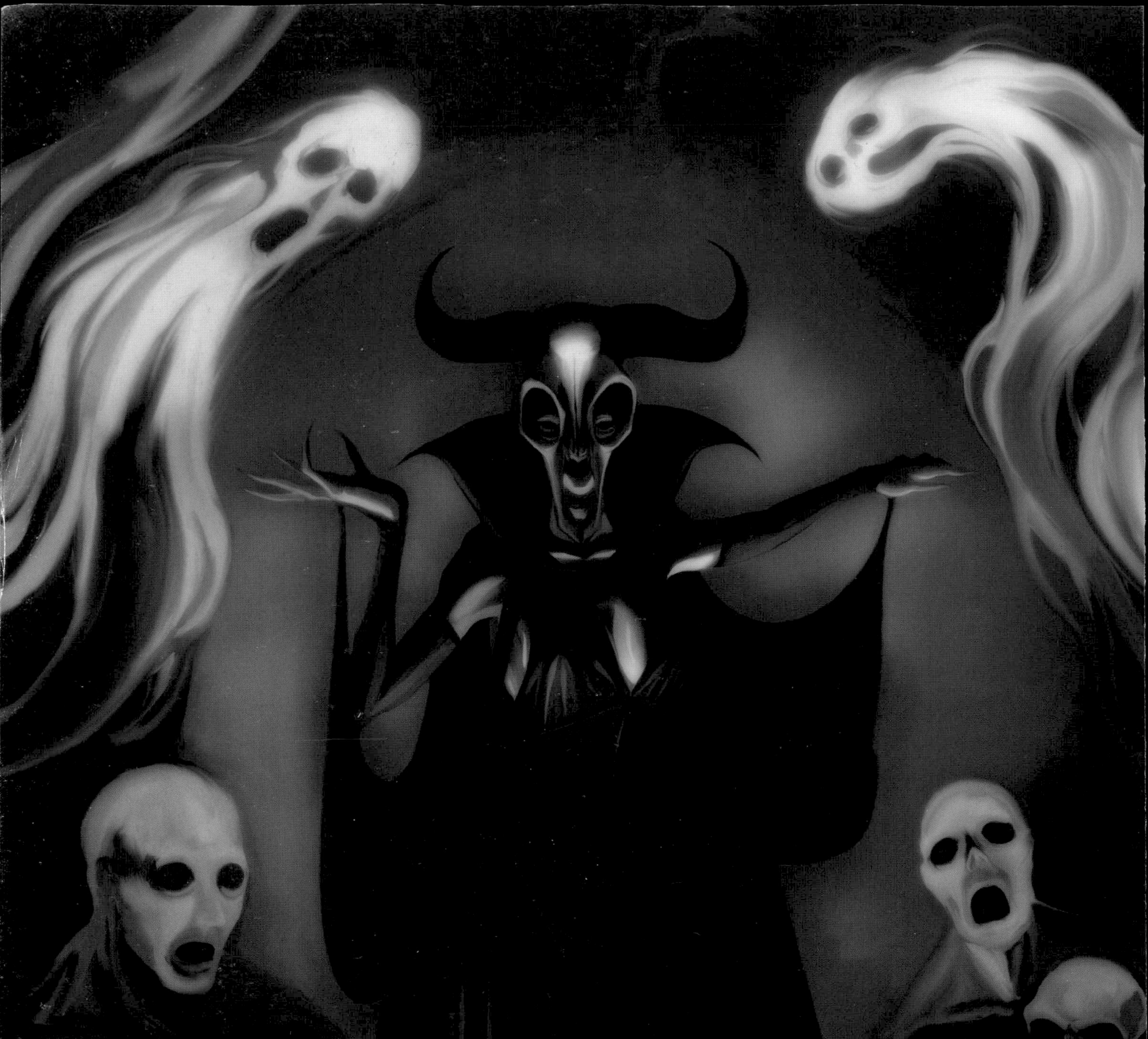

Necromancer

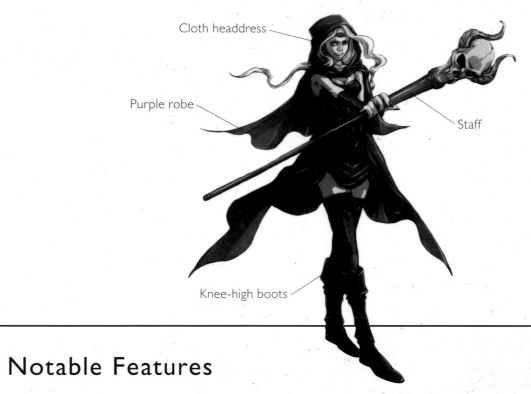

Cloth headdress

Purple robe

Staff

Knee-high boots

➡ Notable Features

- **Human or half-human, dark elf, gnome, goblin or dwarf**
- **May have pale and corpse-like skin and a skeletal figure**
- **May have a long, horned skull with metallic or cloth headdress**
- **Wears long robe in orange, purple, red or dark colors, or tight body suit in animal skin with spikes and armor**
- **Has long nails, dark and hollow eyes, and ferocious appearance**
- **Carries a staff and may wear knee-high boots**

✢ Outline and Origin

Necromancy, a form of black magic that summons spirits or dead people, was used in Homer's *Odyssey* (700 B.C.). In the Renaissance period, necromancy was banned by the church as a dark art, although it was widely practiced in Babylon, Egypt, Greece and Rome. In the Middle Ages, necromancers were generally clergymen who had great knowledge of exorcism, astral magic, astrology and demonology.

In the fantasy world, necromancers use their ability to call on the spirits of the dead to help them fight their enemies. They can also absorb energy from the death of their enemies and make corpses explode. In the process of manipulating death, they can be consumed by it, and therefore, acquire qualities of dead people, like having dark and hollow eyes, pale skin, skeletal bodies and foul odors. They study the method of controlling death; thus, spending most of their lives in dark and hidden places, making them secretive, mysterious and often conniving, but also highly intelligent and learned.

The basic skills of necromancers are their intelligence, endurance and speed, along with their ability to cast spells, prolong life, and to manipulate corpse magic and other forms of magical combat. They use daggers and staffs as their physical weapons.

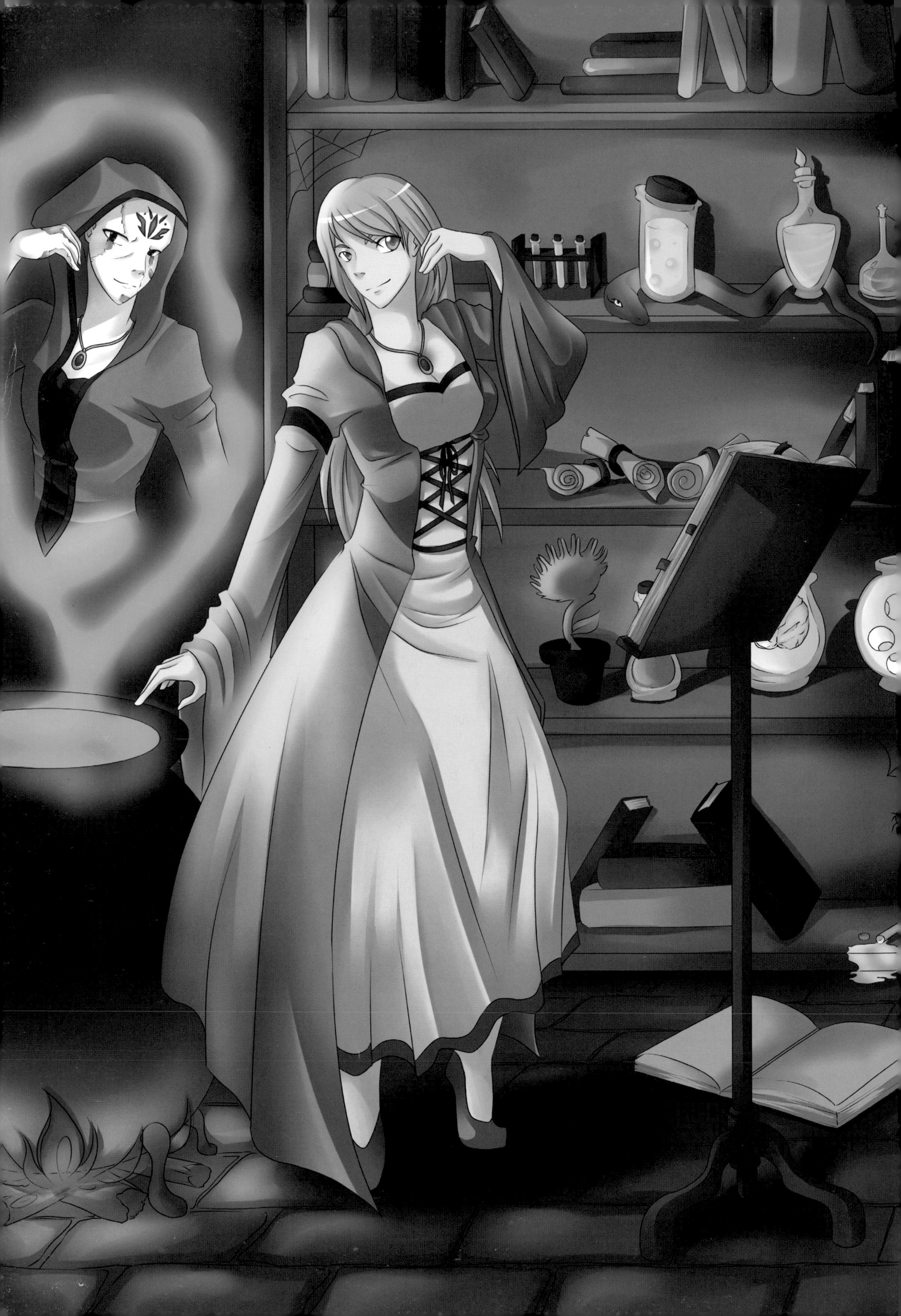

Witch

Female and old, with wrinkled skin

Long nails

Staff

Long, black robe

➡ Notable Features

- Usually female and old with wrinkled, ugly features and a sullen face
- Pale with scars or burns on the body, possibly deformed and foul-smelling
- May have long and dirty nails and messy, long hair
- Wears dirty, loose clothes—usually a black robe with a cape
- Has frightening, melancholy or cross appearance
- Has ability to transform into another being
- May carry a staff, potion, charm or magic book

✛ Outline and Origin

Witchcraft is considered one of the oldest practices in the world. Paleolithic cave paintings show figures performing devilish rituals, frequently through the use of a deformed woman in a circle of followers.

Witches existed in cultures from African to medieval European, South American and Asian, and across most cultures. There are said to be both bad witches and good witches. Bad witches use magic to cause harm or misfortune to others; good witches heal sickness or counteract bad witchcraft.

Witches can communicate with supernatural beings, spirits and demons, and can take on the bodies of both humans and animals. They cast spells by using objects like stones or amulets with inscriptions, molding wax or clay, mixing potions or magical herbs, playing with voodoo dolls, reciting chants, gazing at the mirror, or performing physical rituals. They are wise, cunning, and have a passion for words and mind manipulation.

Witch characters can be humans or humanoids. As fighters, their basic weapons are their charisma and wisdom. They have powers for healing, bluffing, survival, seduction, fortune telling and interpreting astrological signs. They use candles, stones, cauldrons, crystals, cats, songs, mirrors and many kinds of magic to cast spells, such as weather magic, spider magic, serpent magic, mist magic and moon magic.

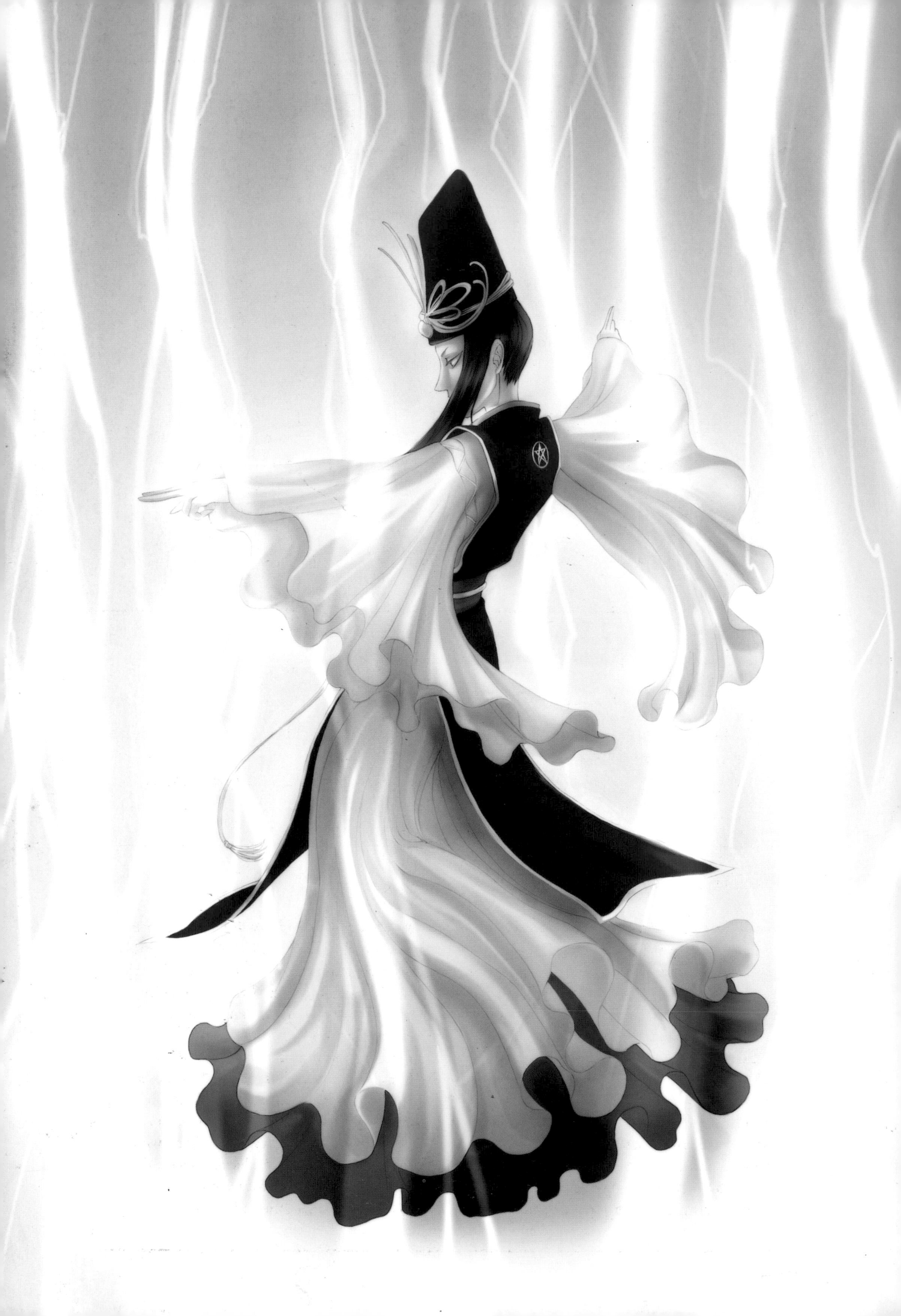

Onmyouji

Half-human and half-fox

Asian

Monk's robe in white and red

Sash

➡ Notable Features

- **Half-human and half-fox, frequently a young male**
- **Asian**
- **Intelligent with mystical powers**
- **Wears Japanese monk clothing or robe in white, black or red and a headdress**
- **Has ability to fight with a sword**

✛ Outline and Origin

Around the 8th century in Japan, onmyōdō,, a form of Japanese esoteric cosmology, was practiced for divination and as a medium for reading astrological signs, calendar making, predicting natural disasters and interpreting good or bad fortunes in life.

Around the time of the Heian period (794-1185), the practice took more advanced steps in using magic and spells to control and fight spirits, ghosts and souls. It consisted of magical aspects taken from esoteric Buddhism and Indian astrology.

Abe no Seimei was known as the greatest onmyouji during the Heian period and served emperors and court officials by providing them with spiritual guidance and advice. Legends told of his background as a half-human, half-fox. He was trained at an early age to study cosmology and the skills of communicating with and avenging the spirits.

Stories of onmyouji have been well interpreted in films and anime. The famous manga novel *Shōnen Onmyōji* is based on a young spiritualist in the Heian period who could fight demons and summon spirits. He had a special affinity with spirits and people who were harmed by the devil. He fought with a sword that he receives as a gift from his grandfather, Abe no Seimei.

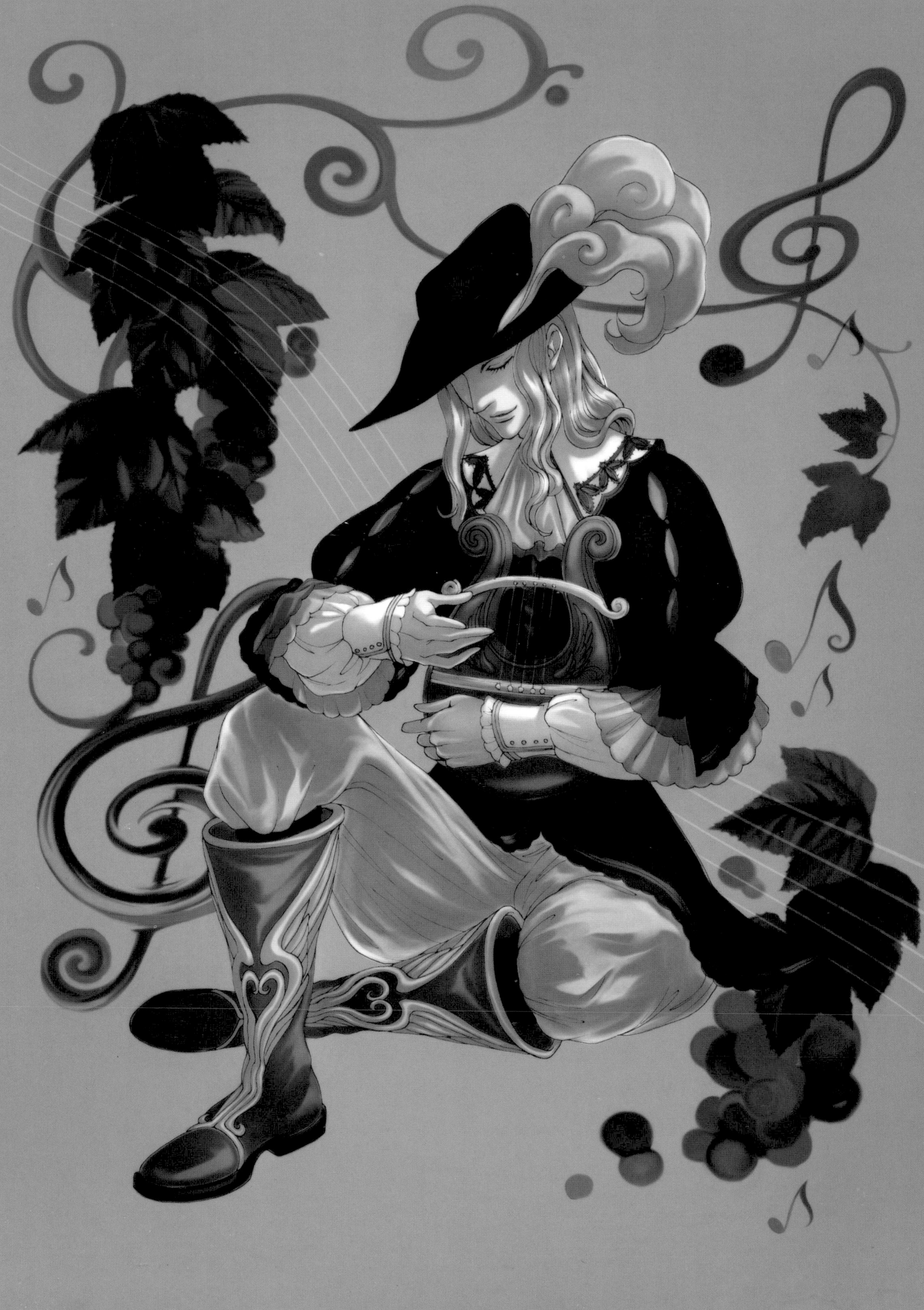

Minstrel

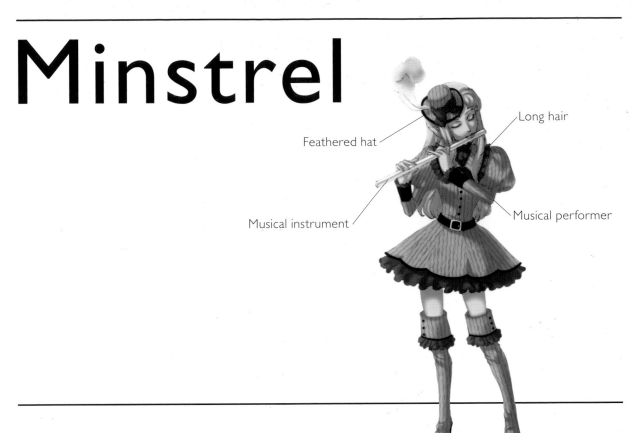

Feathered hat

Long hair

Musical instrument

Musical performer

➡ Notable Features

- Male or female musical performer, usually European
- May wear a loose-sleeved shirt with a vest over a balloon skirt and tights, lightweight tunic and leather boots
- May wear a triangular hat or feathered cap
- Female minstrels have long hair and may wear a long robe or skirt and knee-high boots
- Carries a musical instrument, such as a guitar, violin, harp or flute

✚ Outline and Origin

Minstrels were prominent around the 13th century and onwards in medieval Europe as entertainers who performed songs for royal courts. As poets, they wrote their own lyrics and recited or sang their poems accompanied by instruments, such as harps, mandolins, guitars, flutes, bagpipes and kettledrums. They were often seen at royal feasts and some became jesters skilled in juggling and humor to entertain guests. By the mid-Renaissance period, they were performing in the streets for village folk, and this type of minstrel was later known as a traveling troubadour.

Some fantasy manga portrays minstrels as romantics who seek the affection of those they're in love with; one such story tells of a young boy, a sword-fighting minstrel, who fights monsters and evil beasts.

Another manga story of a minstrel is of a female minstrel mercenary who plays the violin and the guitar very well and uses her music to disrupt battles. In this story, the character's parents were killed by a gang, and she seeks to avenge against the gang with her powerful skills.

The popular minstrel character in fantasy manga fights against the forces of darkness and defeats his or her enemies through songs of power that have different effects during battle. These minstrels have the ability to use magic for healing, fighting enemies and provoking their enemies to hallucinate, which prevents them from using magic.

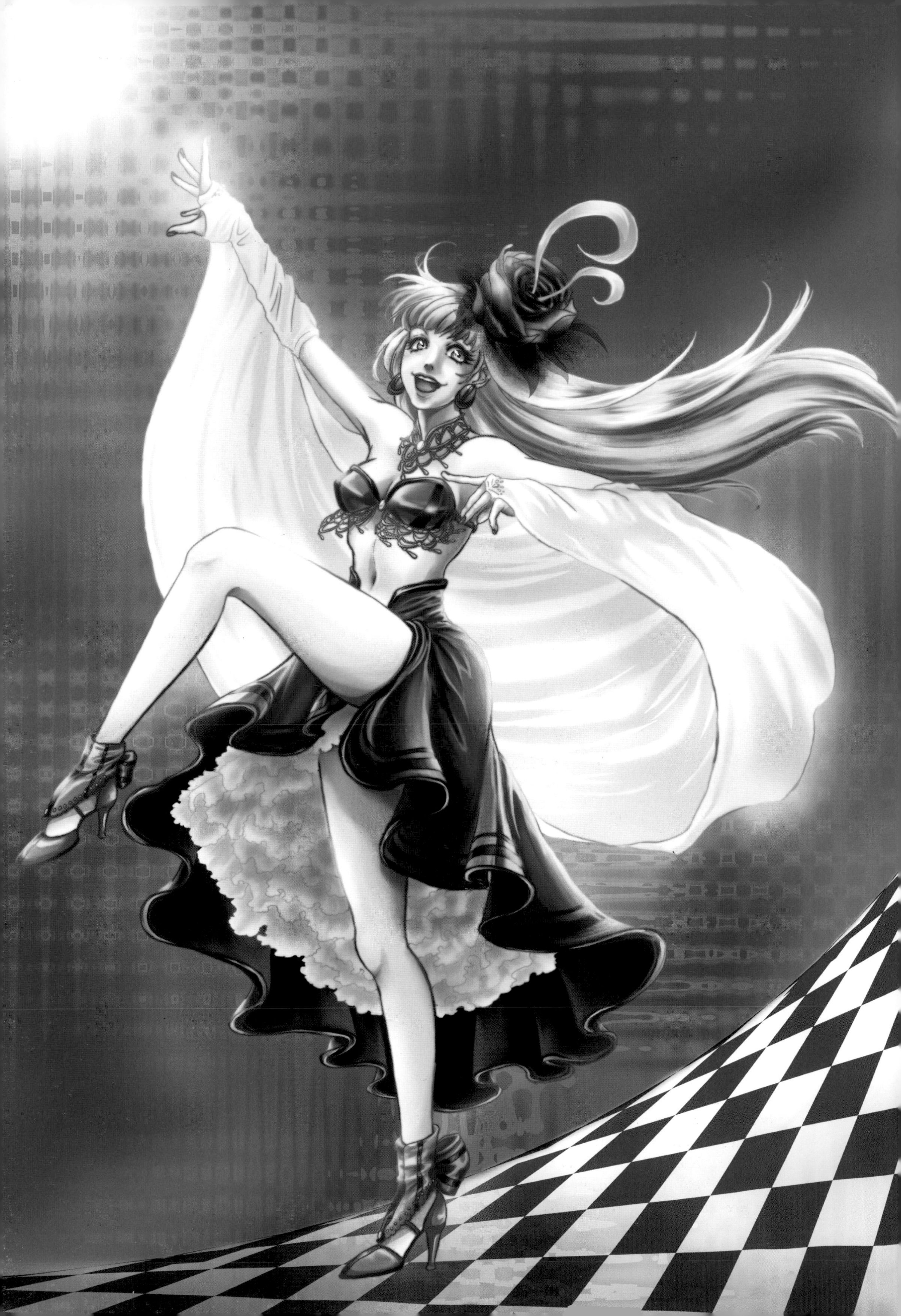

Dancer

Attractive

Revealing and stylish attire

Glittery clothing

Black trousers

➡ Notable Features

- **Attractive performer, usually depicted as a female, who gracefully controls her body**
- **Flexible, agile, creative and expressive**
- **May be a female dance warrior wearing a long dress or revealing and stylish attire, such as open red jacket, black trousers with a green sash or a colorful cocktail dress**
- **May wear jewelry, such as earrings or bracelets**
- **May carry a long ribbon or shawl**

✚ Outline and Origin

The art of dancing can be traced back to prehistoric times where it was captured in tomb paintings found in India and Egypt. It has long been used as a medium for telling stories or serenading lovers. In some tribes it was used in healing rituals. All over the world, in various cultures, dancers were parts of ceremonies, rituals, celebrations and entertainment.

In the world of fantasy manga, the dancer is frequently a female warrior who uses her dancing to distract enemies. She can employ different dancing skills, which have particular effects on opponents. A slow dance, for example, can captivate an enemy's attention and confuse his movements; a polka dance can intimidate an enemy's attack power; changing to a mysterious costume can distract an enemy.

The dancer is highly skilled in high jumps, turns, kicks and in charming, manipulating and distracting a target.

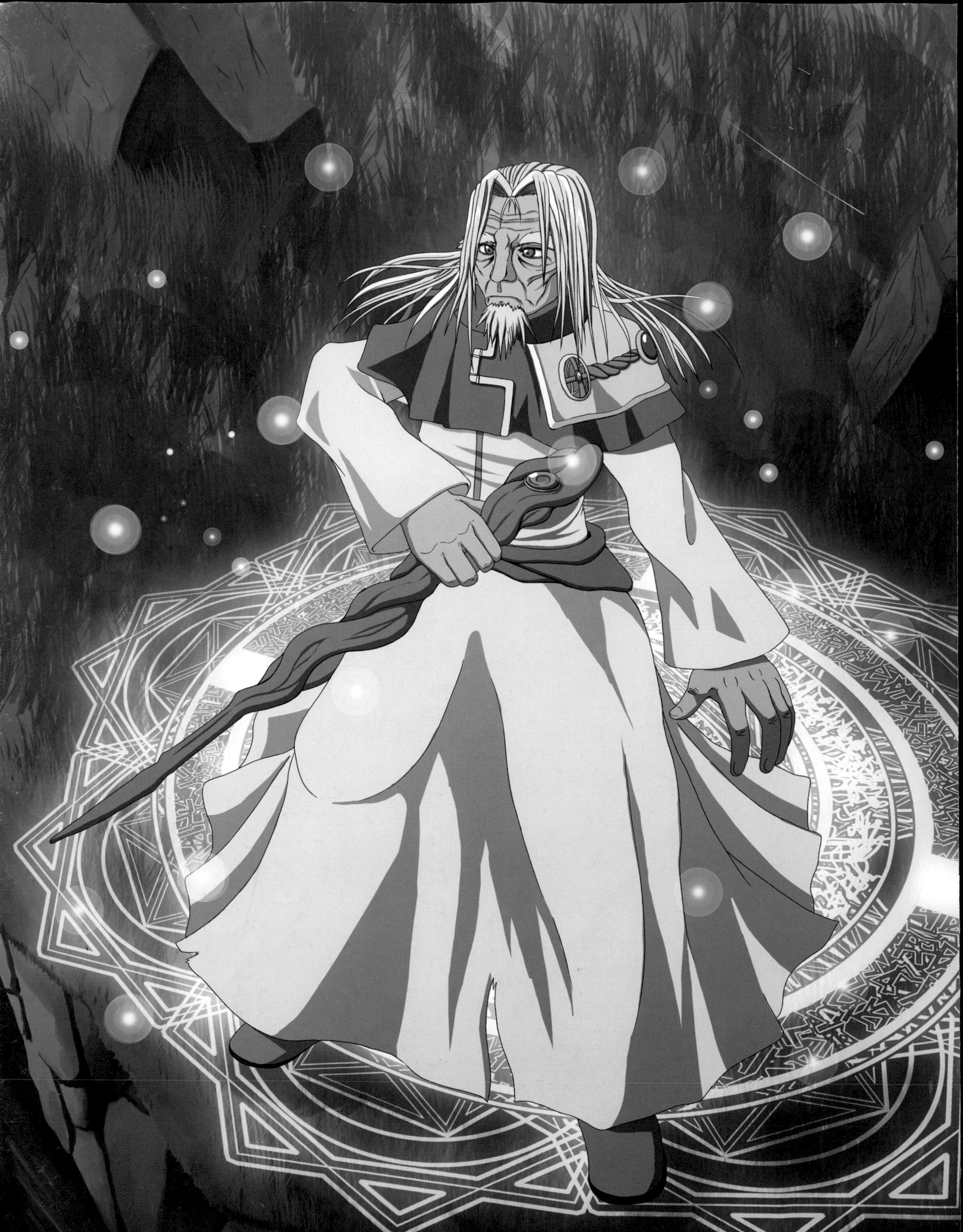

Wise Man

Wrinkled skin

Old man with a beard
and white hair

Stick

Long robe

➡ Notable Features

- **An old man, usually with a beard and white hair**
- **May have wrinkled or weathered features**
- **Physically weak**
- **Highly intelligent, cunning and perceptive**
- **May wear a long robe and carry a stick or dress in a military uniform**
- **Capable of performing black magic (used for evil) and white magic (used for good)**

✚ Outline and Origin

The description of a wise man usually refers to an old man who is similar to a wizard and possesses a great knowledge of all things. The term is associated with the Three Wise Men in biblical literature, referring to the three magi who followed a star that led them to the birth of Jesus Christ. They are depicted as old men with either white or greyish hair and beards or moustaches.

The image of a wise man appears in many literary writings, and is represented by various mythological and historical figures, such as Mentor from Greek mythology, Mimir from Norse mythology, Chilon of Sparta, and Xi Kang, the Chinese author.

The wise man is considered a teacher, mentor, philosopher or scholarly person with a good sense of judgment. In fantasy manga, the wise man, also known as a sage, is known for his impeccable thought process, wisdom, and strong ability to concentrate. He has great skill in acquiring information about an enemy's secrets, and uses spells and magic for healing, removing poison, deciphering codes, and controlling nature and animals. Due to his age, he may be physically weak and incapable of using weapons. He may be seen wearing a magician's robe, vest, feathered hat, armor or a protective ring.

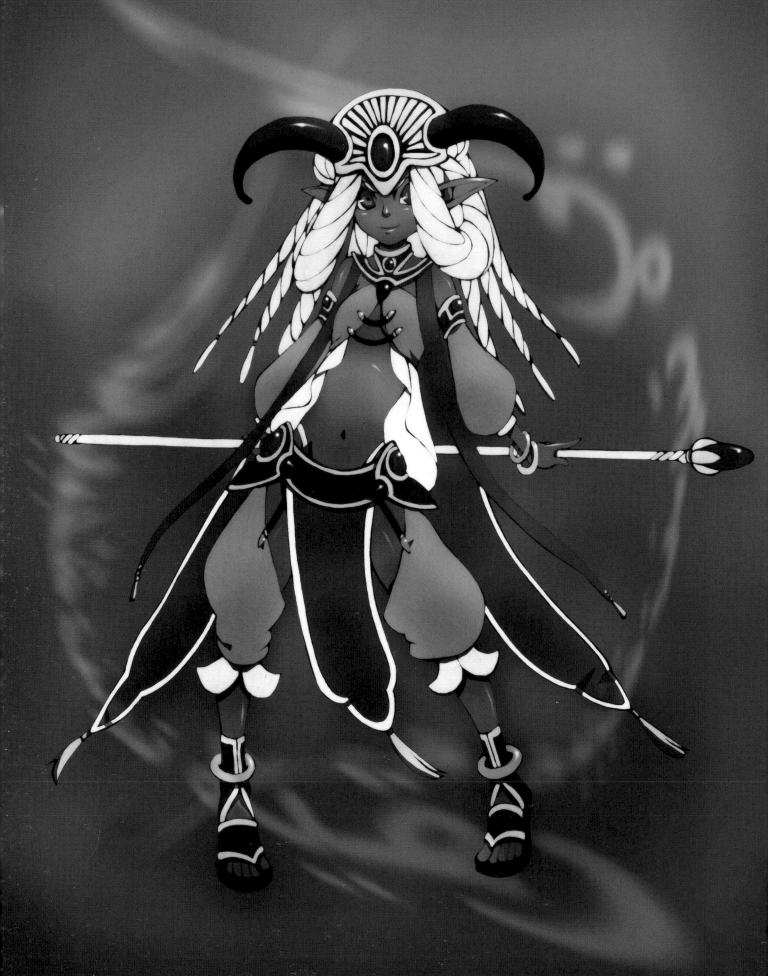

Shaman

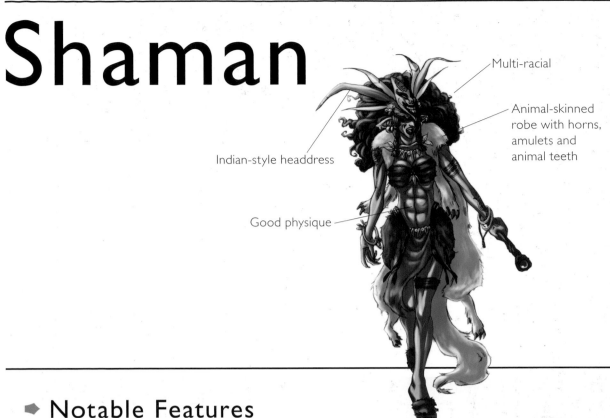

Multi-racial

Animal-skinned robe with horns, amulets and animal teeth

Indian-style headdress

Good physique

➡ Notable Features

- Male or female human, half-human and half-animal, orc, troll, dwarf, goblin or tauren
- Defined muscles
- Strong, boney features, may be bearded
- May have leather or cloth armor, and shield
- May wear a buffalo robe and Indian-style headdress decorated with horns, amulets, the teeth of ferocious animals, stones or jewelry

✚ Outline and Origin

A shaman is a messenger between the human world and the spirit world, a fortune-teller and an omen predictor. He or she may be good or evil, can transcend in a dimension between the living and the dead, can heal diseases through spiritual intervention and can travel though other worlds to guide lost souls. A shaman can also communicate with the spirits of animals. He or she communicates with them in a trance or in rituals where storytelling or singing songs may be present.

Archaeological evidences dating from the Paleolithic age show shamans in buffalo robes, some with animal features, such as those of reindeers, owls, horses, and wolves, sometimes bearded and sometimes dancing. Shamans with birdlike heads that seem to be floating in the air,

like ascending spirit, as well as female shamans surrounded by bones and the skulls of animals, can also be found. Later, shamanism became a part of Greek pagan religion and the Abrahamic religion of the Roman Empire. The rise of Christianity and Puritanism caused the decline of shamanism, as it was looked upon as a form of witchcraft.

The shaman character in the fantasy world is a healer, fortune-teller, and spell caster who sees through the world of spirits and communicates with creatures not visible to humans. He or she is usually an orc, troll or tauren who is dressed in armor and mail gear, and has powerful fighting abilities. It can resurrect itself and other beings, and control forces of nature. It may be slightly slow in speed, but is highly skilled in dark magic.

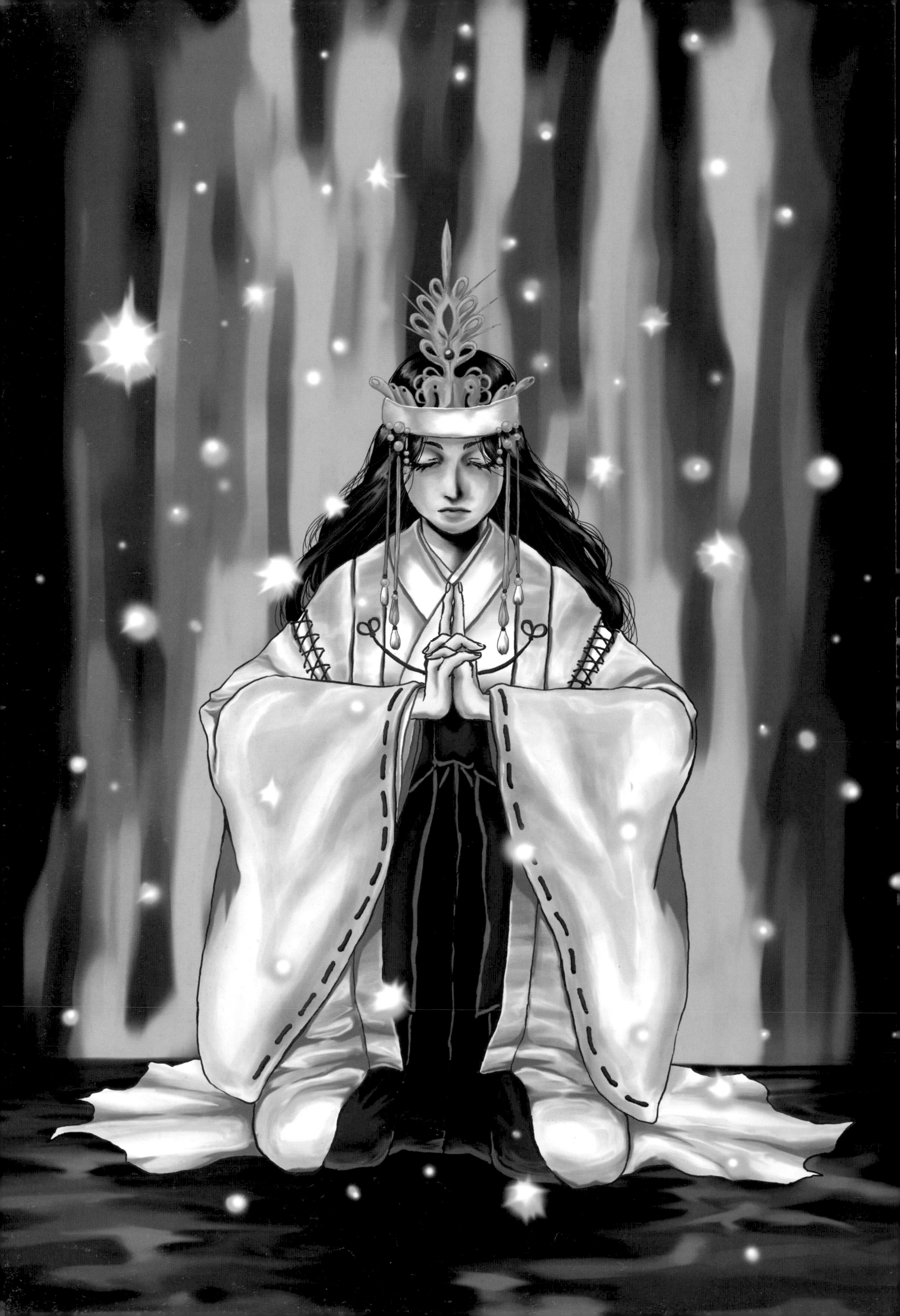

Miko

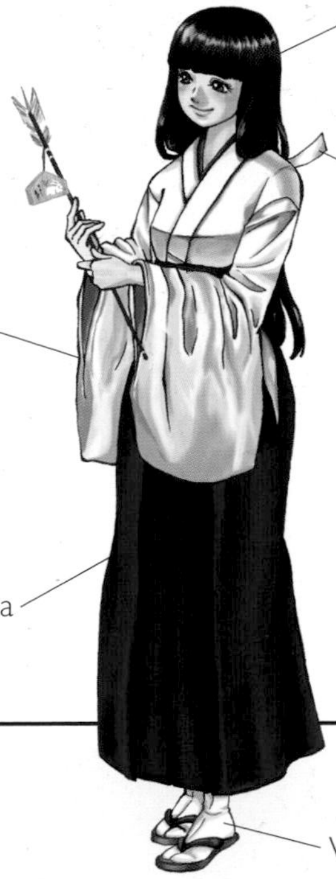
Long, black hair
White hair ribbon
white haori
Red hakama
White tabi socks

Notable Features

- **Japanese features**
- **Has long, black or blue-black hair, brown eyes and a slender body**
- **Wears scarlet red hakama (long, divided trousers), white haori (kimono jacket), white or red ribbons in the hair and white tabi socks**
- **May carry a harai-gushi (wooden stick with attached prayers), ofuda (paper talisman), azusayumi catalpa bow, bells, tamagushi offertory sakaki tree branches, drum, candles, small altar, rice bowl of water or a gehobako supernatural box containing dolls, skulls, and other religious objects**
- **Skilled in martial arts**

Outline and Origin

Miko comes from an 8th century Japanese myth about Ame-no-Uzume-no-Mikoto, a spiritual goddess who performed a shamanistic trance, dancing to trick the sun goddess Amaterasu out of the cave where she hid in the dark out of anger toward her brother. Ame-no-Uzume-no-Mikoto hung heavenly club moss around her like a sash, used a spindle tree as a headdress and binded bamboo grass leaves, then stamped continuously on a sounding board as though she was possessed by a god.

The Miko character is very popular in Japanese manga and "cosplay" or costume play, and is portrayed as a female fighter of evil spirits, demons and ghosts. In many Japanese films and manga, she performs exorcisms to drive bad spirits away. In some role-playing games, she is portrayed as a white witch.

The Miko character is often seen wearing the traditional Miko attire: red hakama and white haori, and red and white ribbons on her hair. She is shy, charming, attractive and brave, and sometimes, serious and temperamental. She is also highly skilled in martial arts, especially jujutsu, which is non-weapon battle that relies on joint locks, throws, strikes, kicks and trapping. She can also raise the dead, and tricks enemies with her supernatural abilities.

"Kuro Miko" refers to the evil version of a Miko—an evil sorcerer who practices black magic and demonology. She wears the Miko attire, but darker in color, usually black-purple or black-gold.

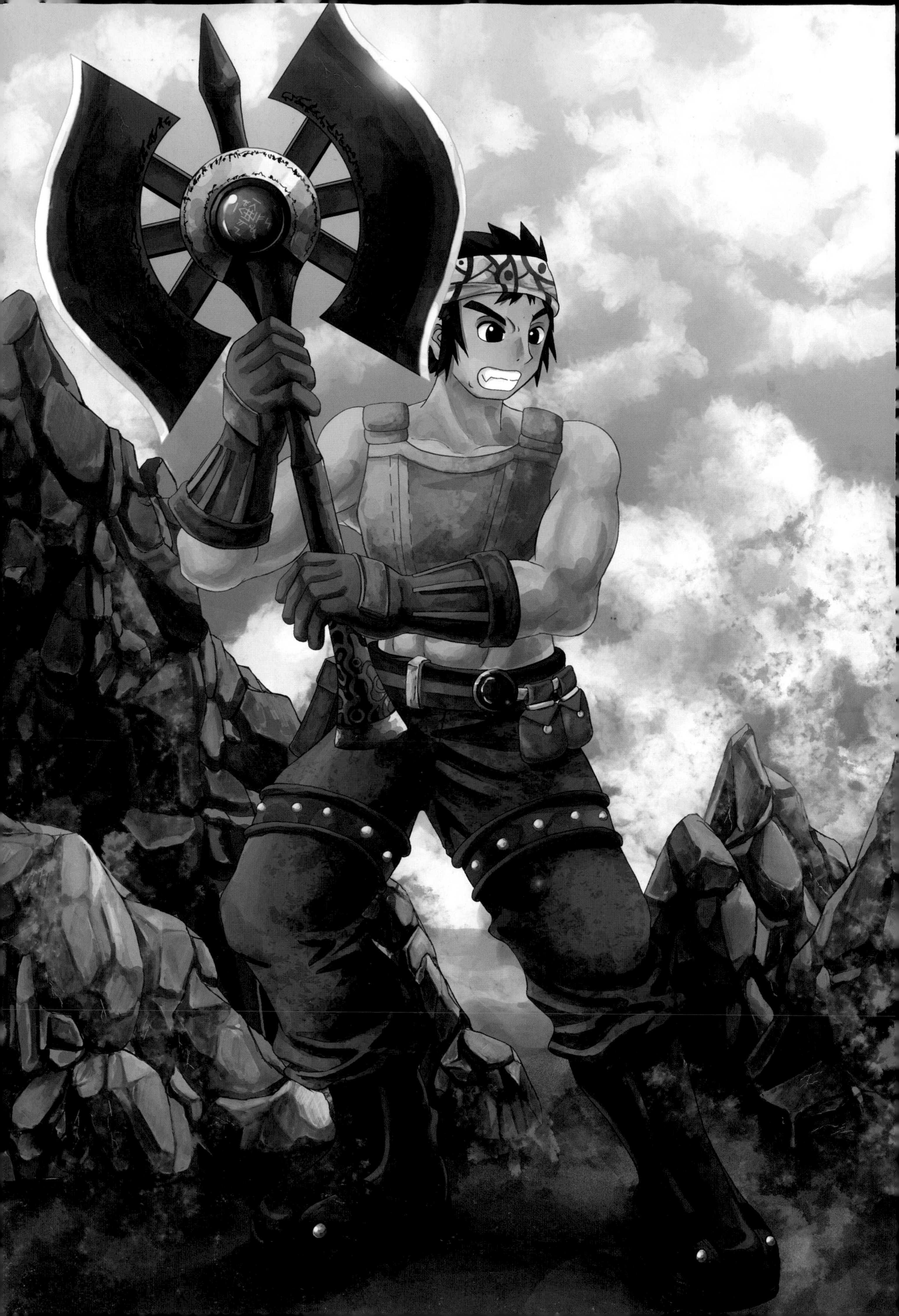

Blacksmith

Muscular

Leather gloves

Working clothes

High boots

➡ Notable Features

- Capable of working with and manipulating iron
- Muscular, strong and can carry heavy objects
- Has patience and high endurance for heat
- May wear worker's clothes or an armor vest and thick, leather gloves, high boots and a steel mask
- May carry a hammer, axe, anvil and pair of tongs

✛ Outline and Origin

There are various blacksmith figures in mythology, such as Hephaestus, the god of blacksmiths in Greek and Roman mythology who created the weapons of the gods; Goibniu, the god of art in Irish mythology who also forged weapons for battle; Gofannon, the god of metal workers in Celtic mythology; and Wayland the Smith; or Völundr, the legendary smith in Germanic and Norse mythology who crafted rings and gems. In the Bible, Tubal-cain is mentioned as an expert in brass work.

Metalwork existed during the Copper and Bronze ages when men smelted, cast, and forged copper and bronze. The ancient Anatolian people discovered the process of smelting iron as early as 1500 B.C. Much later, in the 1800s, armies in the United States and Europe hired blacksmiths to make horseshoes and to repair military equipment. The blacksmith profession, however, has declined since automobiles were invented to replace horses as transportation vehicles.

Blacksmiths in fantasy manga forge weapons using fire, earth, wind and water, and metals and minerals. They can control the level of a weapon's power if they are being attacked or if they are attacking. In addition to creating armor plates, they also create keys that can unlock secret objects. Some of the weapons they can create are cross guards (iron bars), axes, spathas (cavalry swords), and labrys. When blacksmiths reach a superior skill level, they can specialize as armor smiths or weapon smiths.

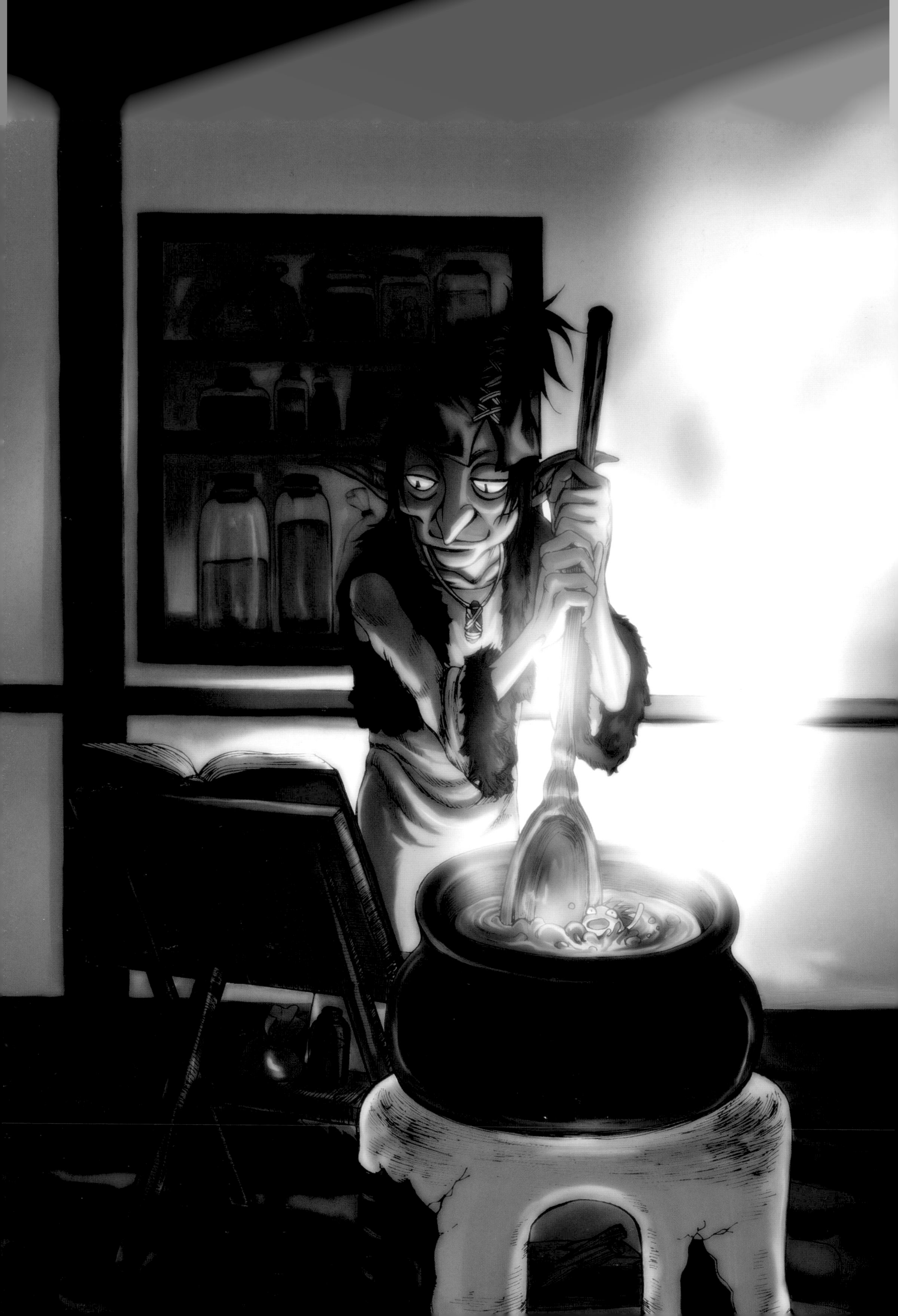

Alchemist

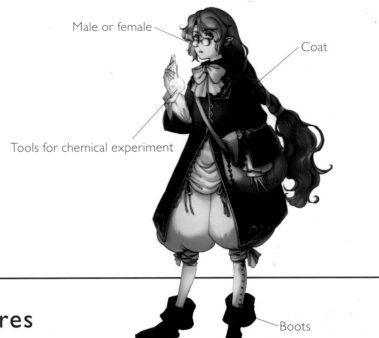

Male or female

Coat

Tools for chemical experiment

Boots

➡ Notable Features

- ◆ **Able to engineer and manipulate gold**
- ◆ **May be male or female**
- ◆ **May be human, half-human, dwarf or goblin**
- ◆ **Intelligent and highly skilled in craftsmanship**
- ◆ **Can possess skills in spell casting**
- ◆ **May wear a robe, light armor, chain mail and boots**

✚ Outline and Origin

The origin of alchemy can be traced from the ancient Egyptian period (5000-400 B.C.) when it was used as a common practice in metal work and mummification. It was also used in the ancient civilizations of Mesopotamia, Persia, India, China, Japan, Korea, Greece and Rome for transmuting metals into gold, curing diseases and extending life. It was considered not only a scientific profession, but also a medium of philosophy and way of attaining wisdom.

In the 14th century when European alchemists focused heavily on transmuting the physical body to create gold for achieving immortality, religious groups' mocked alchemy and banned its practice. Alchemists, however, were already known to have made large contributions in the advancement of chemistry and the distillation of water with their experimentations in metalworking, the production of inks, dyes and paints, leather tanning, and the manufacturing of ceramics and glass. While European alchemists typically focused on the transmutation of metal to gold, Chinese alchemists treated alchemy as a practice of medicine.

Alchemists as fantasy characters mix herbs and chemicals to produce potions, oils, and other liquids known as elixirs to cast spells, to be used for healing or invisibility, or to overpower enemies. Often, they can transmute a range of different materials, but they usually require a Philosopher's Stone to do so. They may also create weapons that are dusted or coated with alchemical gold or other magical elements to increase the level of the weapon's power.

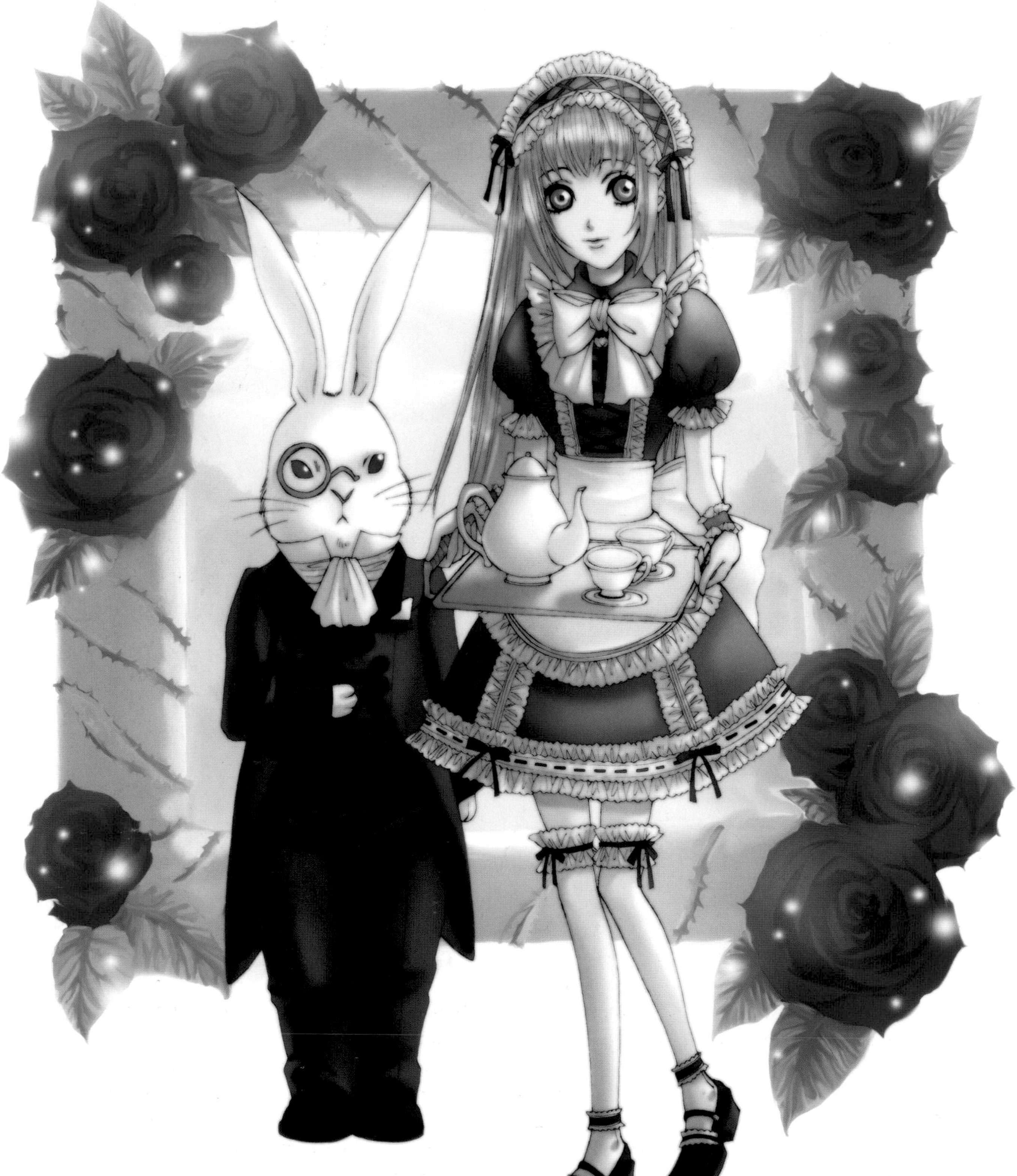

Butler, Maid

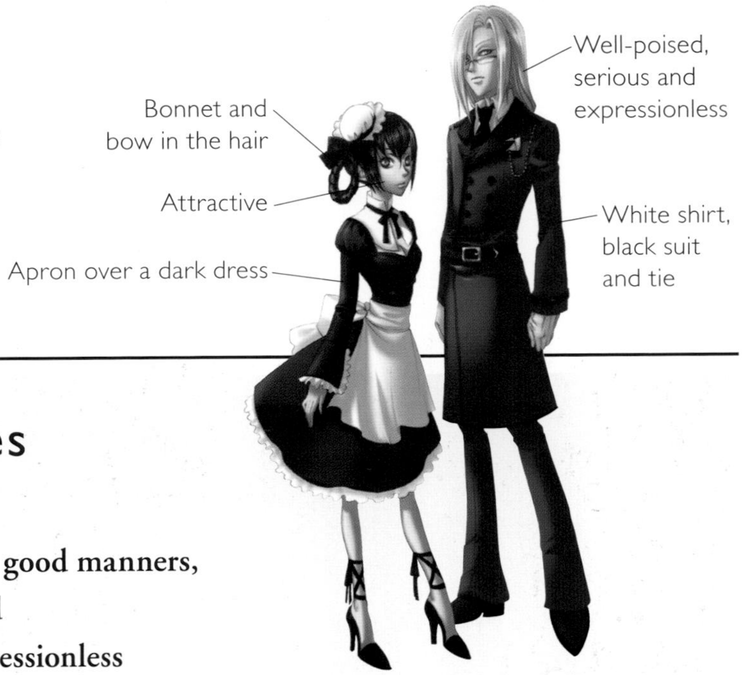
Bonnet and bow in the hair
Attractive
Apron over a dark dress
Well-poised, serious and expressionless
White shirt, black suit and tie

Notable Features

Butler

- **Male servant who possesses good manners, and is polite and disciplined**
- **Sometimes serious and expressionless**
- **Skilled in greeting guests, security and household duties**
- **Wears white shirt, long, black suit and black bow or tie, or military-like uniform**

Maid

- **Female servant who is obedient, orderly, hardworking, patient and helpful**
- **May be attractive and charming**
- **Trained in household duties, carrying out errands and caring for the elderly**
- **Dresses in an apron over a dark dress, sometimes wears a bonnet, ribbon or bow in the hair, and black shoes**

Outline and Origin

In ancient Egypt, servants of pharaohs existed as slaves of nobles. They also existed in ancient Greece and Rome throughout the medieval period. Toward the 17th and 18th centuries, a butler became a common member of the upper class household, especially in Britain, and supervised other servants, greeted guests and constantly served his master and the master's wife. He was, therefore, well trained in household management, accounting, and the general protection and care of the family members.

During the Tokugawa period in Japan (1603-1868), male servants acted as apprentice-clerks, home repairmen, porters, footboys and horse drivers who were hired peasants and dressed in a single piece of loincloth. Some butler characters in the fantasy world are depicted as young men from poor families who work for noble masters. They are skilled not only in household duties, but also in martial arts and fighting with swords. Some butler characters also act as bodyguards to their masters.

Historically, maids functioned similarly as the butlers, but they covered a larger scope of duties, such as cleaning, cooking, laundry, dish washing, babysitting, running errands, such as market-shopping, and acting as companions to their lady masters. In the Meiji era, wealthy households employed butlers and maids and trained them to perform specific skills.

The typical anime image of a maid is influenced by the style of a French maid, and is dressed in a short dark dress, a white, ruffled apron, and white, ruffled bonnet. She is often portrayed as a charmer to men. Other types of maids include the nijiura maid, who is skilled in martial arts. The nijiura maid, like other maids, may appear helpless and obedient, but can be strong and powerful if necessary.

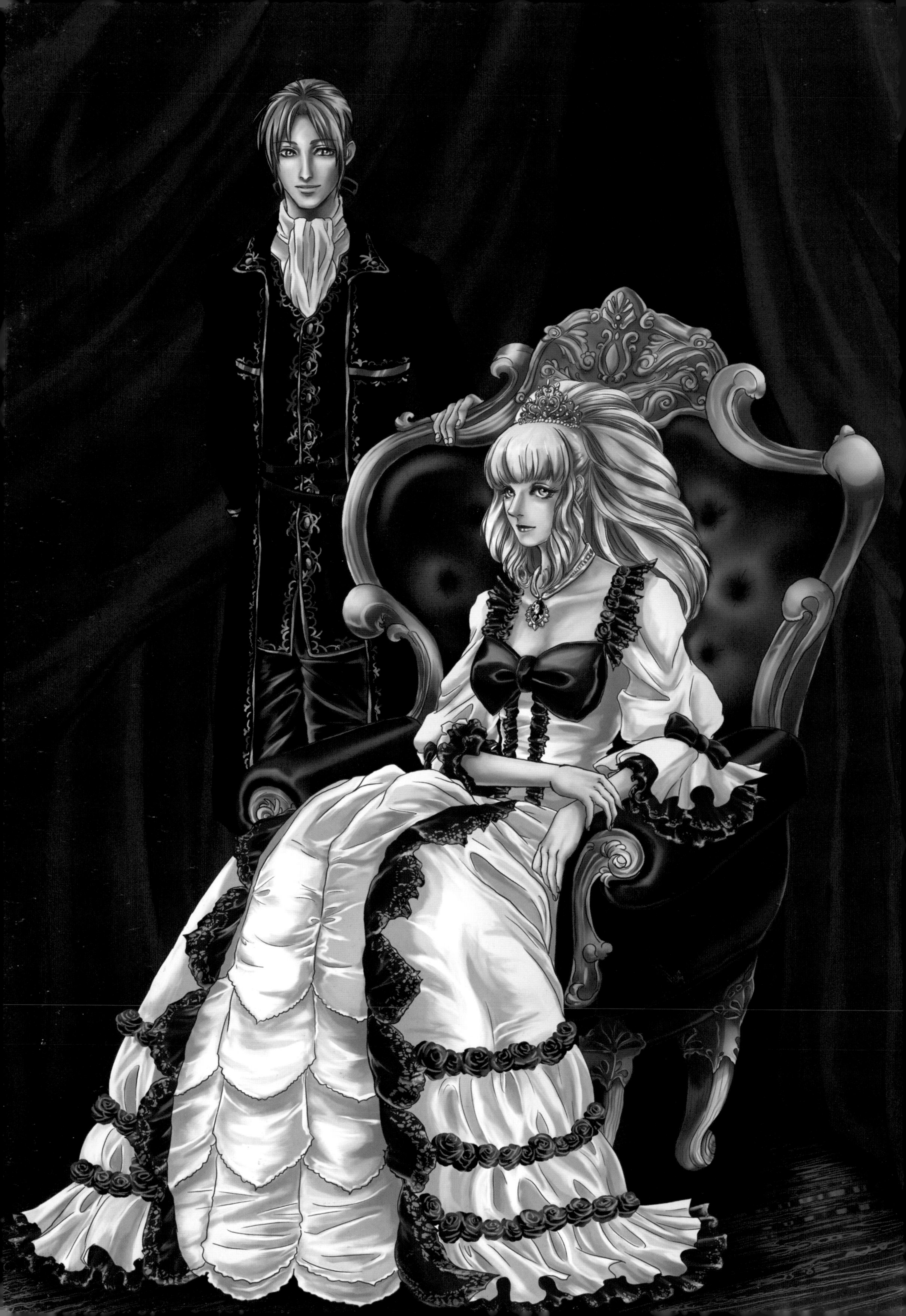

Prince, Princess

Beautiful features · Handsome · Military uniform · Long dress · Sword

➡ Notable Features

Prince

- Handsome, refined and has royal blood
- Intelligent and abides by rules of conduct
- Well-dressed in a robe or military uniform with an emblem or insignia of royal dynasty
- Skilled in hunting, archery, fighting and riding horses
- May carry a bow, sword or spear

Princess

- Has royal blood or married royalty, and is usually beautiful
- Feminine, graceful and charming
- Wears a long dress or robe
- May have similar skills as the prince
- Sometimes seen with a companion or servant

✚ Outline and Origin

A prince can acquire his title by hereditary right (descending from the ruling royal family), by appointment by the pope, by achieving a high military ranking, such as cadets of non-sovereign families, or by having a high rank of nobility.

During the classical period in Europe, a prince could have full control of an entire nation to determine its territories and laws, authorize the minting of money, form armies and declare war against other nations. One of the earliest princes of Japan was Prince Shotoku who established a centralized government in the country during the Asuka period (538-710).

A princess, like a prince, can acquire her title by hereditary right; or she may acquire it by marrying a prince, duke or noble-ranking gentleman among the royal clan. Both the prince and the princess are highly educated. A prince is trained in cavalry, archery, fencing and hunting. A princess is trained in embroidery, singing, dancing and the playing of musical instruments. Both the prince and princess are trained in areas of learning, such as languages, culture, poetry, writing and ethics and both possess good manners. Their specializations are leadership, governance of kingdoms, charm and wisdom.

Princes and princesses in the fantasy world may not possess the superior skills of other characters with special abilities, but they may use their powers of charisma and magic. They are skilled in leading armies in battle and attacking enemies of their monarchies who seek to take over the royal throne.

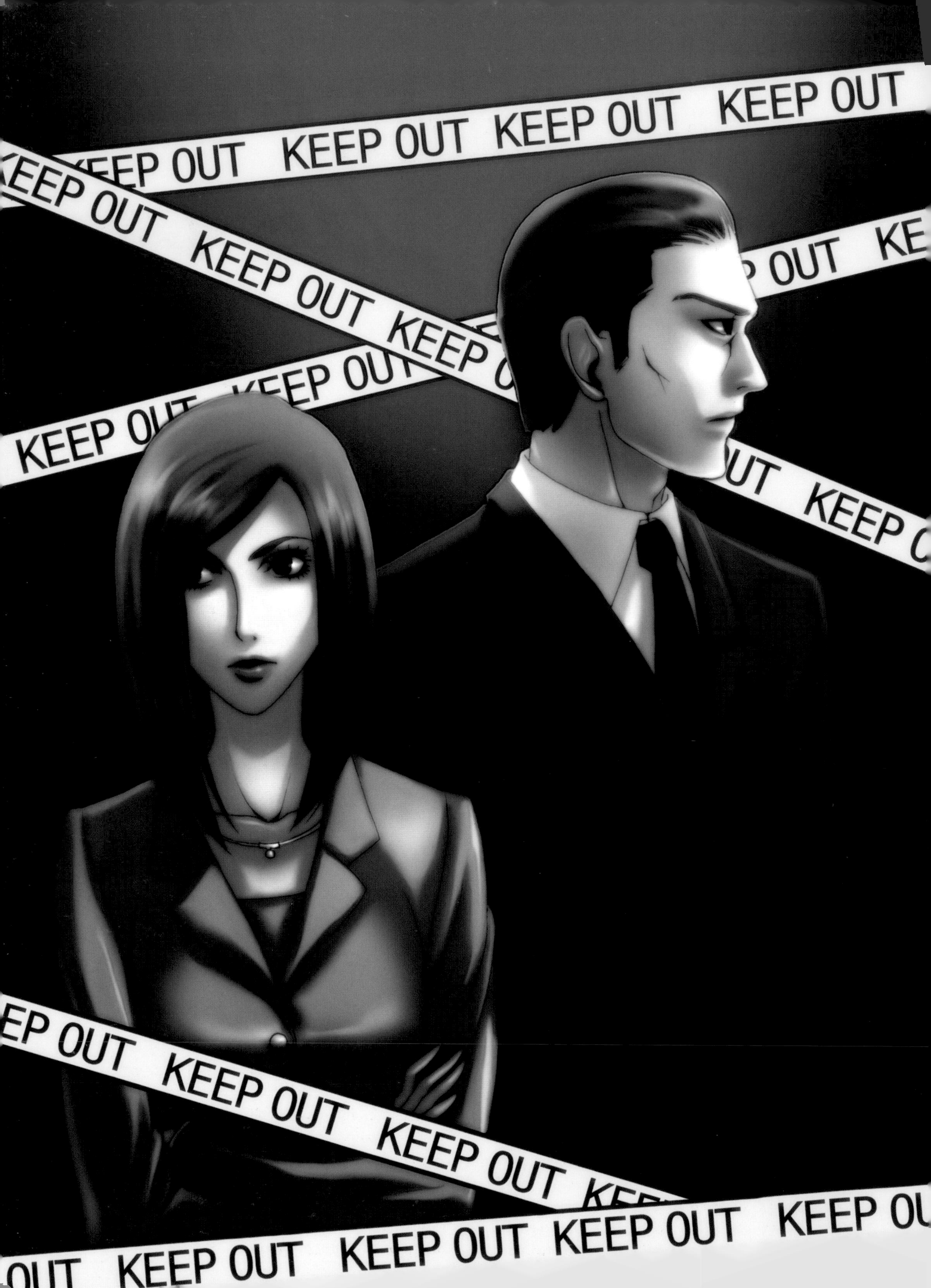

KEEP OUT KEEP OUT KEEP OUT
KEEP OUT KEEP OUT
KEEP OUT
KEEP OUT
KEEP OUT
KEEP OUT KEEP OUT
KEEP OUT KEEP OUT KEEP OUT KEEP OUT

Policeman, Policewoman

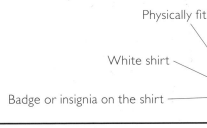

Physically fit

White shirt

White gloves

Badge or insignia on the shirt

➡ Notable Features

- Physically fit, alert, brave and disciplined
- Skilled in military and security tactics
- Paid public official
- Wears dark pants with sewn truncheon pockets and waterproof military-like jacket (usually black, dark blue or grey) with silver or gold buttons, white or light blue shirt, or uniform designated by representing government
- Shirt or jacket shows a badge or insignia
- May wear body armor, cap, tie or white gloves
- Has a belt around the waist to support a weapon
- Policewoman may wear a skirt

✚ Outline and Origin

In ancient Greece, slaves were required to act as police guards to watch over public gatherings that might disrupt order. They arrested criminals and prisoners. During the Roman Empire, the army assumed police duties until 27 B.C. when wards were established and protected by squads.

Throughout Europe and medieval England, local lords and nobles were responsible for maintaining law and order, and crime punishment was dealt with by hanging, mutilation, whipping or blood feuds. As police forces were gradually formed in many nations, the policeman became a model of bravery and protection. Today, policemen and policewomen go through rigid training in weapon tactics,

fighting, criminal arrest and security measures.

In Japan, the police system began following a European style of governance around 1874. They had nationwide control by the 1880s and were respected and feared by villagers. In addition to crime prevention and punishment, they managed fire prevention, public health and land permits.

In fantasy manga, the policeman and policewoman carry out the same roles as real-life police officers in fighting crime and securing justice. They are often depicted as tough, muscular and having very strong personalities suited for combat. They are also highly skilled in using weapons, such as knives and blades.

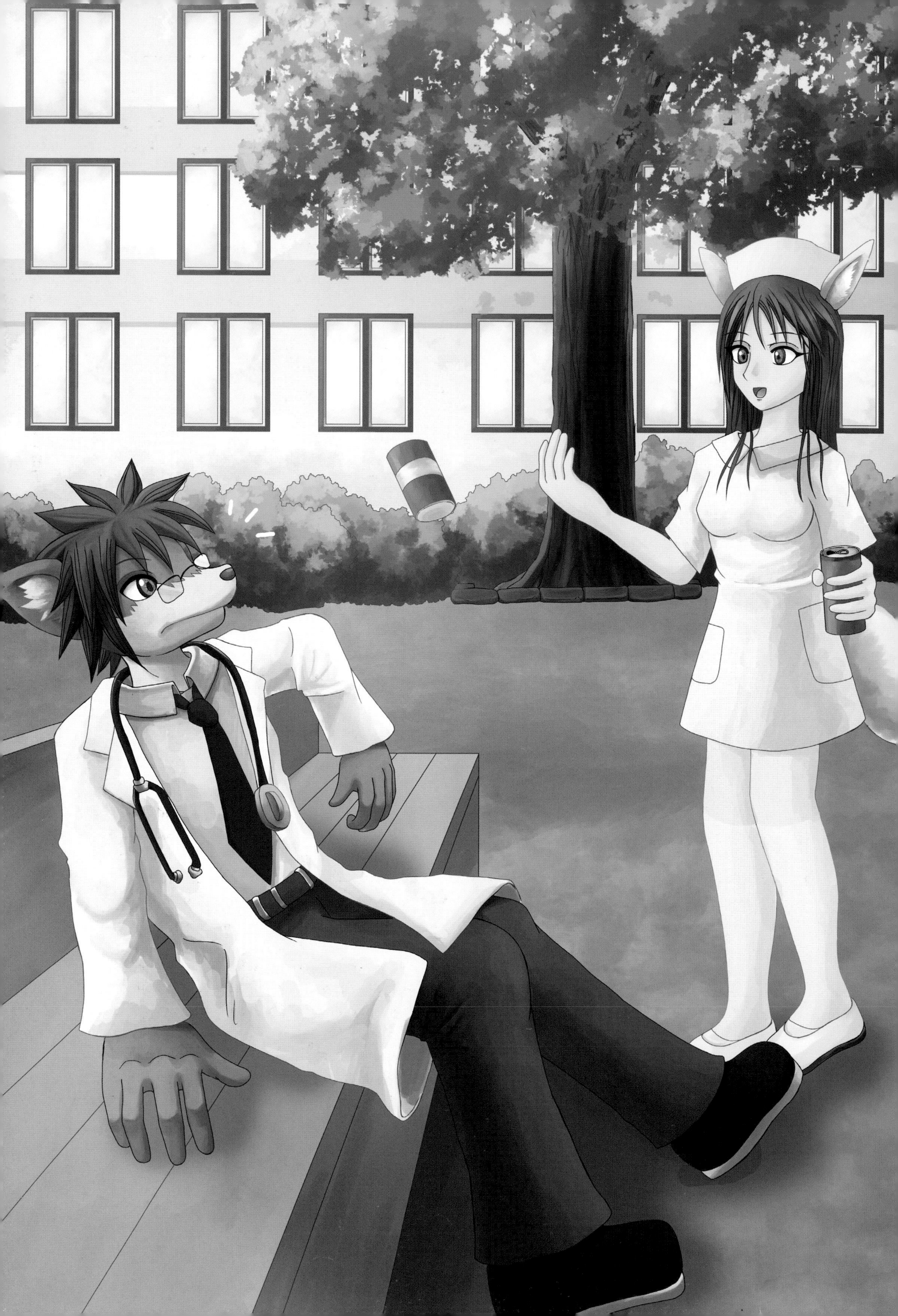

Doctor, Nurse

Doctor
- Stethoscope
- White robe over pants

Nurse
- Nurse cap
- Medical record
- Uniform

➡ Notable Features

- ◆ **Clean, intelligent, patient**
- ◆ **Doctor wears a white robe or gown over white or solid-colored pants**
- ◆ **Nurse wears a uniform dress and a cap**
- ◆ **Either may wear a surgical mask**
- ◆ **Either may carry a stethoscope around the neck or hold a medical record**

✚ Outline and Origin

Spiritual healers and shamans were known to be the first doctors in prehistoric times. They combined religion and nature, prayer, ceremonies and herbs for curing illness. In ancient Egypt, doctors were priests who used religious practices together with healing powers bestowed on them by the gods for remedies. Later, Egyptian doctors studied anatomy and practiced surgery. Greek doctors followed the path of Egyptian medicine, but separated spiritual and physical medical treatment. As early as the Roman period, female doctors existed to care for other women. Medical training spread in Europe from the 11th century, together with the rise of medical schools and universities. In Japan, ancient doctors used Chinese medicine, herbal treatment and acupuncture.

Before the 15th century, the nurse was associated with a wet nurse, a female expert in breastfeeding. Later, she also took care of sickly or elderly people.

Nurses are frequently hired by nuns and armies and play significant roles during war. The traditional nurse uniform was adapted from a nun's habit when nurses were called "sisters" during the 19th century. It usually consists of a white or light-colored dress, an apron and a nurse's cap.

Modern-day illustrations of doctors and nurses also depict the style of the white dress and cap uniform. In the fantasy world, however, the doctor may also wear a black cape, and a witch doctor may appear in various forms and attires. Doctors in animation games are designed as intellectual characters (like real-life doctors), though they typically have stronger personalities and may have abilities to fight or use spells. Nurses, on the other hand, are portrayed with very feminine roles; they cure the sick and easily attract men. They are not usually skilled fighters.

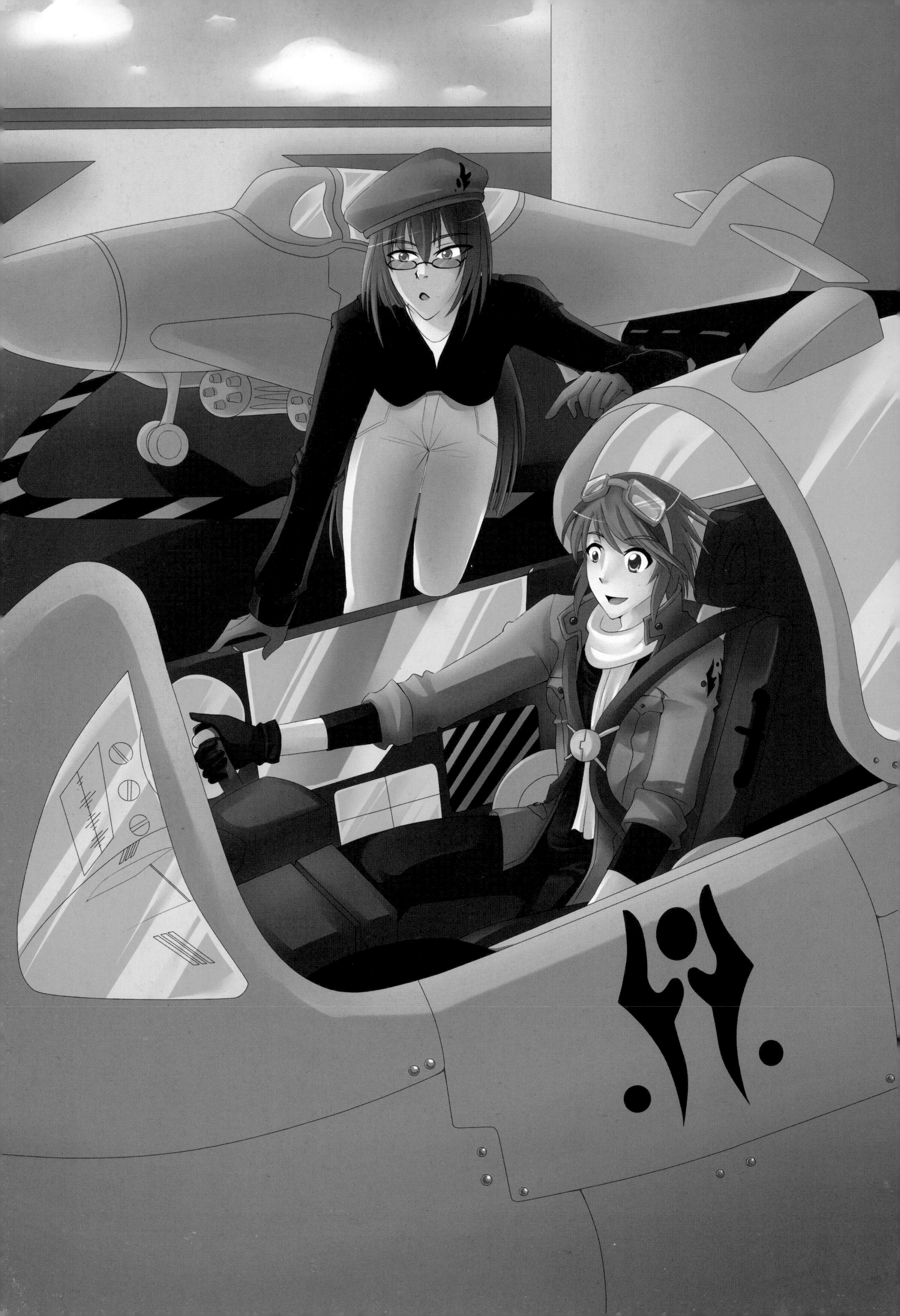

Flight Attendant, Pilot

Pilot
Suit or military-like uniform with epaulettes

Flight Attendant
Clean and well groomed

Tall

Suit-skirt ensemble

➡ Notable Features

- **Clean, well groomed, and has a pleasant and accommodating personality**
- **Alert, disciplined and well-mannered**
- **Pilot is brave and has no fear of flying**
- **Flight attendant is patient and attentive to passengers**
- **Wears suit or military-like uniform with epaulettes, brass buttons and beret or cap**
- **Female flight attendants may wear suit-skirt ensemble**

✢ Outline and Origin

Around the 14th century, English and American marines first designated duties to chief stewards who were given ranks on board merchant ships. Later, this tradition was adapted to passenger airlines.

Flight attendants, also known as stewards and stewardesses, first took their roles in 1911 on board the Zeppelin LZ 10 Schwaben. The flight attendants' duties cover customer service, baggage handling, passenger security and safety, and emergency and evacuation control during flight turbulence or accidents. Therefore, they need to be highly trained in emergency measures and physical injuries or illnesses that could occur during flight.

In 1908, Louis Blériot, a French aviator, was given the first certificate for flying an aircraft as a certified pilot. Today, there are licenses for pilots that fly military planes for combat and pilots that fly passenger airplanes for civilian travel. There is also pilot licensing for commercial aircrafts, which was established by the American civil aviation in 1930. Commercial pilots focus on safety and aviation maneuvers across geographical borders. All pilots need to have good eyesight and a sharp understanding of climate conditions and their implications on air travel.

In Japanese fantasy manga (like in real life), there are both male and female military, civilian and commercial pilots. Many animations portray pilots as fighter pilots who travel across space colonies and attack other planets. They may be humans, humanoids or robots that undergo pilot training and are highly skilled in military combat and the use of weapons. They may fly sophisticated airships, Zeppelins, jets or fighter planes. They may dress in fashionable military suits or with armor, arm guards and helmets. Flight attendants may act as assistants to pilots and be trained in fighting or they may act as independent characters. In some cases, stewardess characters are portrayed as feminine muses who have sad experiences that compel them to fly and escape to other worlds.

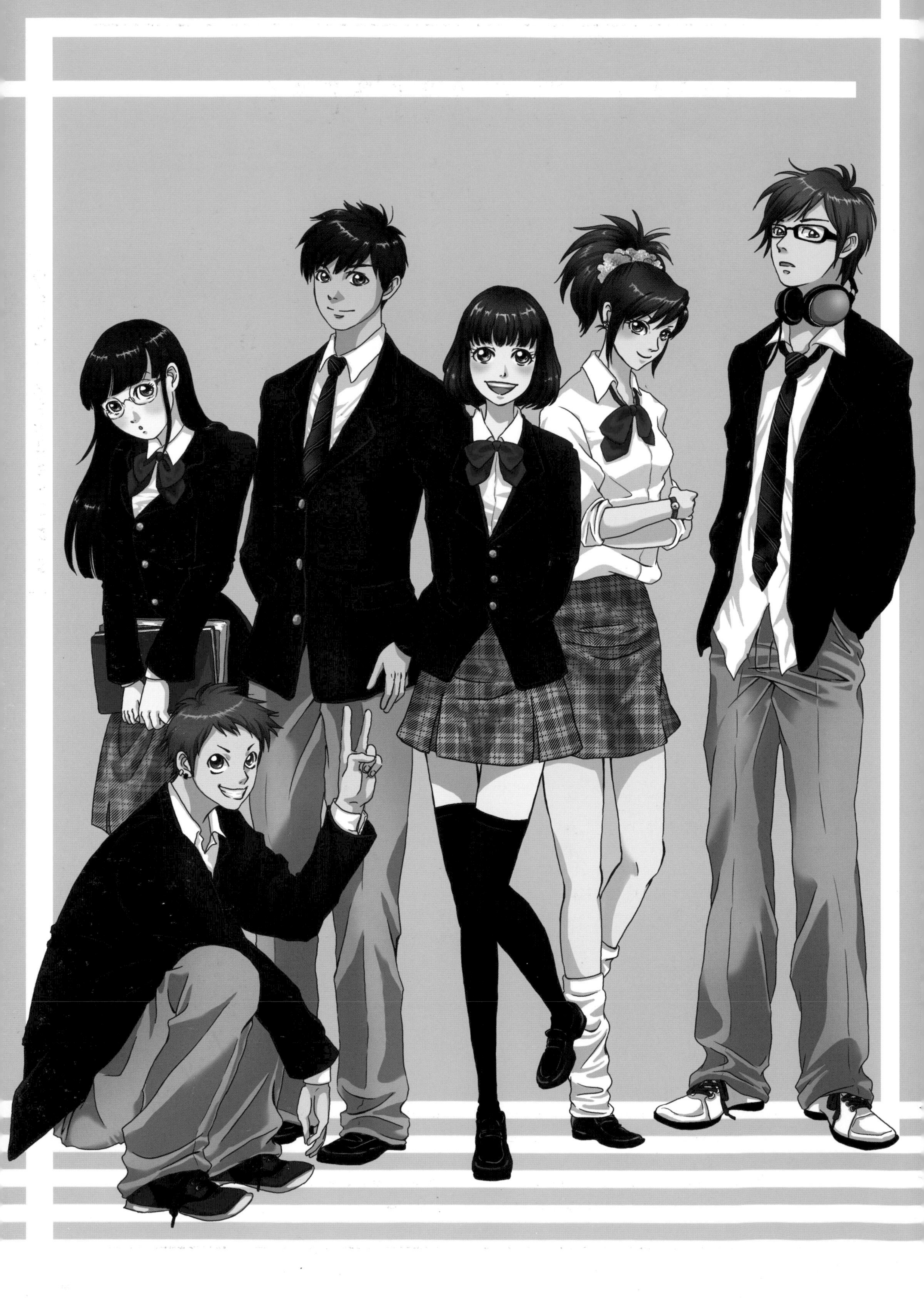

High School Boy/Girl

Short hair

Sailor-type uniform

Gakuran uniform

Dark-colored schoolbag

Leather shoes

➧ Notable Features

- Teenager between 13 and 18 years old
- May have short or long hair; a girl's hair usually styled in a ponytail or pigtails
- Boy character wears white shirt and red, blue or grey striped tie, dark blue, grey or black blazer with school insignia on the breast pocket and tailored trousers; or traditional gakuran black top-to-bottom buttoned uniform with high collar and matching cap
- Girl character wears dark blue, grey or checkered skirt and blazer with school insignia on the breast pocket; or sailor-styled simple white shirt with red or blue sash
- Wears black or brown leather shoes or white sports shoes
- Carries dark blue, black or brown leather schoolbag

✛ Outline and Origin

The first school to open a secondary education or high school program was established in the United States in the 19th century. In Japan, the pre-war system of secondary schools was replaced with the current three-year middle school and three-year high school adopted from the four-year American system.

Some high school boys can be rough, aggressive, dominating, hyperactive, have short attention spans. They may be more inclined to sports and games than studying and may bully or tease girls, and form groups. Others may be overly studious, serious and quiet, and avoid peer interaction. Similarly, high school girls can be loud, talkative and domineering or passive, obedient, studious, friendly to teachers and more diligent than boys.

High schools girls may pay detailed attention to their hairstyle, facial appearance, hand care and clothes. They are frequently conscious of attracting the attention of high school boys, and may quarrel out of jealousy or peer pressure.

High school boy and high school girl characters in animation follow teenagers' behavioral patterns in real life. In manga, however, some are portrayed as having special powers, such as the ability to read minds or cast spells.

Some Japanese manga stories depict differences in rich and poor social classes. Bullying, violent scenes and suicide are also common plots in Japanese fantasy manga. Not all Japanese fantasy manga shows characters asking for help when they need it.

TIMELINE OF PROFESSIONS FROM MAGIC TO SCIENCE

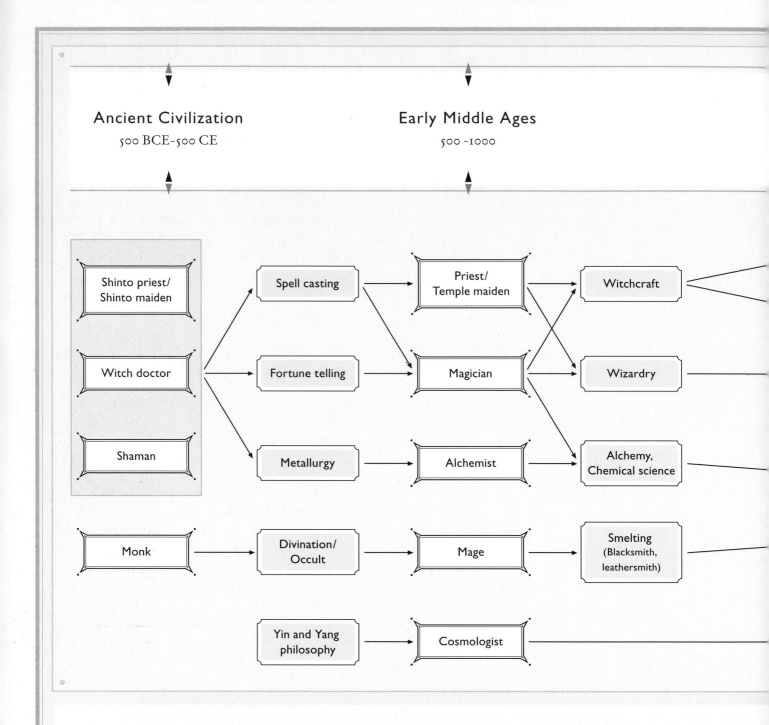

Ancient Civilization
500 BCE-500 CE

Early Middle Ages
500 –1000

Shinto priest/
Shinto maiden

Witch doctor

Shaman

Spell casting

Fortune telling

Metallurgy

Priest/
Temple maiden

Magician

Alchemist

Witchcraft

Wizardry

Alchemy,
Chemical science

Monk

Divination/
Occult

Mage

Smelting
(Blacksmith,
leathersmith)

Yin and Yang
philosophy

Cosmologist

✧ Prehistoric to Ancient Civilization:

Since the beginning of mankind, tribal societies have depended on the powers of natural science and religion for healing sicknesses, driving away evil spirits, and summoning gods, spirits, and the natural elements (earth, water, wind, and fire) for good harvest and protection from enemies. People who could use such special abilities were shamans, early magicians or sorcerers.

✧ Ancient Civilization:

In Ancient Greece and Rome, temple priests and maidens possessed extensive knowledge in astrology, climate and natural forces, which enabled them to use medicinal herbs for various rituals. Priests, hence, became the first prototype magicians in the Classical age, and were especially active in Hellenistic religion (300 BCE-300 CE) when magic and superstition were combined. People relied on oracles, charms, astrology, and symbols to cast spells.

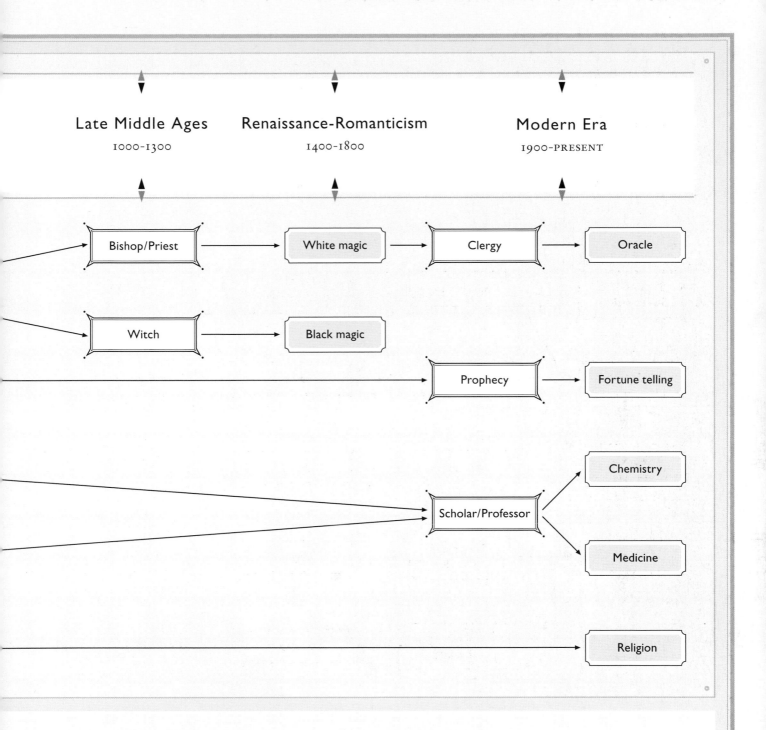

Late Middle Ages
1000-1300

Renaissance-Romanticism
1400-1800

Modern Era
1900-PRESENT

Bishop/Priest → White magic → Clergy → Oracle

Witch → Black magic

Prophecy → Fortune telling

Scholar/Professor → Chemistry

Scholar/Professor → Medicine

Religion

⟡ Middle Ages-Renaissance:

With the spread of religious doctrines, many churches abolished magical rites rites as declaration of heresy, and magic practitioners were labeled as harmful witches or devils who were tried in court or put to death. By the coming of the Renaissance period and Industrial Revolution, science began to influence tools and methods of magic. Alchemy became the source of metal composition, creation of potions and other chemicals that were widely used by magicians in the attempt that the fusion of science into their profession would escape heretic implications.

⟡ Baroque-Modern Era:

Natural sciences, occultism and superstition were all fused with witchcraft and sorcery, and the Witchcraft Act of 1735 allowed magicians to have spiritual powers to continue their profession. Magic and science continued to evolve together until the 20th century with the creation of magic guilds and organizations. Cults all over the world arose with more enhanced practices of magic, both based on potions and chemicals and religious spirits.

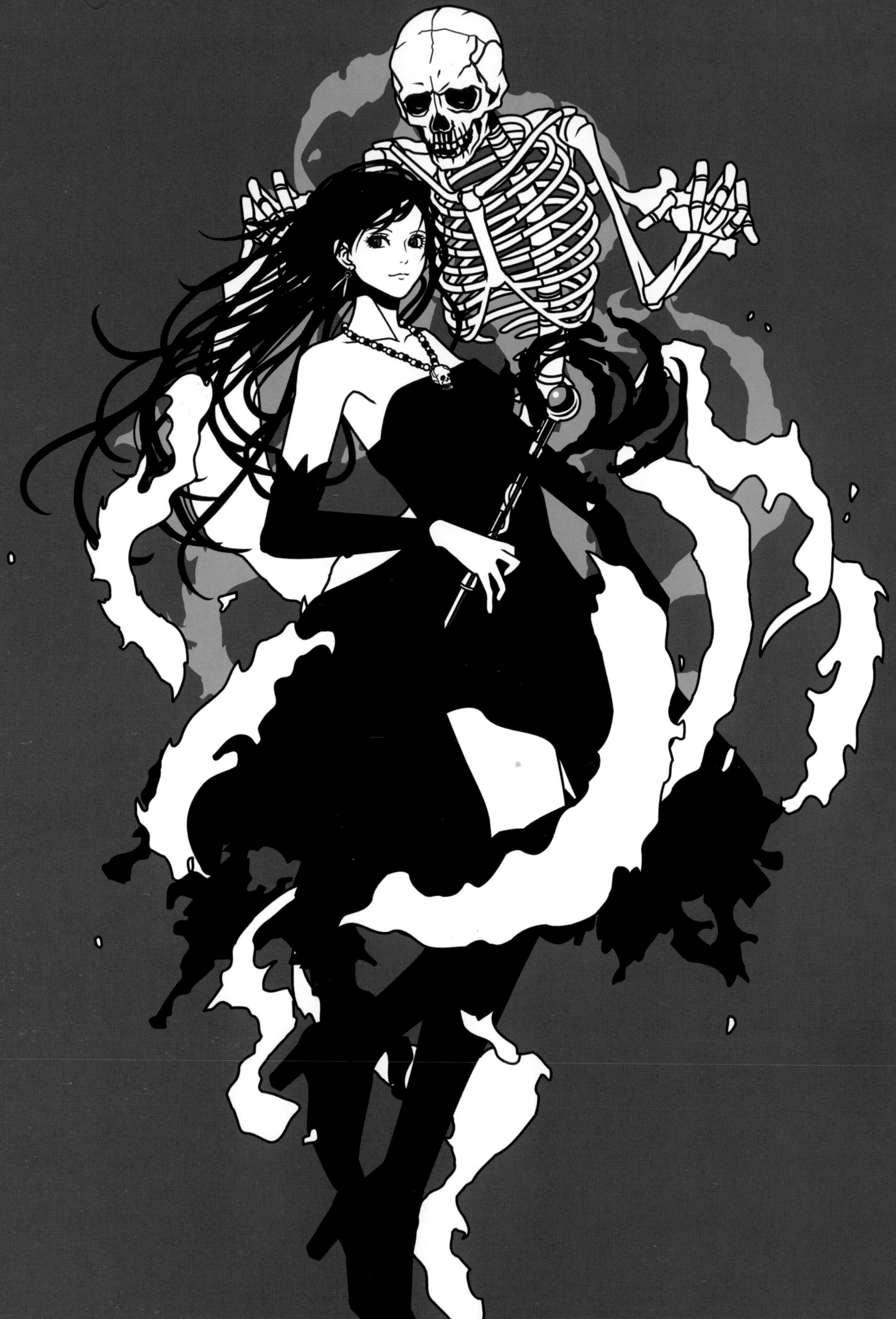

Chapter

技

GIKOU

Practicing Your Superpower

巧

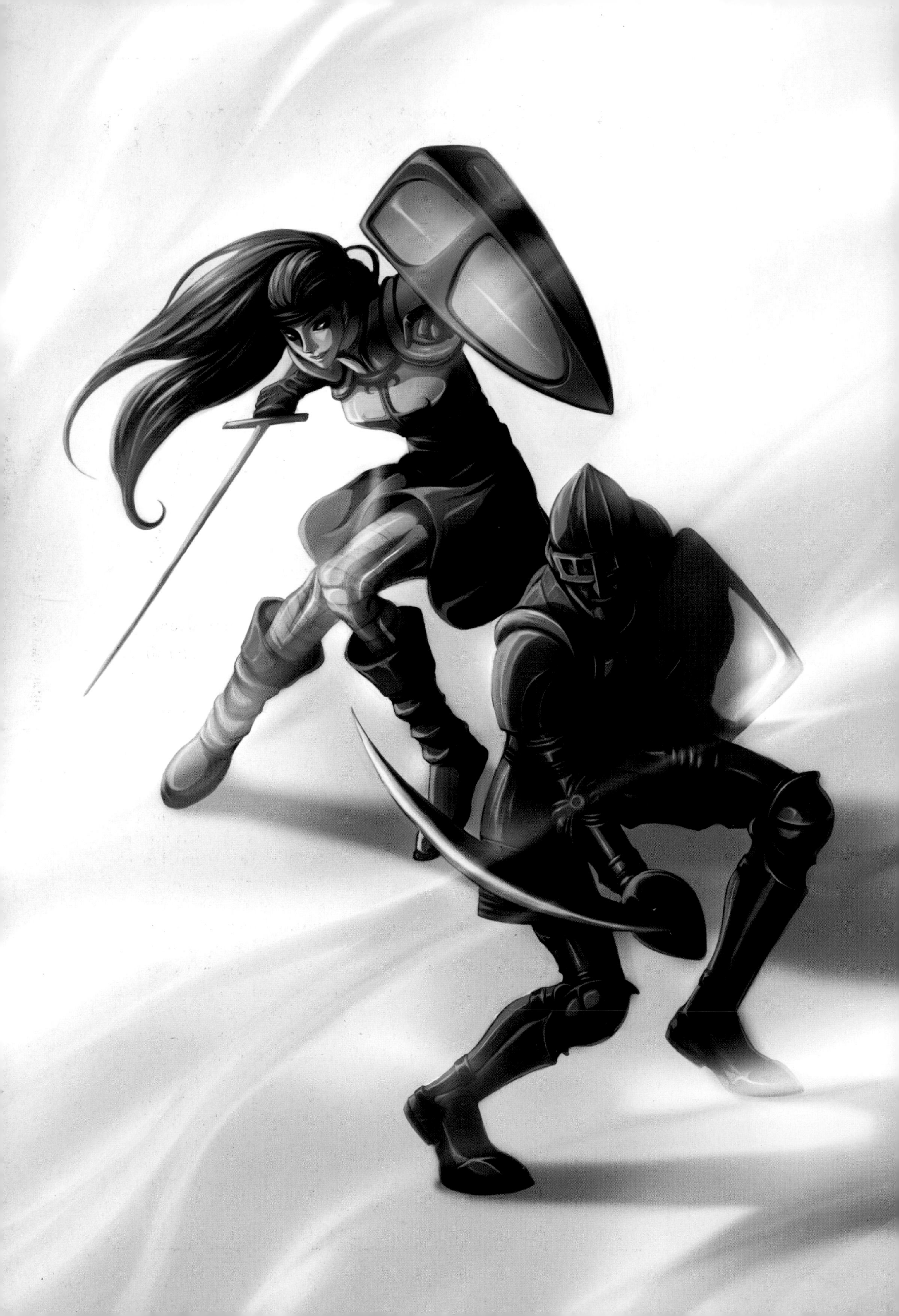

Swordsmanship

Sword thrust — Helmet

Full body armor — Saber

➡ Notable Features

- Skill using the art of the sword
- Types of weapons: double-edged sword (jian), single-blade sword (dao), Japanese wooden sword (bokken), bamboo sword (shinai), unsharpened sword (iaitō), Japanese metal sword (shinken), saber, gladius, spatha (straight sword with a long point), waster (practice sword), arming sword, rapier (slender sword with intricate handle), side-sword, small sword and flame sword
- Swordsman is muscular with rugged features, bulky body, sharp and strong eyes
- Attire: full body armor, helmet, arm guards, metal or leather boots with spikes, long cape or robe, tight trousers or skintight suit

✚ Outline and Origin

The origin of the word swordsman comes from the Latin term gladius, meaning sword, associated with Roman gladiators who were trained fighters that dueled against each other in front of spectators during the Roman Empire. Swords were first used as hunting weapons as early as the Bronze Age around 3300 B.C.

Around 1190 B.C., the first evidence of fencing as a match was seen in a carving in an Egyptian temple, showing men in masks and weapons with judges. But it was not until 1450 when European fencing guilds were formed.

Spain developed the first fencing technique around 1471. By 1500, the Italians started to use the rapier, holding it with the right hand, and the dagger or a small shield with the left hand. They invented the various fencing positions, and by the 16th century, fencing had become a popular skill for dueling.

Swordsmanship spread quickly across China, Japan, Korea and the Philippines, in Arab countries, and across the European continent. The sword is a prominent tool in Asian martial arts, especially the Chinese double-edged sword and the Japanese metal or wooden sword. Swordsmen are strong, powerful and highly trained in warfare tactics using various types of swords. Members of noble families are frequently given lessons in sword handling and fencing.

Fantasy heroes of swordsmanship can increase their energy level through the power of their swords. Their swords can lift heavy objects, cut stone or steel, swing at high speed and release powerful blasts. Swordsmen are characters known for their defensive strength, vitality, and dexterity. They are capable of using shields in addition to their swords, and some have the ability to use magic or spells. Dragon slayers and knights are examples of characters who rely on their swordsmanship.

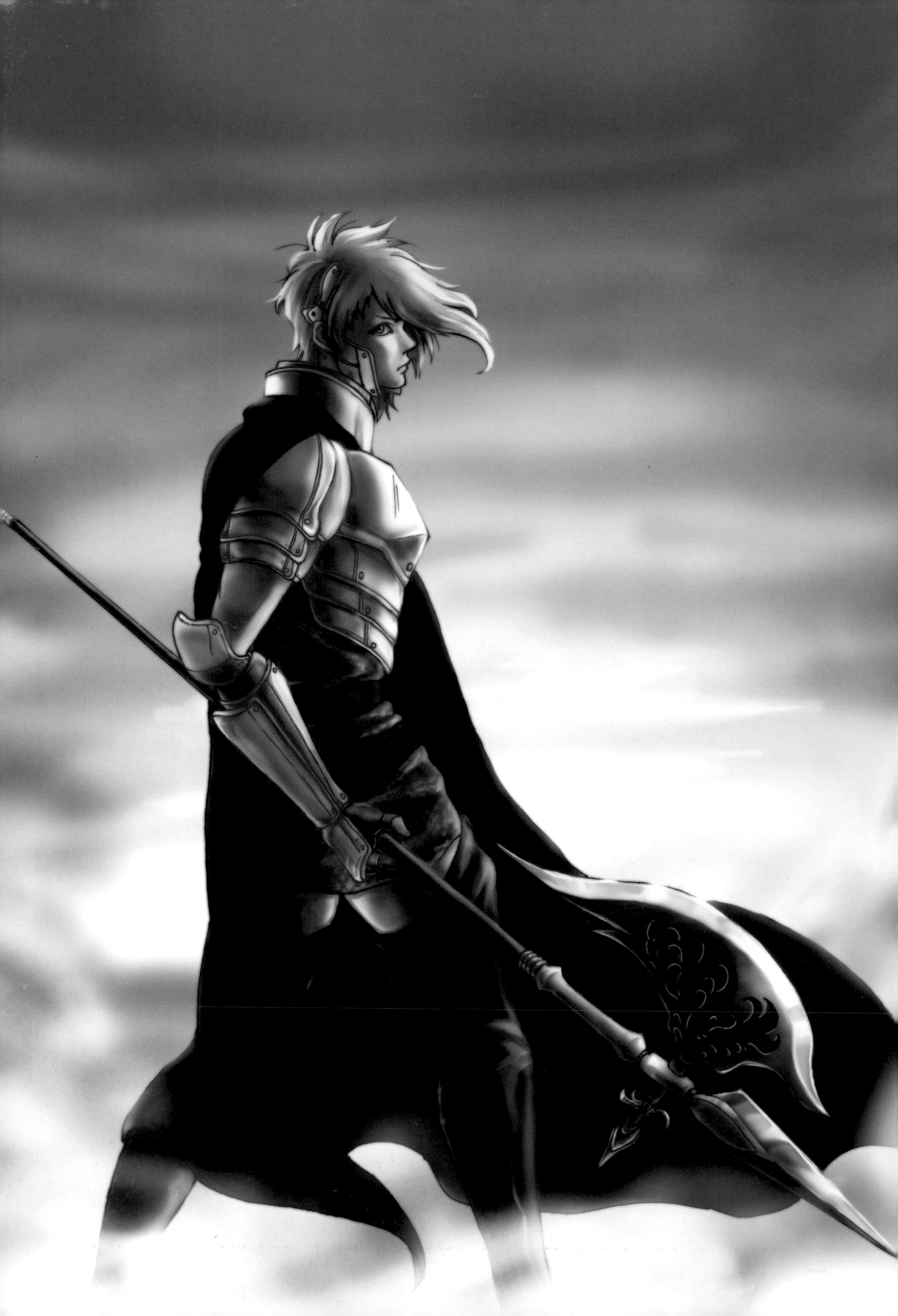

Spearing

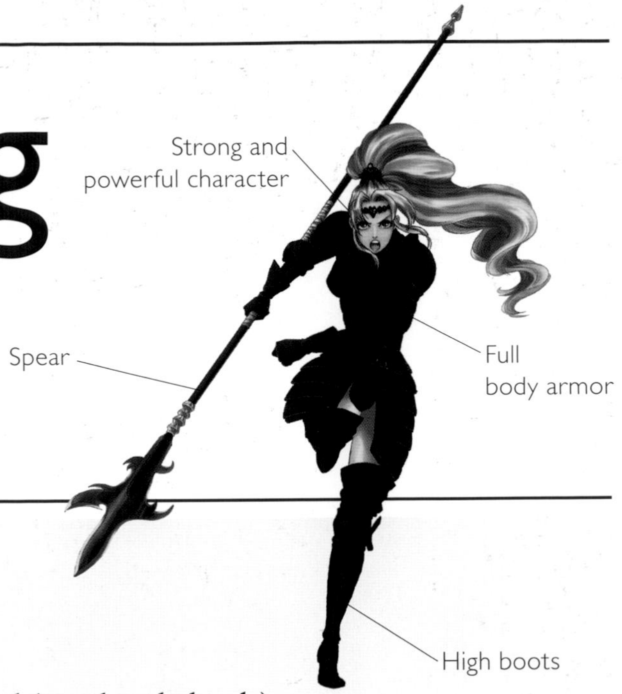
Strong and
powerful character
Spear
Full
body armor
High boots

➡ Notable Features

- Skill using the art of the spear
- Types of spears: bamboo spear, halberd (two-handed pole), naginata (Japanese pole with a curved blade), sarissa (ancient Greek long pike), hasta (early Roman spear with an iron head), xyston (ancient Greek pointed stick with a metallic tip), kontos (long and wooden cavalry lance), pollaxe (polearm with an axe or hammer head), spontoon (half-pike) or dangpa (Korean three-ponged spear)
- Spear fighter or spearman is strong, powerful, quick, alert and well-focused
- Attire: long trousers, tunic with chain mail and a vest over the shirt; or long cape and belt around the waist to hold a dagger or short spear, and metal helmet; also commonly worn is full body armor and high boots, or martial arts attire (loose tunic and loose trousers)

+ Outline and Origin

Wooden spears were first used as hunting weapons more than a million years ago. Neanderthal and Paleolithic humans made spearheads out of stone. By around 15000 B.C, spear-throwers, such as atlatls were used in spear fighting. The lance, halberd, naginata and pike were the early ancestry weapons used for combat, and javelins were specifically used for throwing, as they are lighter and finer.

The Mesopotamian, Egyptian and Greek warriors used short spears, and around 7th century B.C., infantries were formed with soldiers carrying shields and 9-foot spears with iron heads and bronze butts. Spear fighting dominated the Roman period, and until the 2nd century, all legionaries fought with a pilum (heavy javelin with an iron shank).

All European armies throughout the Middle Ages, including the Vikings, employed spears and shields. Cavalrymen were also seen on horses holding lances and tucking them under their armpits, which became the common lance technique for spear combat while mounted on a horse. Spears were also very powerful weapons in Asia among Chinese spearmen who used them for group attacks, and Japanese samurai who preferred them over swords around the 11th century.

The spearman in the fantasy world is a powerful mercenary who can cause great physical damage with his spear. He can attack two enemies at the same time, and is highly skilled in using a lightning spear, which easily makes opponents miss turns. While he may have great attack power, he can be weak in magic defense. While spearmen are frequently human, there are also orc spearmen as well as humanoid spearmen.

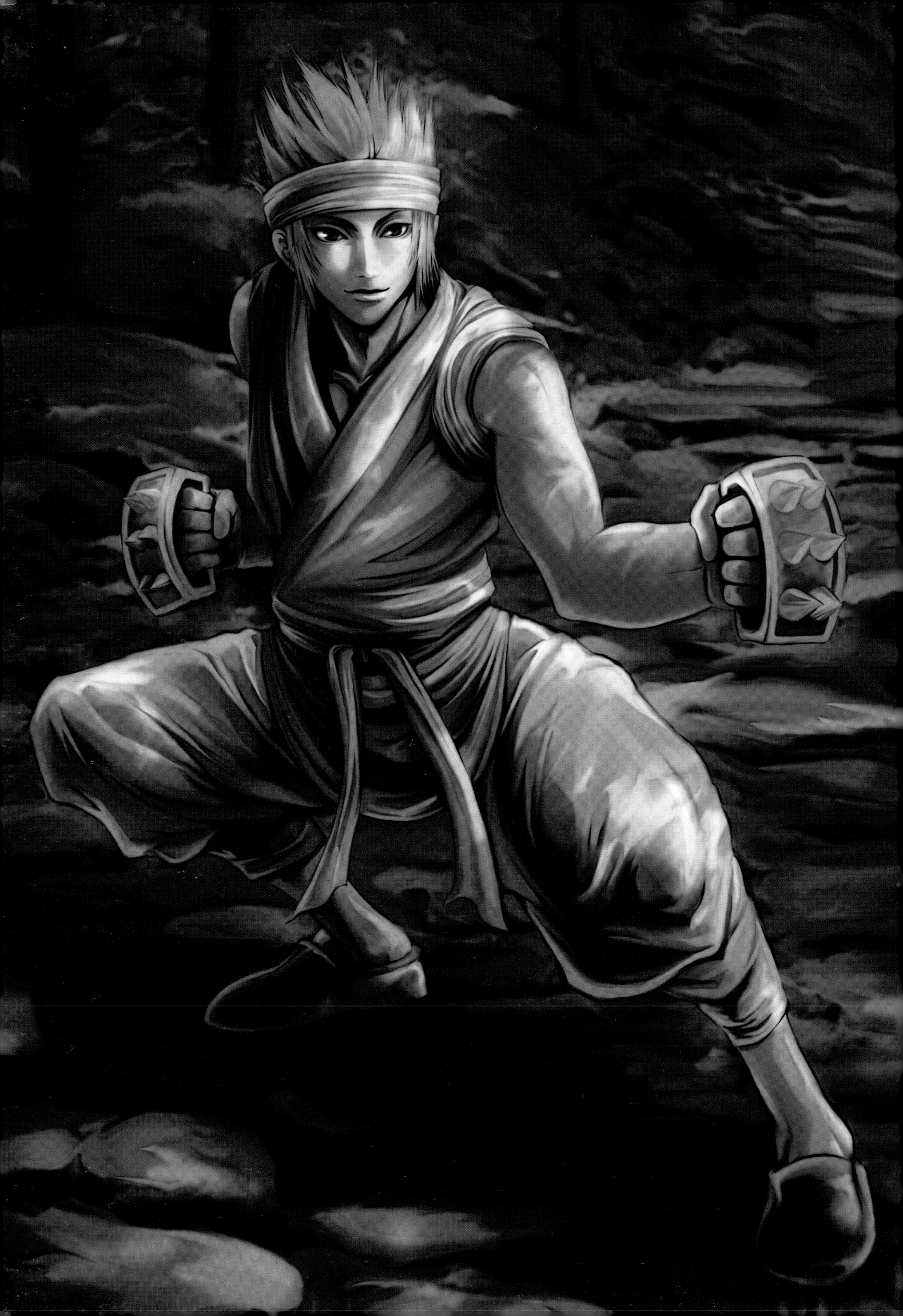

Knuckle Use

Fierceful eyes

Iron claws

Loose half-trousers

Shoe studs

➤ Notable Features

- Skill of knuckle fist fighting
- May be bare-knuckle boxing or brass knuckle boxing with knuckle dusters, iron claws, rings, cestus (ancient battle gloves), blade handle, weighted-knuckle gloves, and iron stirrup or tekko
- Knuckle blows may be accompanied by kicks, swings, jumps and turns
- The knuckle fist fighter is muscular with fierce eyes and a rugged appearance
- Attire: bare top and loose trousers; colored sleeveless vest over plain or white sleeveless shirt, rugged pants; long body tunic with leather or cloth belt around the waist; or martial arts attire with a cloth headband

✚ Outline and Origin

Early evidence of fist fighting can be found in relief carvings from Sumer, Egypt, Assyria and Minoa around the 3rd millennium B.C. Around 1500-900 B.C., archaeological findings of men fighting with gloves were found. Ancient Greek warriors were known for joining boxing competitions. Around the 9th century B.C., Theseus, the Greek ruler, was said to have invented fist fighting by having two men sit face to face and beat each other with their fists until one of them died. Eventually, men involved in fist fighting fought each other while standing and wearing gloves with spikes.

Bare-knuckle fist fighting is combat boxing without the use of any weapons. Unlike street fighting, it abides by the rule that one cannot strike an opponent who has fallen on the ground. The first recognized bare-knuckle fighting champion is the English prizefighter James Figg who received his title in 1719. Brass knuckles, also called knuckle dusters, are made of metal shaped to fit the knuckles. They produce a more forceful punch and can cause massive tissue damage and bone fractures. They originate from the Roman cestus, ancient battle gloves used by Roman gladiators that were sometimes covered with spikes, studs and iron plates. The Greeks also used a version of them that were made of leather thongs. In Japan, kobudo or Okinawan martial arts introduced the tekko, a fist weapon designed like a stirrup with iron backing. It emphasizes blocking or shielding, receiving weapon blows without injury and striking opponents forcefully.

In fantasy games, a mastery of knuckle fighting requires expertise in several techniques, such as hell fist (a knuckle attack performed while a character is moving forward), twin fist (a double punch with a powerful blow), flame kick (a strong spin kick), wind kick (a double spin kick), crescent kick (a back spin kick), and energy boom (an energy driven blow from the palm).

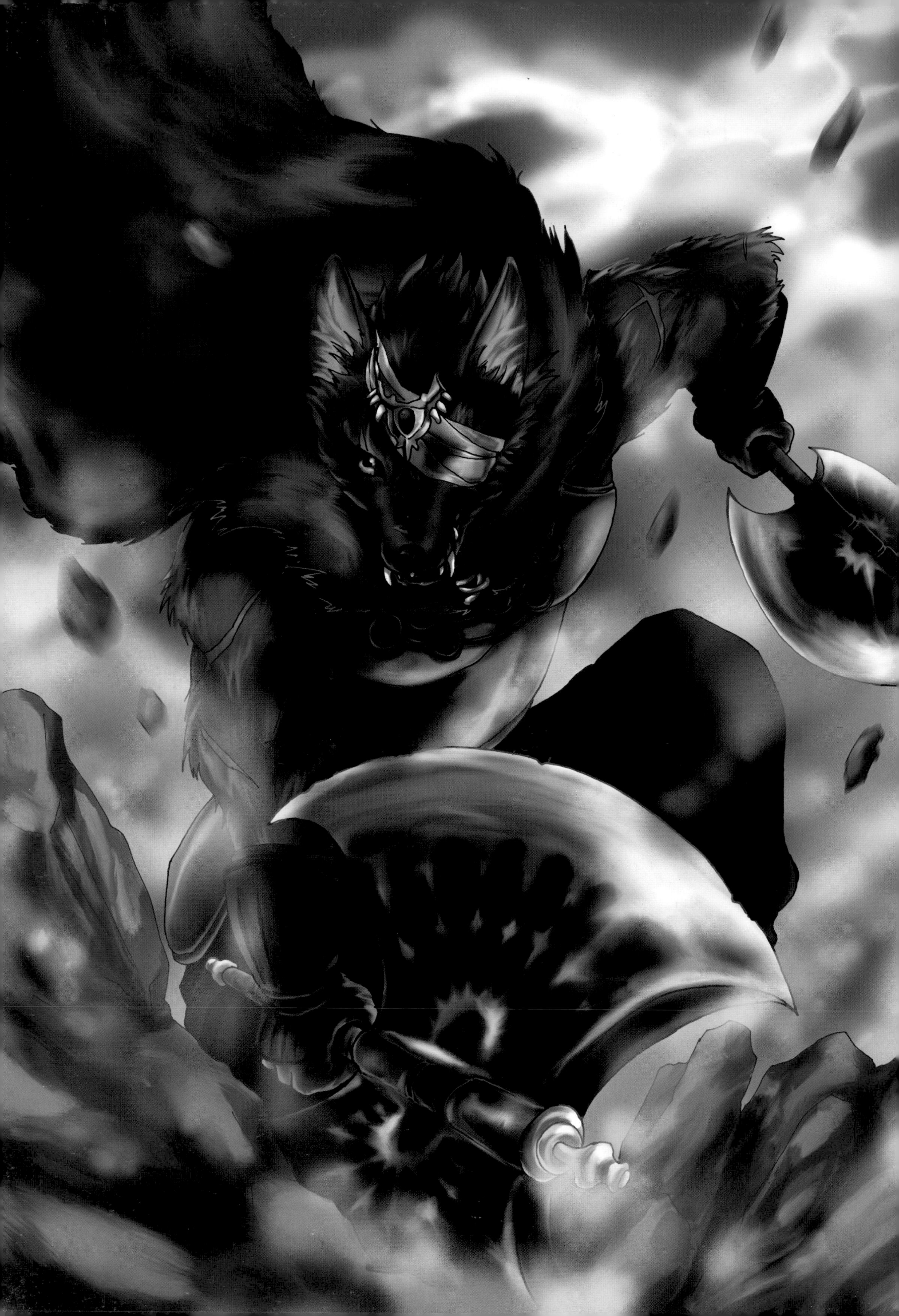

Blunt Instrument Use

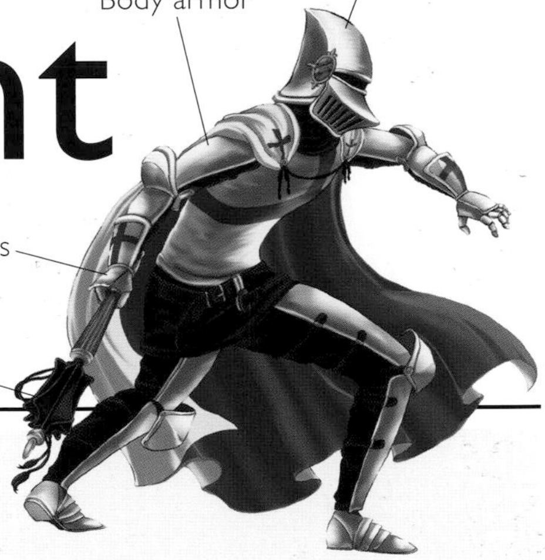
Helmet
Body armor
Powerful hands
Flanged war mace

➡ Notable Features

- **Skill of striking forcefully, usually with a rounded or squared-edged object**
- **Types of blunt weapons: club, hammer, bat, cane, axe, nightstick, baton, chain lock, brick, mace, staff or weight stone**
- **Fighters may be character classes of: rogues, priests, shamans, druids, knights, paladins, barbarians, crusaders or warriors**
- **Fighters are heavy, stocky, and have powerful hands**
- **Attire: long trousers; cloth, leather or mail armor; cloth or leather gloves with spikes; headdress; heavy boots**

+ Outline and Origin

Using blunt instruments is one of man's instinctive actions when fighting. These blunt instruments become weapons when used to forcefully strike an opponent's head, neck, chest, abdomen, legs or other body part, and cause severe bone damage by a single blow, which is referred to as blunt force trauma. Examples of physical damages caused by such a trauma are an internal hemorrhage, internal organ damage, eruption of the liver or intestines, severe eye injury, and surface wounds that can result in death.

The early Egyptians used clubs in combat, which were made of strong wood that could smash the head. The degree of the striking force can depend on the size of the club—the bigger the club, the greater the damage. Later, the club evolved into a mace, which is usually a wooden club with a stone head in the form of a disc and was first used in predynastic Egypt (5500-3100 B.C.). Pharaohs and kings were seen holding mace weapons as symbols of power. In the Middle Ages, the mace was designed with star spikes attached to a chain for greater speed and force.

In the fantasy world, blunt instruments are popular one- or two-handed crushing weapons. The most common one-handed weapons used as blunt instruments are maces. Some types of maces are the spiked mace, flanged war mace (wire-wrapped or spiral-gripped), and dowel pin mace (with corrugated, spikes on the head). Maces may be made of iron, steel, silver, glass, ebony, and sized to be used by humans, humanoids, dwarves, elves, rogues, priests, shamans and druids.

The most common two handed blunt instruments are battle axes which can be enchanted or unenchanted, swords, pole arms, staves and hammers. The staff has a small ball or decorated shape on one end, and is often used by knights, paladins and warriors. Hammers can be sledgehammers or riders' hammers with thick, metal spikes.

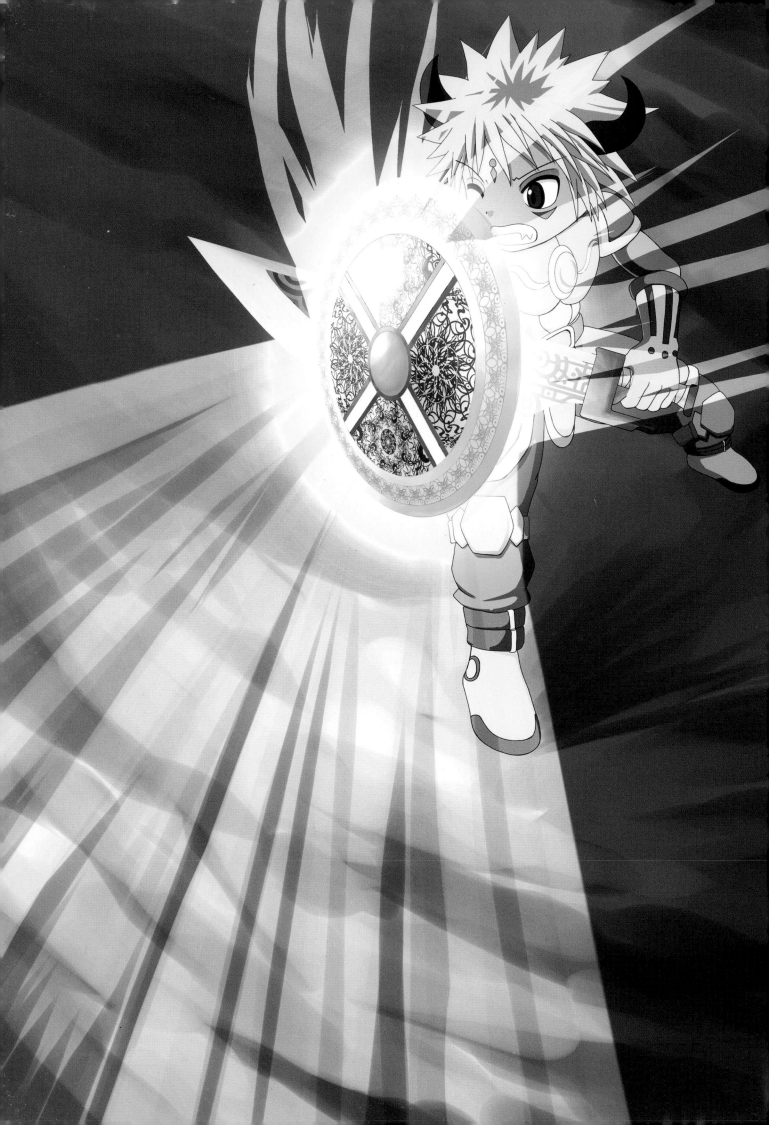

Shield Use

Spear

Strong and fierce

Battersea shield

Heavy boots

➡ Notable Features

- Skill in using a shield for combat
- Types of shields: Yetholm shield (copper alloy shield with domed boss), Battersea shield (bronze shield with repoussé decoration), aspis or hoplon (wooden dished shield), scutum (rectangular semi-cylindrical shield), kite shield (teardrop-shaped with leather straps), heater shield (flat iron-shaped wooden shield), heraldic shield (qval, round or diamond-shaped with a crest), pavise (large, convex shield), buckler (small shield gripped by the fist), targe (large shield with enarmes), parma (round, iron-framed Roman shield), Ishlangu (large, lightweight shield), riot shield (used by police), divine shield (used by paladins), lightning shield (used by shamans), mana shield (with magic) and fire shield
- Shield users may be paladins, shamans, knights or warriors
- Attire: heavy body armor and helmet, and may carry other weapons in addition to the shield, like a spear or sword

✚ Outline and Origin

During the Bronze Age and Iron Age, shields were used to block hand weapon attacks. They were made of wood, metal or animal skin. The Yetholm shields of the Bronze Age (1200-800 B.C.) came from Britain, Ireland and Denmark, and were characterized by rings of dots with a domed boss at the center. The battersea shield originates around the 1st century B.C., and was decorated with repoussé (ornamented metalwork) and enamel, but was not known as a strong combat shield.

There are light shields for lightly armed warriors who focus on speed and sudden attack, and large, heavier shields with straps for heavily armored warriors who need them to protect their entire bodies. Egyptians used large and small round shields made of a variety of materials; Greeks used round, bowl-shaped shields made of wood. In the Middle Ages, knights were known for using kite shields, heater shields

and bucklers.

In fantasy manga, fighting with shields involves tactics for defense and dodging (reducing the chance to be hit), or using spells and magic. Shields for defense strategies are suitable for warriors and paladins, while those with spells and magic are made for shamans or holy paladins. Power word shields, for example, are reflective shields used by priests and can cause mental pressure or pain suppression. Divine shields have protection spells that help the paladin to gain time before casting his spell; they also prevent damages like falling and drowning. Lightning shields are used by shamans, and they consist of three lightning balls that will strike an enemy. Mana shields absorb all kinds of physical and magical damage, and are therefore, widely used by magicians and other spell casters. Other shields used by spell casters are ice barriers and fire shields.

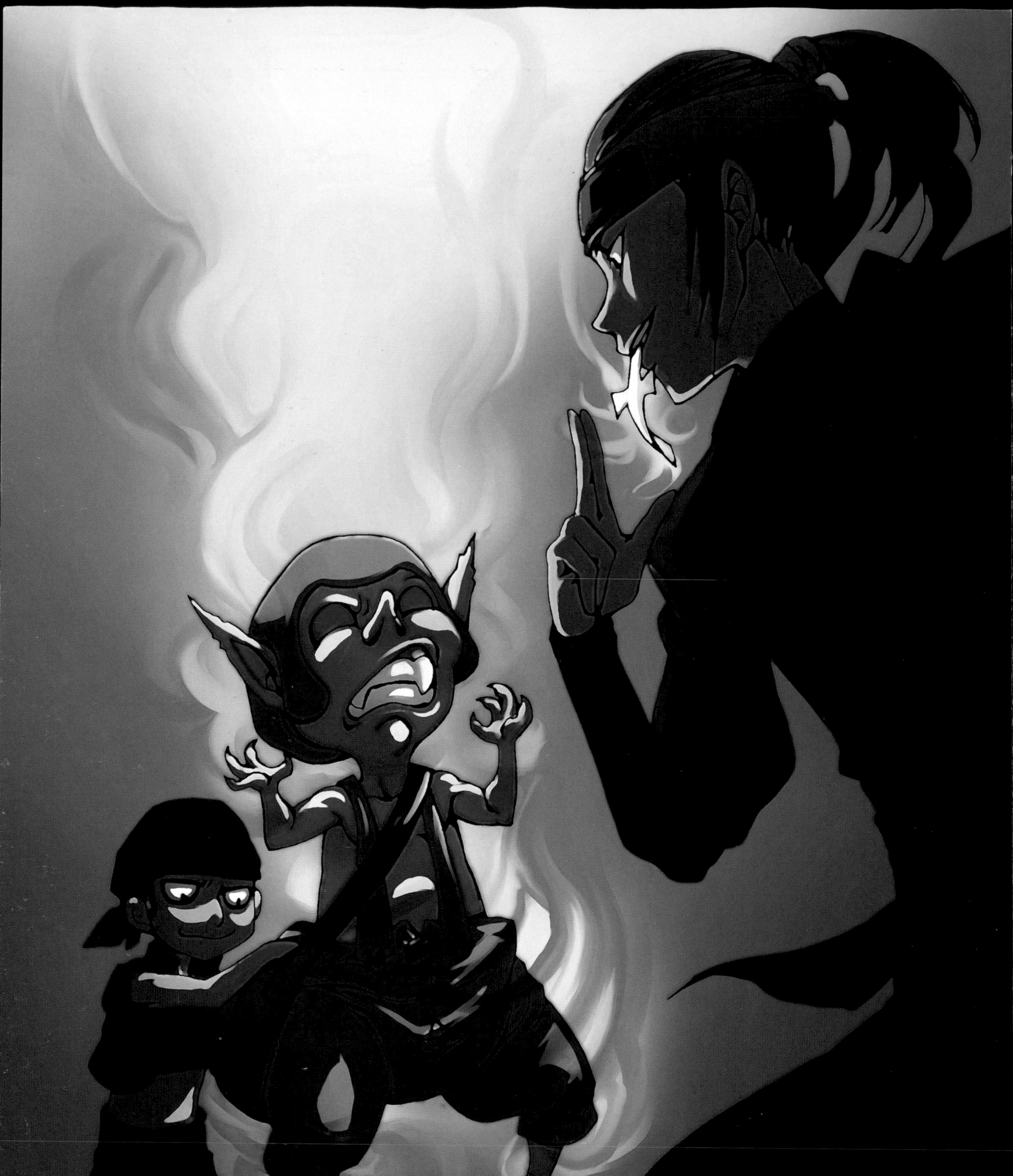

Stealing, Hiding, Ninja Art

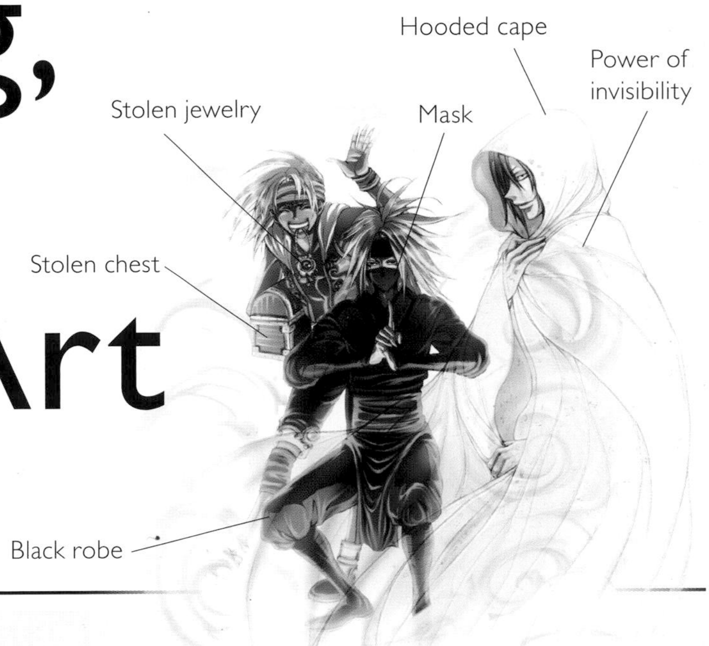
Hooded cape
Power of invisibility
Stolen jewelry
Mask
Stolen chest
Black robe

➡ Notable Features

- **Skills in taking items from others secretly (stealing), using the power of invisibility (hiding), and mastering ninja combat strategies (ninja art)**
- **Stolen and hidden items: potions, gems, junk boxes, coins, weapons and documents**
- **Stealing skill users may be rogues and thieves; hiding skill users may be gypsies and thieves; ninja art skill users are ninjas, thieves and assassins**
- **Attire (stealing and hiding): leather or cloth armor, black clothes, hooded cape or robe, mask; may carry sword, mace, fist weapons and ranged weapons**
- **Attire (ninja art): traditional attire of ninja (loose black robe with belt, body armor or tight body suit with mask); may carry swords or spears**

✚ Outline and Origin

Thieves and rogues excel in the skill of stealing. They may be humans, dwarves, gnomes, elves or ethereals (astral spirits). They steal coins, gems, treasures, healing potions, poisons, documents and other items from monsters and enemies. Stealing can be target-based, which gives the rogue or thief higher chances of succeeding, or done randomly, wherein one cannot pre-determine what to steal. Thieves may use a disguise to hide their appearance, or the power of stealth (deception skill) for distraction and pick pocketing.

The skill of hiding may invoke the power of invisibility, but enemies can use a "detect hidden" skill, "reveal" spell or "tracking" skill that can spoil this strategy. By using stealth power, the character hiding can move to other places without being seen. This skill requires a high degree of dexterity and intelligence.

Ninjitsu or ninja art is practiced by ninjas who are highly trained in gathering secret information, disguise, non-detection, escape, use of medicine, explosives, poison, and weapons of archery or swordsmanship. Ninja art skill users can perform death strike, animal transformation, Ki (life force energy of martial arts) and surprise attack, backstab, shadow jumps and mirror image. They may carry swords, maces, or bows and arrows, and use shuriken darts and smoke bombs.

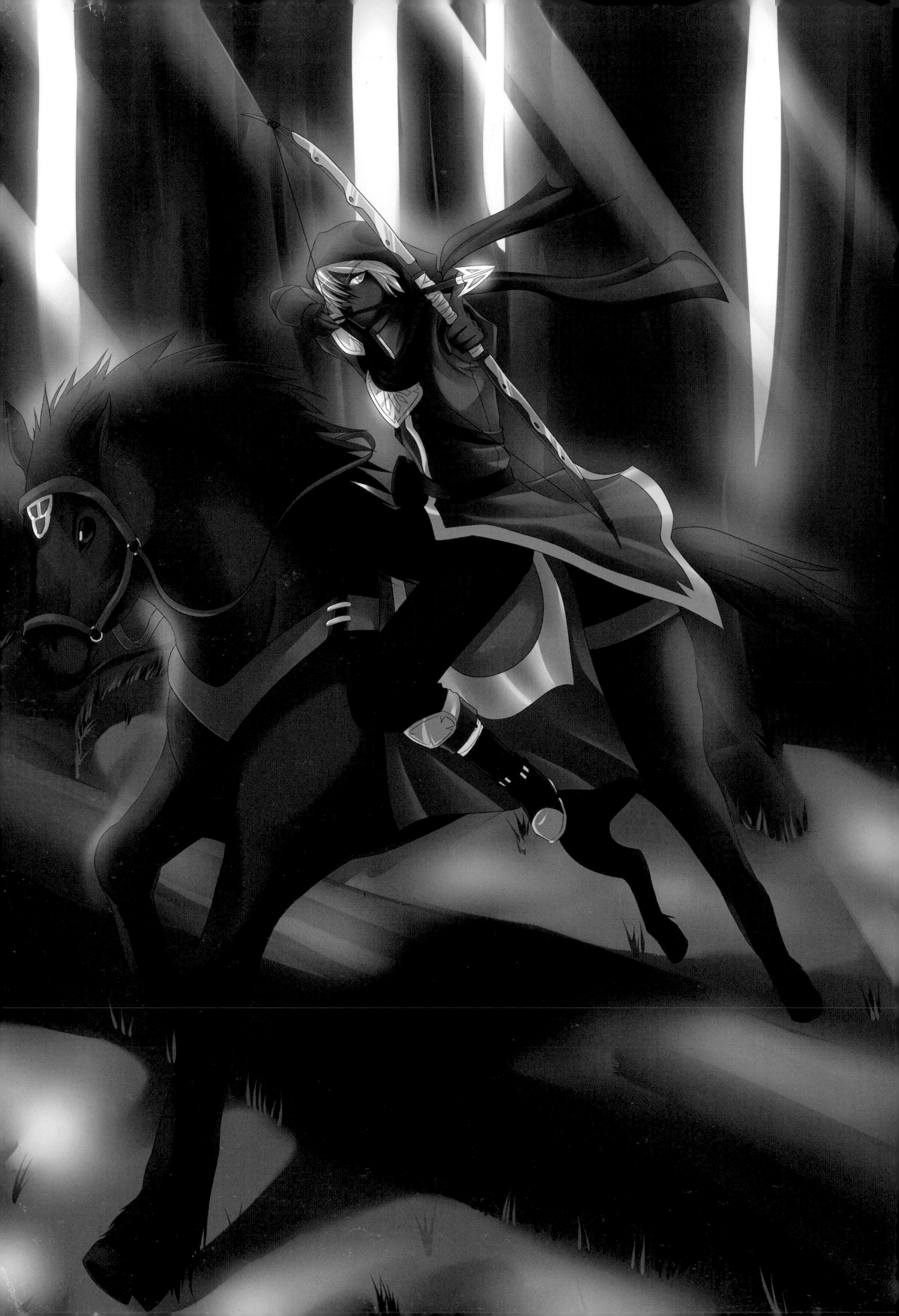

Archery

Bow and arrow — Pandaren — Arm guard — High boots

➡ Notable Features

- Skill in using bow and arrow for combat
- Types of bows: composite bow (different materials laminated together), crossbow (mounted on a stick), orcish bow (one-handed, crude), slayer bow (modified with gears for slayers), elven composite longbow (two-handed with serpent arrow), lightweight short bow (magical), recurve bow (tips curved away from the archer), decurve bow (curved or curled arms at the ends facing the archer), deflex bow (curved or curled arms at the base), self bow (made from single piece of wood), flat bow (with non-curved, flat limbs)
- Types of arrows: rough arrow, sharp arrow, razor arrow, feathered arrow, jagged arrow, ice threaded arrow (bright blue glow), ice blade arrow, footed arrow (inlay or "footing" at the head of the shaft)
- Archer may be human, elf, pandaren (humanoid panda), orc, goblin, dwarf or gnome
- Attire: bracer or arm guard and a chest guard, glove or thumb ring, long hooded gown or long jacket and hat, layered shirts or vests, loose trousers fit at the knees, and tucked in high-laced boots, and may ride on a horse

✛ Outline and Origin

Bows have existed since the Paleolithic or early Mesolithic period. Around 9000-8000 B.C., most arrows were made from pine and had long foreshafts; there were also arrowheads made of stone in Africa. Among the earliest self-made bows were those made of elm that had flat arms; these were found in archeological ruins in Denmark. Archery is known to have been prominent in early Egypt, and widely used by Persian, Indian, Korean, Chinese and Japanese armies.

Archery is included in a fighter's skill set that also includes fencing, mace use and swordsmanship. It may be a weak skill, but because of its long-range element, an archer does not have to be too close to his enemy, which can be a monster, ogre, rotten corpse or other non-character player, and therefore attack by surprise. An archer, who can be human, elf, half-elf, half-orc, dwarf or humanoid, must have steady aim, dexterous fingers, and mastery of the special moves of the bow and arrow he is using. There are also night elf archers who have great speed and power of dark vision and stealth.

Different types of bows and arrows have their own power levels, and an archer must be familiar with them. A moving shot, for example, that allows archers to fire while in motion, can be used with a heavy crossbow. A paralyzing blow is a special move that stuns the enemy, leaving him unable to move and attack. A double strike can be used with a repeating crossbow. A lightning arrow can be used with a magical short bow.

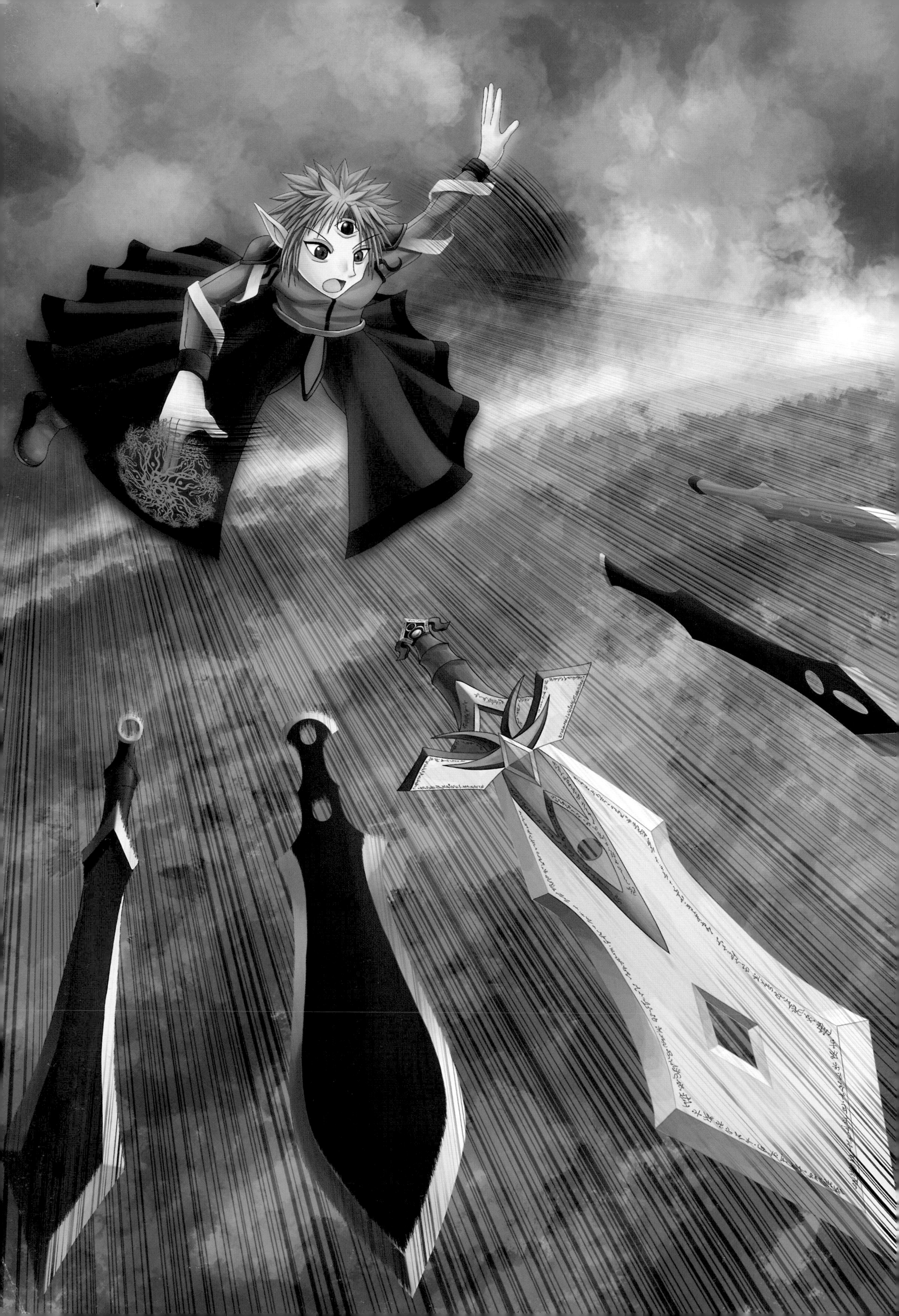

Weapon Throwing

Quick, alert and well-focused character

Cloth attire

High speed throw

Metal discs

➡ Notable Features

- Skill in throwing weapons for combat
- Types of thrown weapons: axe, shuriken, blade, dart, knife, dagger, harpoon, boomerang, cyclone blade, glaive, spear, sling, tomahawk, throwing cutter, hammer, club, stick, chakram (metal disc), dragon beard hook and arrow
- Weapon throwers may be rogues, hunters, warriors, knights, warlocks or gargoyles
- Attire: cloth, leather or mail armor, shield, ring, necklace, cloak

✛ Outline and Origin

Weapon throwing was one of the first types of long-range warfare. The oldest wooden throwing spears are 400,000 years old and were found in Germany. A javelin is a kind of throwing spear that dates back to the Paleolithic period. Throwing clubs were used as early as 6000 B.C. in Africa, and there were also prehistoric throwing axes made of stone and wood. Sumerians, Egyptians, Assyrians, Greeks and Romans have all used spears, axes, clubs, daggers and slings for throwing during battles.

The technique of weapon throwing relies on reaching specific ranges for specific weapons. The shortest range is reachable with the underthrown technique, followed by a middle range with the perfect range technique, and a longer range with the overthrown technique. Different types of throws are also suitable for different weapons. Boomerangs can be used with a heavy concussion throw; cyclone blades with a moving shot; and glaives with a mortal strike. Throwing knives or special throwing knives poisoned to cause extra harm allow a fast attack speed. Axes have a slower speed because of their weight. Darts are very fast weapons; they can be made of iron, bronze or steel.

Many fighters prefer weapon throwing to other forms of ranged combat because it does not require supplementary ammunition. Rogues use weapon throwing most effectively, and they can reach the highest level of a deadly throw, which causes intense physical damage or death to an enemy.

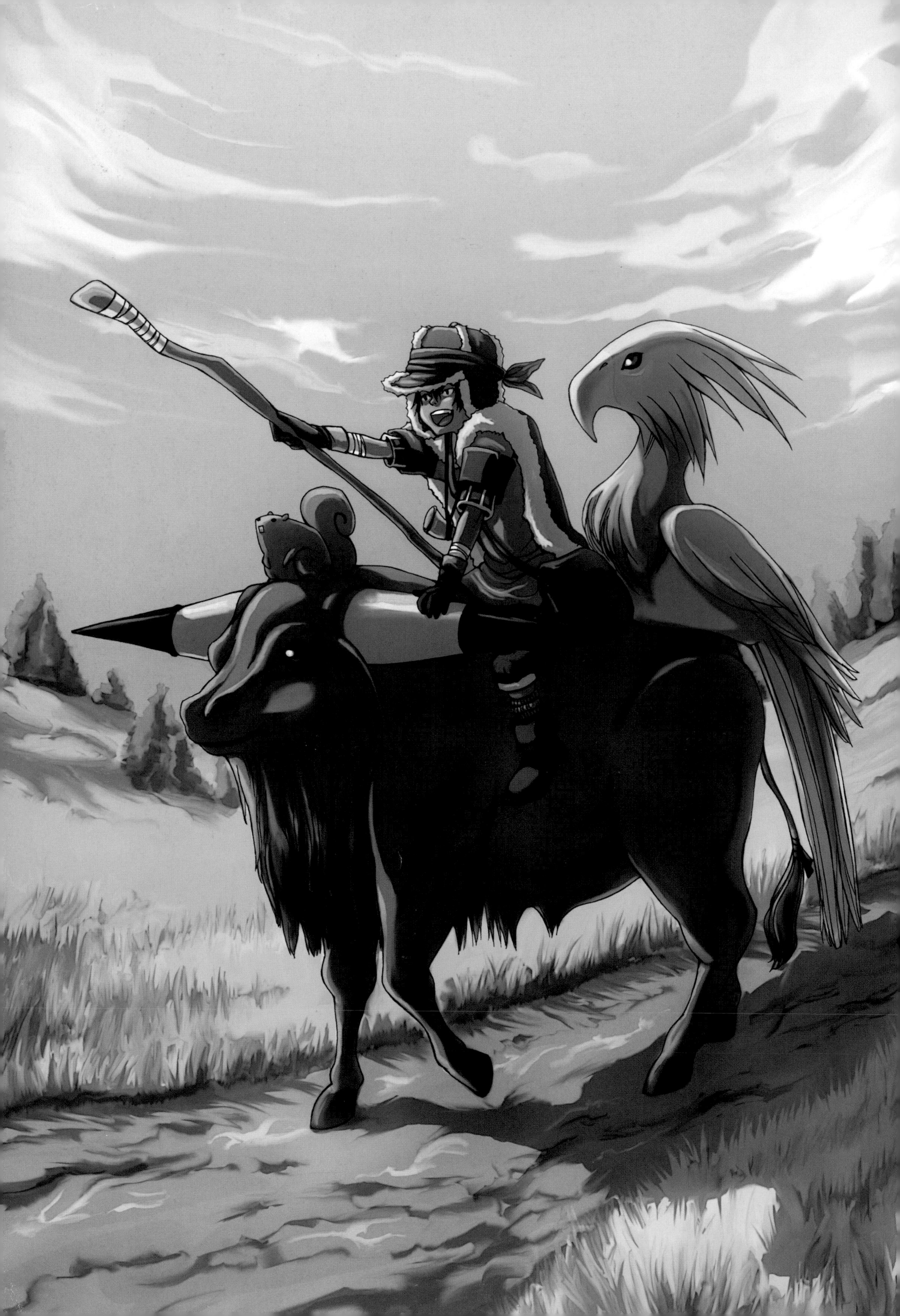

Animal Taming

Wild animal

Tamer is friendly and close with animals

Leather attire

Fighting weapon

➡ Notable Features

- Skill in training, commanding and controlling animals, magical beasts, reptiles and insects
- Types of controllable creatures: dragon, fire steed (golden horse), unicorn, nightmare (fallen horse), ridgeback, dire wolf, bull, grizzly bear, polar bear, walrus, cow, goat, pig, sheep, forest ostard (large bird), snow leopard, panther, fox, rune beetle, dragon hawk, gorilla, hyena, serpent, spider and moth
- Animal tamer may be a beast master, hunter or warrior
- Attire: leather, cloth or mail armor, and carries axe, crossbow, sword, dagger, pole arm, staff or other fist weapon

✚ Outline and Origin

Taming and training animals, such as dogs, cats, goats, sheep, horses and cattle, can be traced back to 13000 B.C. In ancient Egypt, wild cats were trained to guard shops and protect them from rats. From around 9000-4000 B.C., wild pigs, sheep, horses, cows and goats were domesticated for agricultural purposes. Horses were used for assistance in plowing fields, and later for transportation and battle. Other animals were trained to behave in a calm manner toward humans, to eat an affordable diet, to mate and breed, and to survive harmoniously with other animals.

Beast masters, hunters and warriors are the the most well-known animal tamers. They have patience, will power and the physical strength to overtake the animals they are taming. Most animals must be paralyzed to be tamed. This can be done by fighting them until they are almost dead, using a freezing trap, using a polymorph (to transform the animal into a sheep so that it wanders around and cannot attack), hibernating tactics (to cause the animal to sleep), or a "holy nova" light effect that weighs down the animal and nearly causes it to explode.

To command an animal, a master may use specific orders, like follow, stop, come, stay, guard, kill, drop or release. When taming animals for combat, a master will rely on skills, such as magery (spellcasting), musicianship (using music as a buff), stealthing, healing and archery. A tamer may use animal summoning to call an animal from one location to another. Individual animal breeds have particular required skill levels to be considered trained. Unicorns and fire steeds, for example, require more training than cows, wolves, pigs or sheep as they have a higher level of fighting potential.

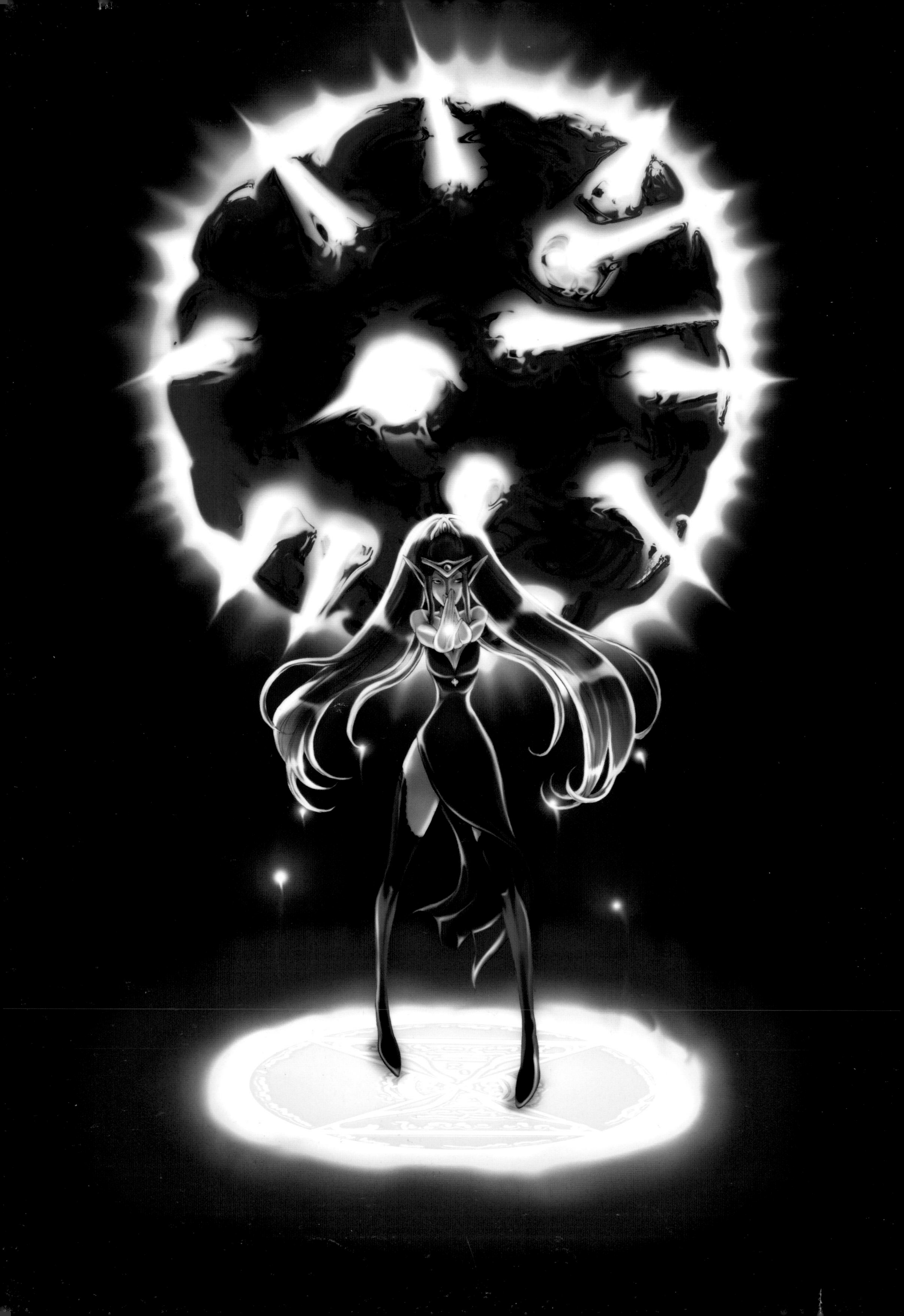

Fire Sorcery

Magic rod

Fireballs

Character has high level of endurance and energy

High boots

➤ Notable Features

- Skill in using fire for magic and casting spells
- Types of fire magic skills: fire bolt (throws darts of fire), inferno (creates wild fire), blaze (creates fire on the ground), fireball (throws balls of fire mixed with energy), firewall (puts up a block of flame), enchant (uses a fire-powered weapon), meteor (calls out a falling star from the sky), extinguish (puts out fire), ignite (creates a flame), fire shield (creates a ring of fire around an enemy) and explosion (creates a huge fire attack)
- Fire sorcerers may be humans, night elves, shamans and others
- Attire: armor, shield, gloves, boots, amulets, charms and rings
- Equipment: wand, rod or staff

✛ Outline and Origin

Fire, one of the basic elements of the earth, symbolizes both life and destruction. In rituals and in sorcery, it is a medium for cleansing or purification, and also a result of punishment or suffering. In mythology, Agni was the Hindu god of fire that carried a flaming spear and rode on a chariot pulled by fiery horses. Through his power with fire, he was able to make people immortal and purify their souls, and burn a forest to restore his own energy. Another legend of fire dates to 1441, when the wife of the Duke of Gloucester melted a wax image of King Henry over fire to ruin the king's life.

Fire sorcerers must have excellent spell casting abilities and a high level of strength, endurance, dexterity and energy. They may use black and red candles, a pentagram, a rod, staff, wand, talisman and reagents, such as volcanic ash, pig iron, brimstone, or demon's bones. The pentagram is used for indicating the strategic position of the candles, weapons and reagents. When the candles are lit and the proper words of power are recited, the fire spell can be created. A wand can be used for the fire skills of "extinguish" and "fire bolt;" the rod can be used for the "fire shield" skill; the staff can be used for the "explosion" skill.

In fantasy manga, a fire sorcerer can pull a falling star from the sky to strike his or her enemy. Effectively manipulating a fire bolt is a primary skill that a fire sorcerer must master before moving on to the next level of sorcerership.

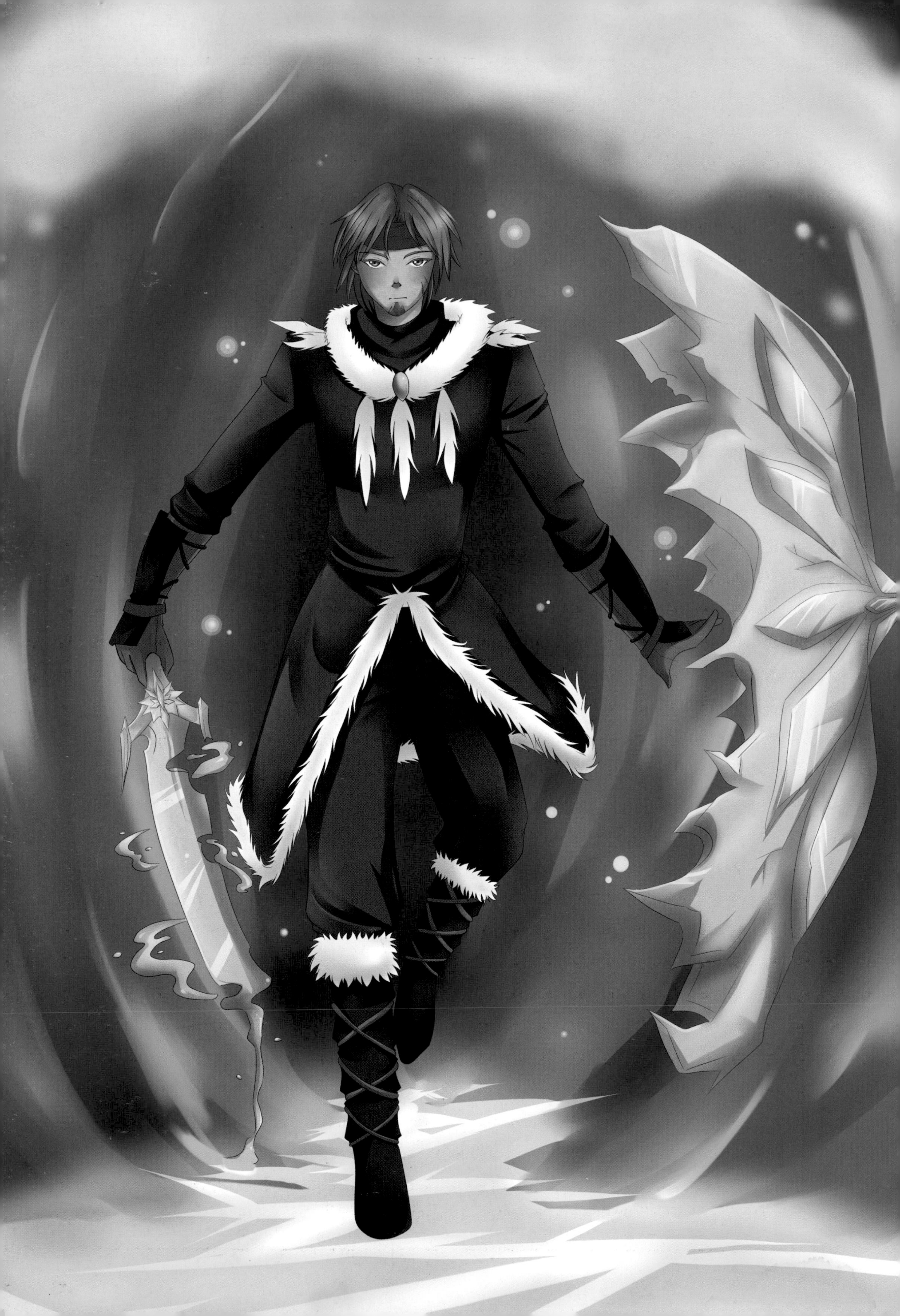

Water/Ice Sorcery

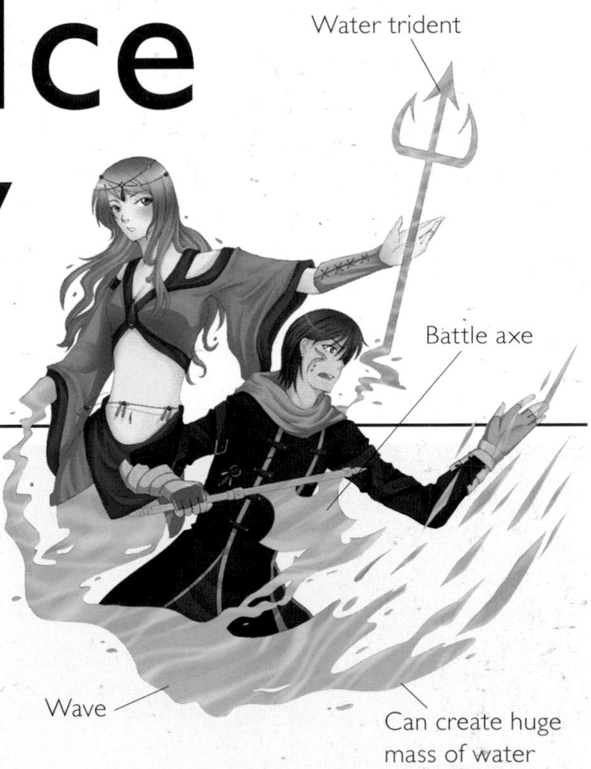
Water trident
Battle axe
Wave
Can create huge mass of water

➡ Notable Features

- **Skill in using water or ice for magic and casting spells**
- **Types of water and ice sorcery skills: wave (moves huge mass of water to drown an enemy), bath of cleansing (washes away poison), ice touch (creates frost on any object), splash (startles an enemy), armor of frost (creates a shield of ice frost), frozen burst (ice explosion to freeze an enemy), ice prison (freezes an enemy's legs), wall of frost (straight line of ice wall), and breath of ice (sorcerer breathes ice on enemy's wound)**
- **Water and ice sorcerers may be shamans, alchemists, necromancers, ninja snowmen or other elementalists (summoners of elements of earth)**
- **Equipment: ice sword, ice blade, glacial blade, wand, staff, axe grip, hammer grip, bow grip, shield**

+ Outline and Origin

Since ancient times, water has denoted heavenly or miraculous powers due to its association with cleansing, healing and purification. In ancient Greece and Rome, fountains and springs were known to be mystical and were worshipped for medicinal cures. In 1553, a doctor in France was said to use a white cloth and clean water while chanting words to perform cures. Sorcerers and witches in the 19th century used water, not only for cleaning away poison and evil, but also for restoring a person's health and strength; they believed that lakes, rivers, and snowfields contained magical power.

Sorcerers use transformation spells, like liquidization (causes the body to flow like the lake or ocean), freeze (freezes an enemy) and ice touch (produces chill on any object), to change and weaken an enemy's physical being and combat abilities. Water enchantment spells, like harmony (calms the person's mind), lunatic fever (storm of emotional rage), and skin of painlessness (melts the mind to detect physical pain), make the person erratic or insane. Ice alchemists may use "ice make" spells, such as geyser (freezes the ground with a tower of ice spikes), snow tiger (creates a tiger made of ice) and shield (creates a half-dome of ice block). The combination of water and ice spells is cold damage, and is effective especially when the enemy uses fire damage. The spells can cause shivers, bitter chills, icy veins, and ultimately death.

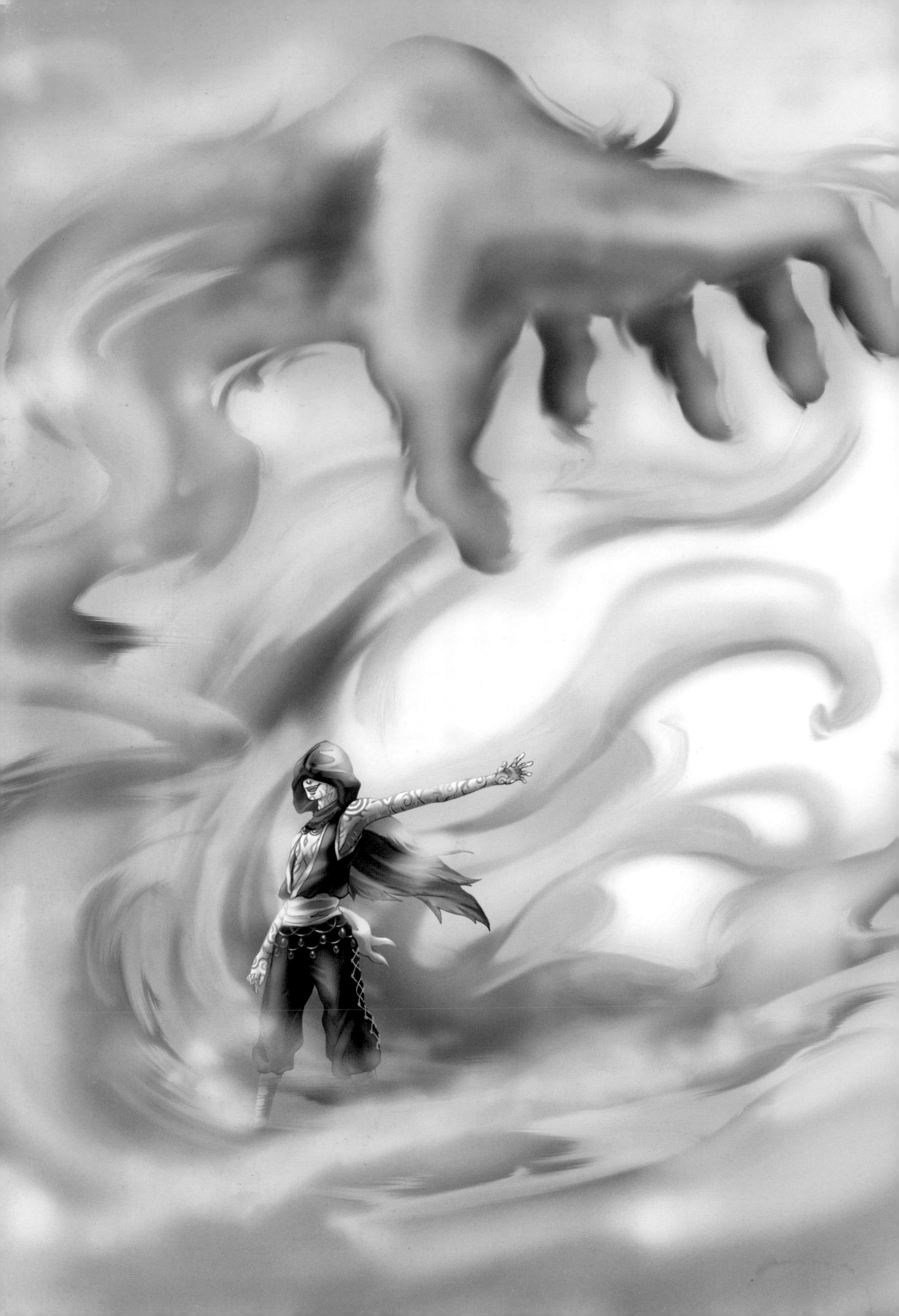

Earth Sorcery

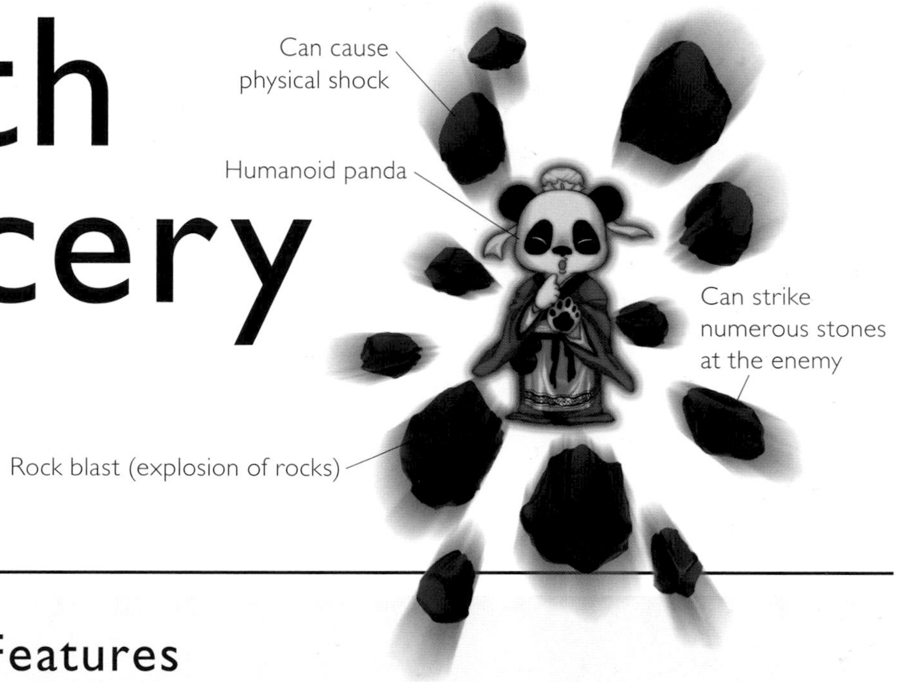
Can cause physical shock
Humanoid panda
Can strike numerous stones at the enemy
Rock blast (explosion of rocks)

➡ Notable Features

- **Skill in using elements of the earth for battle or destruction**
- **Types of earth sorcery skills: gust (uses wind to attack an enemy), earthquake, stalagmite (causes a rock to fall on an enemy's head), quicksand, dust (causes a dust storm), earth churning (causes the earth to spin violently), ash blast (creates an ash storm that can cause blindness), eruption (causes eruption of the ground), unsteady ground (causes the ground to move to knock down an enemy), stone striker (throws numerous stones at the same time), corrosive blast (fires an exploding acid projectile) and rock blast (releases a magical rock that explodes)**
- **Earth sorcerers may be warriors, pandarens (humanoid pandas), elementalists (summoners of elements of the earth), geomancers (humanoids using magic) or taurens (huge, muscular humanoids)**
- **Equipment: stone, ash, soil**

+ Outline and Origin

Dating back to the Paleolithic and Neolithic ages, archaeological evidence points to shaman-looking beings that used mysterious powers to summon spirits to shake the ground or cause blizzards and other earthly phenomena. This form of magic was performed for healing illness, calling for protection against evil, praying for rich harvests and offering a sacrifice. There have been tales about the Roman poet Virgil who had the magical powers to create a river, and mythological figures, such as the Greek Gaia and the Egyptian Geb, who were the goddess and god of the earth and could control all matter on earth.

Earth sorcery is commonly practiced by elementalists who perform magic using dirt, stone and other earth elements. Their spells can cause physical shock, blindness, weakness or a sudden knock down. An earth magic spell, such as the "deadly swarm," can summon deadly insects to attack a target; an ash blast can create a whirlpool of ash to blind or trap an enemy; earthen shackles can cause the earth to shake violently; eruption allows the ground to erupt or explode; a stoning or stone strike causes numerous stones to strike or block the opponent; a meteor strike pulls a meteor from the sky to hit the earth.

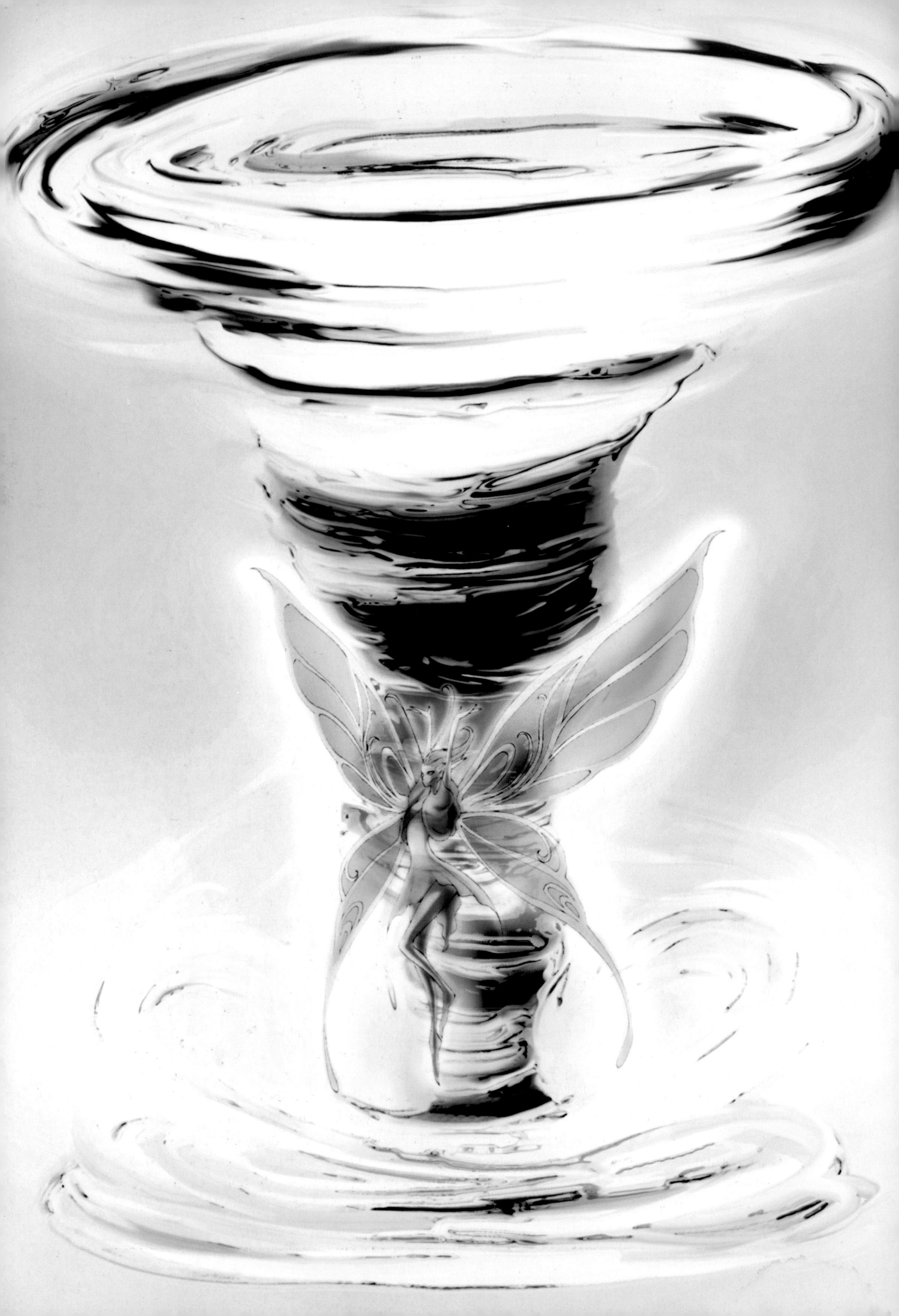

Air/Wind/ Lightning Sorcery

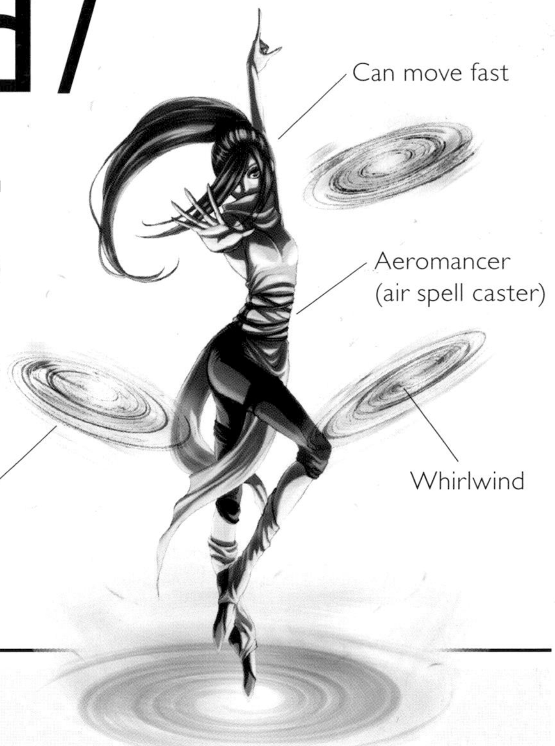

Can move fast

Aeromancer (air spell caster)

Whirlwind

Can create fast blowing wind to capture the enemy

➔ Notable Features

- Skill in using air, wind or lightning for magic and casting spells
- Types of air, wind and lightning sorcery skills: blinding flash (air explosion that causes blindness), gust (gust of wind causes cold damage and knockdown), windborne speed (fast blowing wind captures an enemy), healing breeze (heals wounds), lightning orb (lightning orbit strikes an enemy) and thunderclap (massive lightning strike dazes an enemy)
- Air, wind and lightning sorcerers may be aeromancers (air spell casters), mages, elves, alchemists, wizards, warlocks, necromancers and other elementalists
- Equipment: air wand, air staff, lightning spear, lightning sword

✛ Outline and Origin

Air, wind and lightning sorcery have been practiced since the time of the ancient Greeks and Romans. Egyptians and other cultures also used air spells for healing or raising the dead. The north wind god, Boreas, was the god of the wind, death and change. He could cause destruction and coldness by changing the forces of the wind suddenly. Eurus was god of the east wind, associated with renewal of life and intelligence. He could summon the rain to bring good harvest and positive change in the villages. The south wind god was Notus who created ferocious winds that cause cursing and deception, but also love and passion. Zephyrus was the west wind and healing god who brought love and fertility to the people.

There was also Zeus, King of the Gods, who struck the earth with lightning to show his anger.

Air, wind, and lightning magic can cause blindness, exhaustion, physical and mental weakness and a sudden knockdown. This magic may have the effect of illusion, such as a static trap (hides a trap); shadow (makes the spell caster invisible); enchantment, such as reflection (creates mirrors in an enemy's mind); or obedience (controls an enemy's mind); motion, such as fist of wind (moving wind knocks down the enemy), or teleportation (moves the enemy to different places). Lightning damage is also a very powerful tool and is used with an air wand or air staff to produce shock effects.

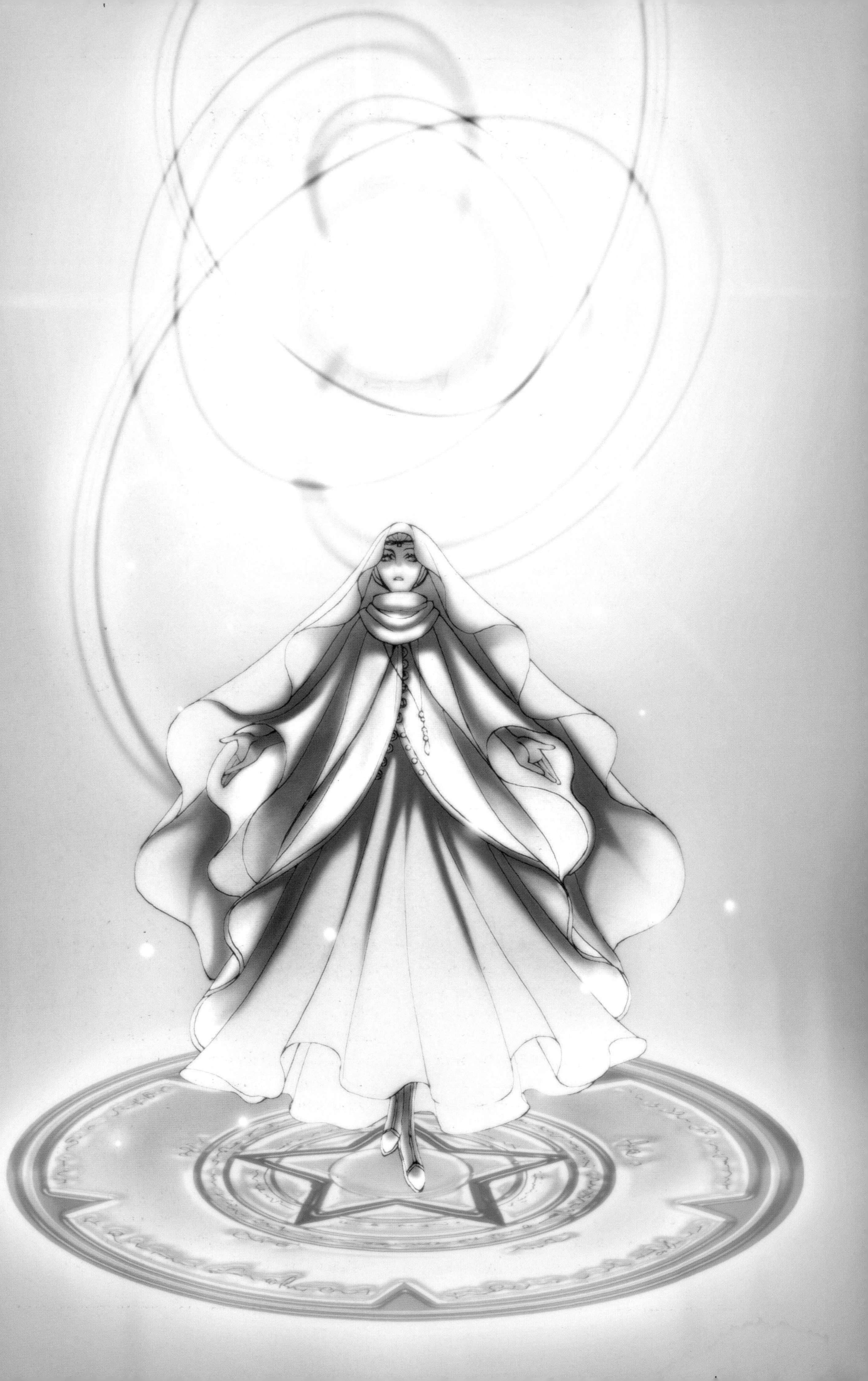

White Magic

Sacred-looking ——

Holy nova
(explosion of sacred light) ——

Priestess

Long robe ——

➡ Notable Features

- Skill in healing and aiding based on sacred techniques, prayers, faith and a belief in gods, spirits and the powers of nature
- Types of holy abilities: blessing of sanctuary (blessing a target to reduce injury), holy shield (uses shield with holy power), holy shock (strikes a target with holy energy), holy fire (wraps an enemy in sacred flames), holy nova (explosion of sacred light around the spell caster), redemption (resurrects a dead target), repentance (puts a target in state of meditation) and holy resist (gives energy to mortals and purifies ghosts)
- Holy magic practitioners are paladins, shamans and priests
- Equipment: shield, axe, mace, staff, wand, cloth armor

✚ Outline and Origin

Healing magic is referred to as white magic, as opposed to black magic that serves evil purposes. The magic of healing using sacred power is considered a divine magical practice because it relies on a faith in gods, spirits and symbols of nature. In the mid-2nd century, neoplatonists (religious and mystical philosophers following Plato's teachings) used meditation to connect with the divine world. Healing had been practiced by neo-pagans and was considered a mode to transform the body's energy fields, and a way to use sound, breath, touch and movement to acquire holy powers. In the Renaissance period, there were remedies such as chanting prayers that fought sicknesses caused by fairies, and healing by touch to channel a person's energy.

In fantasy, healers use holy light and shamans summon the powers of nature to carry out spells. A priest may whisper prayers to obtain power from divine gods or can use spells to aid wounded allies or to attack enemies for vengeance. He can use a resurrection spell for raising the dead or a cure disease spell for removing disease. Similarly, the paladin uses his aura and buffs, and mixes warrior and holy abilities. He uses blessings, such as a blessing of might (increases power), or a blessing of wisdom (increases knowledge) that increase the combat strength of friendly targets. He may also use hand spells (placing the hand on the target), such as a hand of freedom (allowing the target free movement) or hand of protection (securing the target from physical danger) spell.

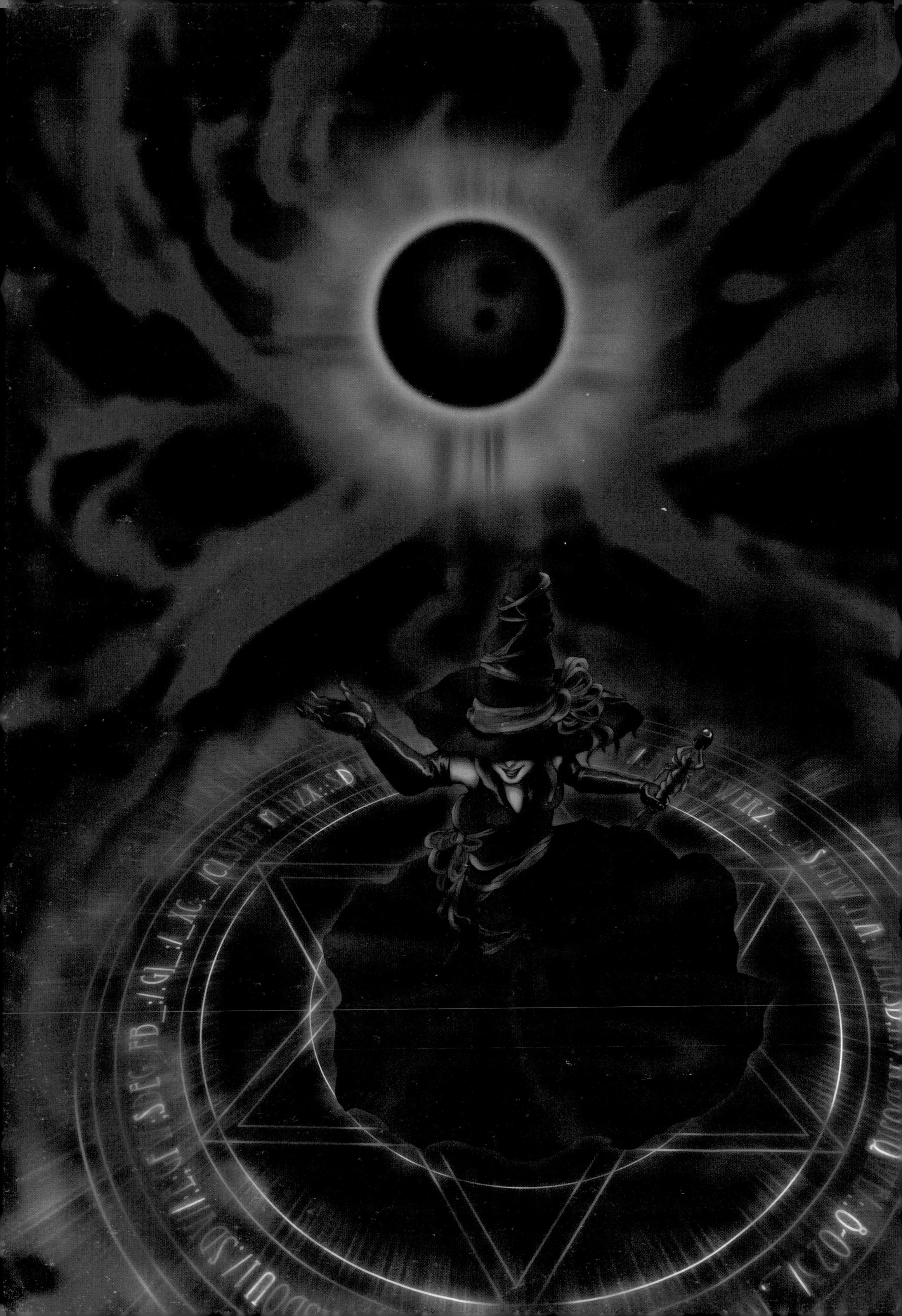

Black Magic

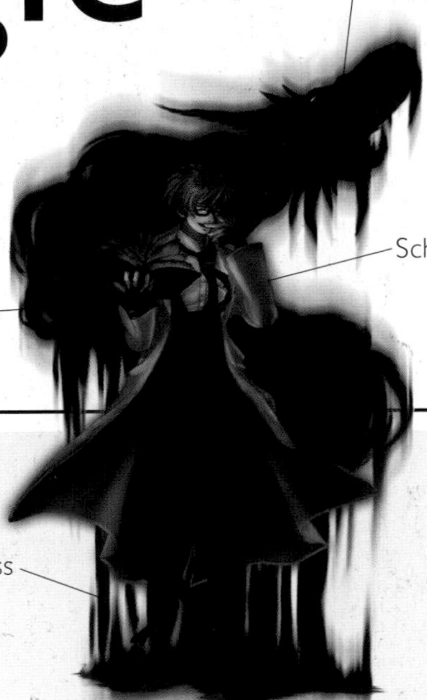
Dragon-like shadow
Scholar
Gloves or gauntlets
Creates darkness

➡ Notable Features

- **Skill in using spells for harmful or evil purposes**
- **Types of black magic spells: flare (fire damage on an enemy), aqua (water damage on an enemy), sleep (puts an enemy to sleep), poison, paralyze, prism (uses earth elements for damage), curse, force (causes physical damage), balus rod (light that strikes the palm and attacks a target), blast ash (black void turns the body to ash), dark claw (magical energy balls that disintegrates matter), disfang (dragon-like shadows that bite an enemy), hell blast (creates darkness) and stun (prevents an enemy from attacking)**
- **Black magic practitioners include black mages, dark knights, scholars, red mages and wizards**
- **Equipment: belt, ring, gloves, gauntlets, axe, staff, shield**

+ Outline and Origin

Like white magic, black magic has its roots in neo-pagan practices and ancient rituals that use the power of spirits. Evil witches were known to recite chants and use potions, amulets, a strand of hair and other objects to cause harm to people who disagreed with their ways or whom they were jealous of. A tale from around 1144 describes children in a forest in England who were cursed by a lord who practiced black magic. There are also rumors that Shakespeare himself used black magic in his writings to provoke witches to put success spells on his masterpiece, *Macbeth*. Demonology was used in the Middle Ages to protest against conservative Christian practices, and those who practiced it had mystical abilities to cause sickness, inflict evil thoughts on someone and even cause death.

Dark magic spells are usually carried out by selfish motives to damage a target's strength. Many of the spells draw out the strong qualities of a target, and then transfer them to the spell caster. The black mage is a very powerful caster of black magic, and his spells can quickly destroy his targets. He can use spells, such as blind (blindness), flood (water damage), freeze (ice damage), quake (earth damage), gust slash (wind damage), sunburst (light attack), viper bite (poison use), spirit taker (possession of the dead's spirit) and shadow stitch (cripple target to the ground until it vanishes).

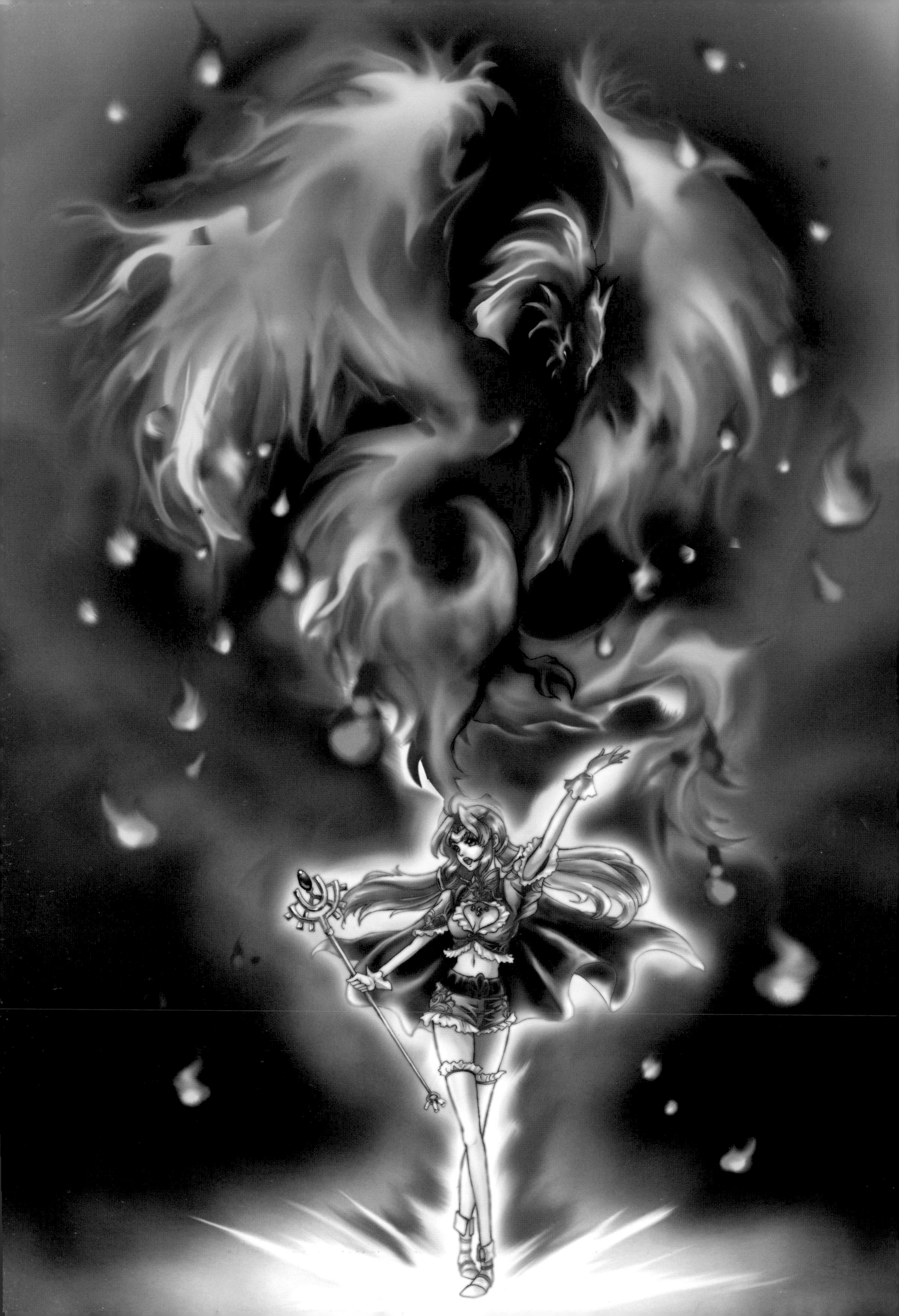

Summon Magic

Can summon an earthquake

Can raise a golem from the earth

Bracer

Staff

➡ Notable Features

- Skill in calling demons, spirits or other creatures to cast spells
- Types of summoning spells: inferno (summons creatures from the sky), raise skeleton (summons the dead to fight), clay golem (raises a golem from the earth), revive (resurrects a monster), undead legion (turns a corpse into a skeleton to fight monsters), summon elementals (summons fire, water, earth and air elementals), and army of the dead (summons ghouls)
- Summon magic practitioners are warlocks, paladins, necromancers, druids and sorcerers
- Equipment: ring, bracer, tiara, necklace, cape, staff, belt

✚ Outline and Origin

Summon magic provokes the power of demons, evil spirits and the dead to perform spells. In the 13th century in Europe, nigromancy (black magic) was heavily practiced, which enabled people to gain wealth or seek vengeance by enlisting the help of demons. There were also corrupt priests and monks who used chants and prayers to summon the dead.

Spell casters use a meeting stone, which is a giant thumb-shaped rock that summons other targets to the spell caster's location. Using summon magic may provide white and red mages to help summoners improve their healings skills sand buff enemies; or it may aid samurai with meditation and spirit taker skills; thieves with sneak and attack skills; or the bard with a mage's ballad skill (singing skull). Summon magic may also be used to summon different kinds of avatars, like titans (giants), garudas (avians) and elementals, or spirits like the fire spirit or ice spirit.

Apart from spirits and creatures, summon magic can dictate elements of nature to perform spells, such as fist of wrath (summons a fist with magical powers to cause physical damage), earthquake (summons an earthquake) or arcane armor (summons an energy shield to trap a target).

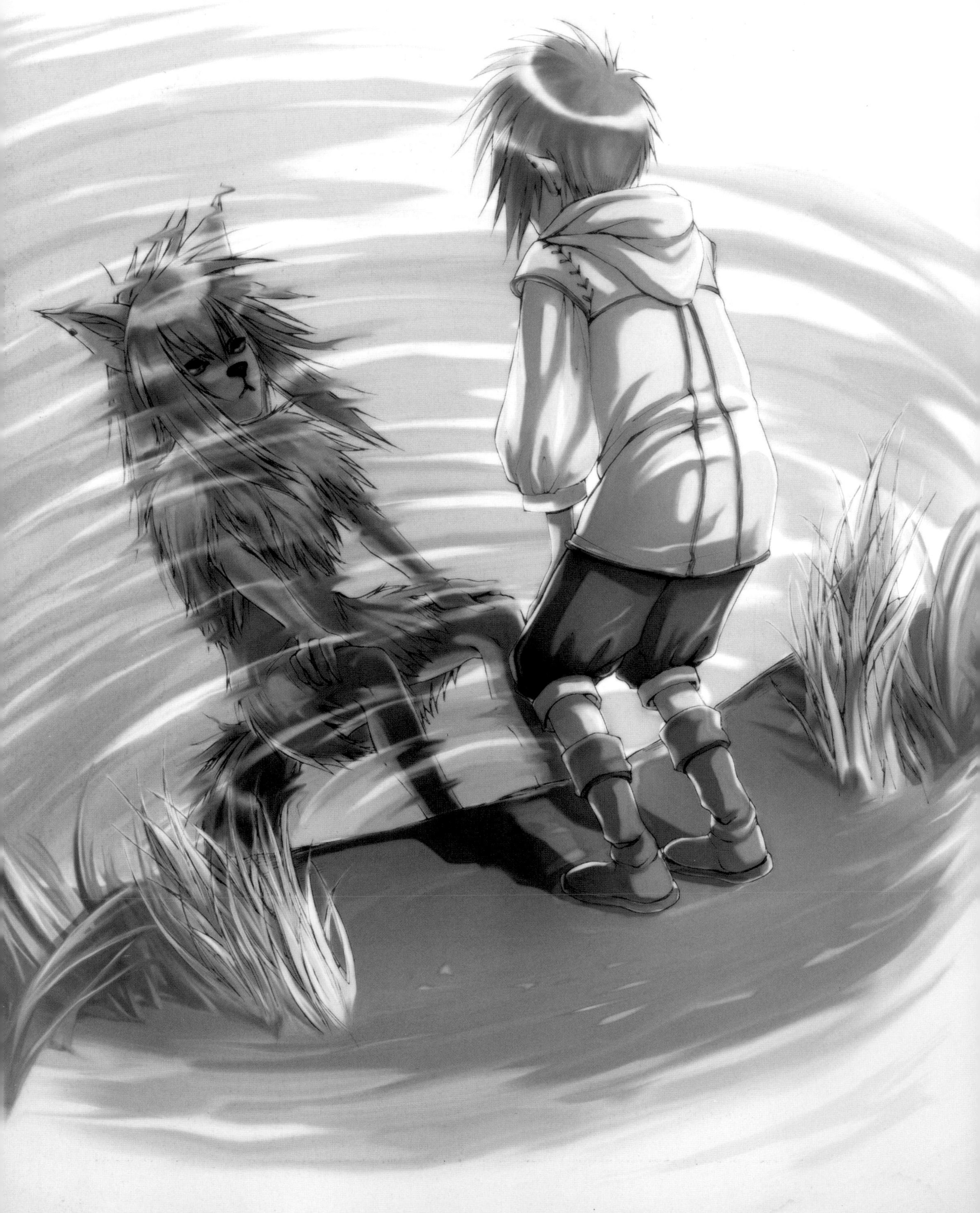

Transformation Magic

Can alter the face

Can stretch or deform the body

Can change the sex of the creature

Can change the body into a hairy creature

➡ Notable Features

- Skill in altering the forms of creatures, objects and other matter
- Types of transformation spells: gender (changes the sex of the person or creature), fictitious character (turns the character into a fictional character), invokio amulet (makes the person wearing it become younger), Satan soul (transforms a target into a demon with wings), polymorph (transforms an enemy into an animal), beast soul (changes a body into a hairy monster), arborare (transforms a target into a tree), elasticity (stretches or deforms a body), inorganic (transforms a target into an inorganic substance), liquefaction (changes a target into liquid) and other spells designated by the names of objects and creatures the target is to be transformed into
- Transformation magic practitioners include mages, wizards and sorcerers
- Equipment: bracelet, ring, sword, armor

✛ Outline and Origin

Transformation abilities were practiced by many Greek and Roman mythological figures. Arachne was a human weaver who was turned into a spider; Medusa, a human was turned into a monster with a head of snakes; Zeus transformed himself into a bull, swan, gold matter and other forms; Vertumnus, the Roman god of seasons, transformed himself into an old woman. In Celtic mythology, Pwyll, prince of the Dyfed county, was transformed into Arawn's (king of the otherworld's) body shape and Math, king of the Gwynedd kingdom, transformed flowers into a woman. In Japanese folklore, yokai, which are mystical animals, can shapeshift their bodies into other creatures.

Transformation magic is a superior-level skill that can only be performed by the best mages. It is used as a buff to deceive an enemy or to increase one's power. A transformed creature can enter the territory of an enemy or fit in its group. A termite transformation, for example, can allow a character to attach itself to a steep surface; a crocodile transformation can allow a character to attack by biting; a bee transformation can allow a character to fly anywhere; a snowball transformation can revive a character's energy by rolling in snow; a T-Rex transformation can frighten an enemy; a candle transformation can brighten up an area. Other transformation spells transform beings into other races. A caster that uses an orb of deception tool can transform a target into a blood elf, dwarf, druid or gnome.

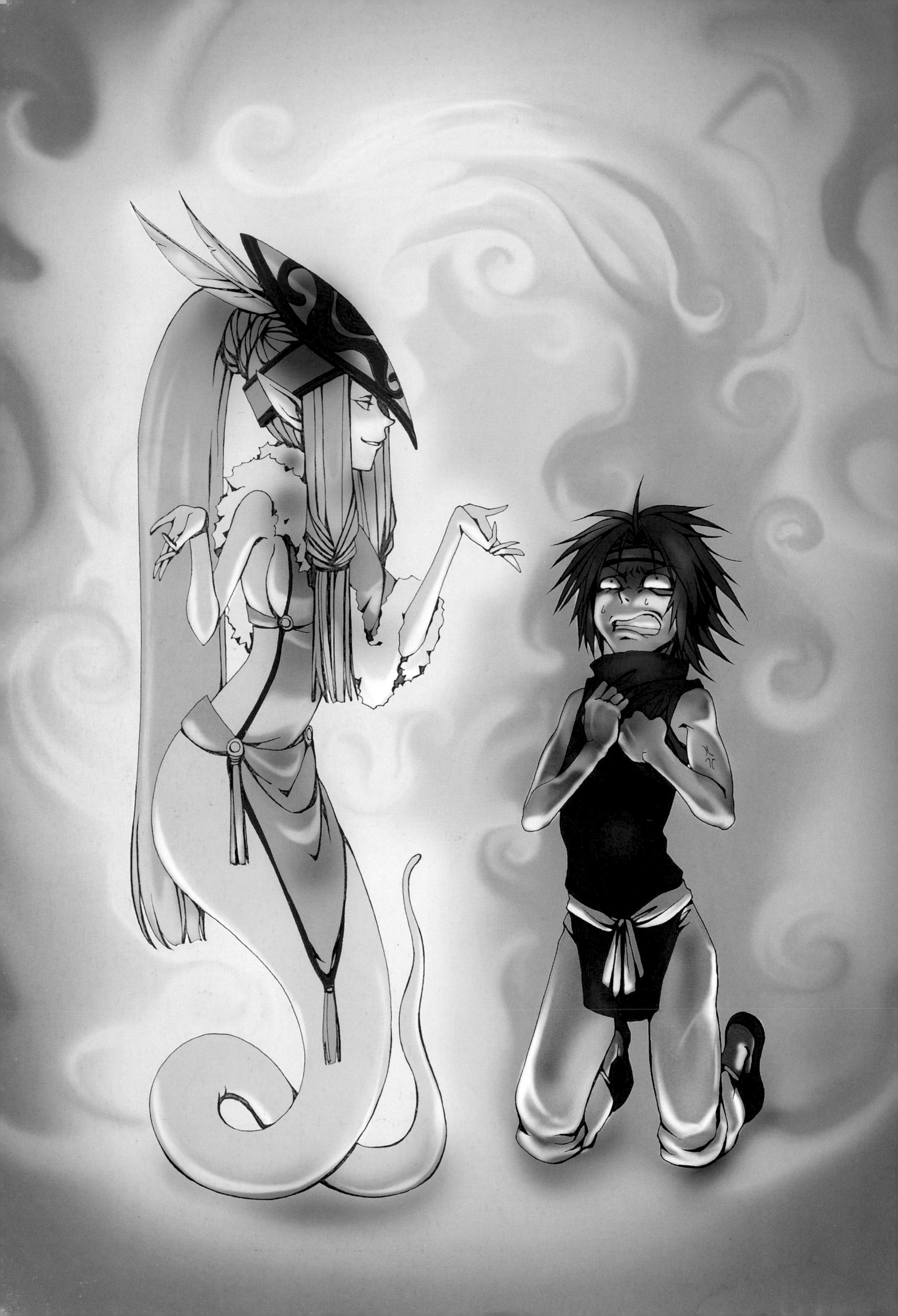

Prayer Magic

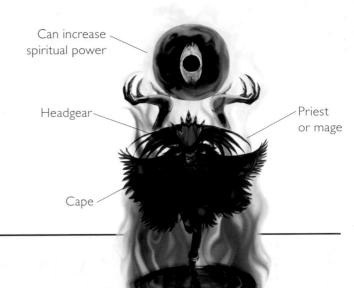

Can increase spiritual power

Headgear

Cape

Priest or mage

➡ Notable Features

- Skill in using prayers for spells and combat
- Types of prayer skills: thick skin (increases defense power), burst of strength (increases strength), clarity of thought (increases attack power), sharp eye (increases range ability), mystic will (increases magic ability), rapid restore (counteracts negative effects of spells), rapid heal (restores life), protect item (protects against curses), protect from summoning, protect from melee, chivalry (increases the user's attack and defense skills), redemption (heals users), smite (drains out enemy's prayer ability), augury (increases the accuracy of magic), spirit (increases the user's spiritual power), fortitude (increases stamina), shadow protection (increases resistance against shadow creatures) and mending (gives a healing buff)
- Prayer magic practitioners are priests, white mages and bishops
- Equipment: jewelry, robe, armor, headgear, gloves, cape, mace, cane, spirit shields, holy book, amulet of glory, god's stole, monk's robe, white boots, fire cape and weapons, such as iron mace and a godsword (sword capable of powerful attack)

✛ Outline and Origin

Gods from ancient Mesopotamia and Egypt communicated with heavenly bodies for protection, good harvest or forgiveness through prayer. People also used prayers in their everyday lives in the form of chants, recitations, and written scrolls. Judaism, Christianity and Islam include prayers in their teachings and rituals. Some Christians pray to saints in hope of miracles. Witches and sorcerers use prayers in the same manner to perform healing or black magic.

In fantasy manga, users of prayer skills obtain special blessings from gods so that their holy energies can be increased. Prayer magic usually requires the act of burying bones (remains of the dead dropped by monsters), such as burnt bones, monkey bones, dragon bones and other animal bones that are offered to altars where prayers can be "reused."

Bishops are well known for using prayer spells and prayer staves, such as the cura spell (fires a sphere of positive energy) and cure staff for healing; dispel spell and bless staff for removing a magical ability; holy spell and Nirvana staff for causing holy damage; aero spell for causing wind damage; and water spell for causing water damage.

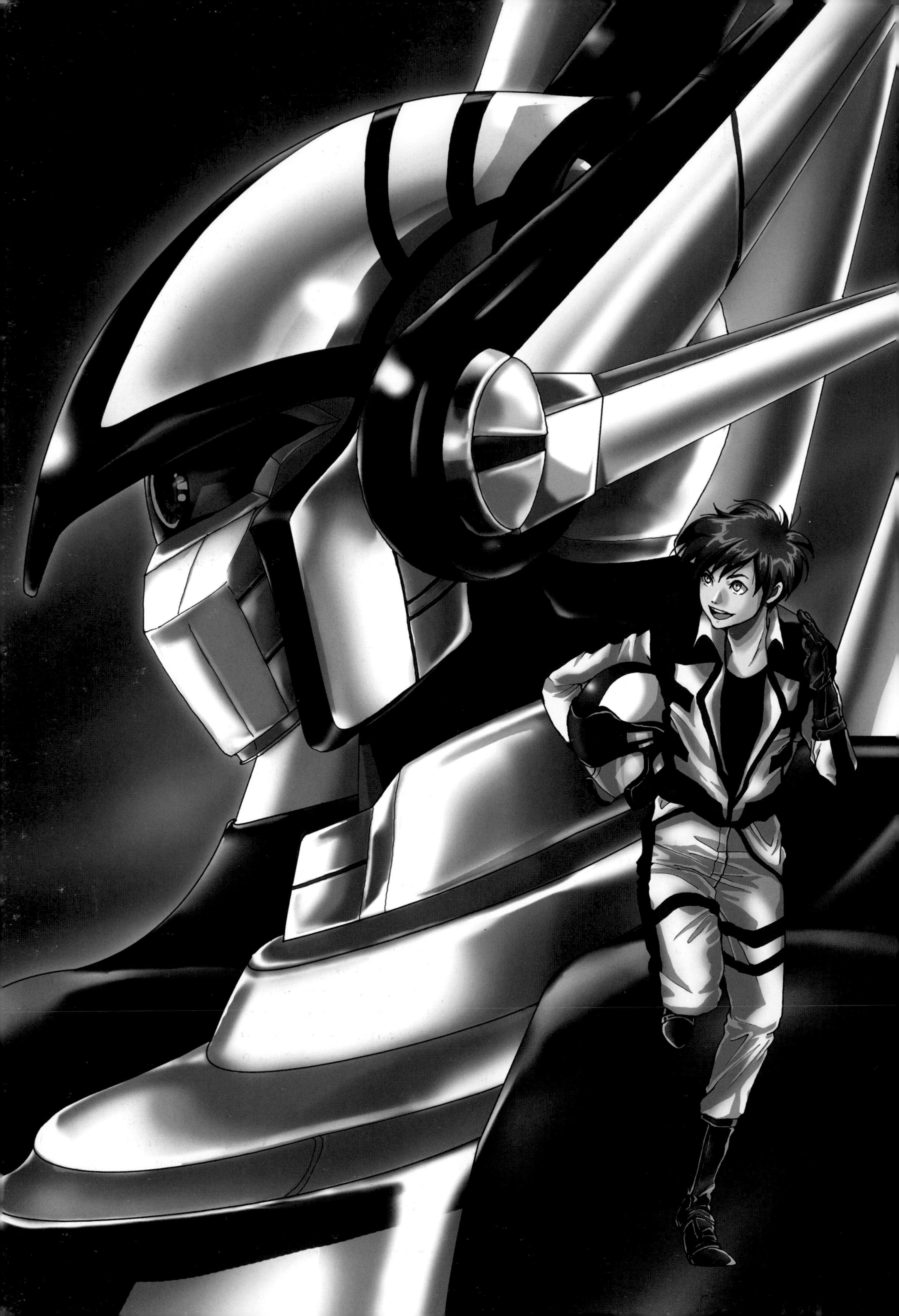

Robot Control

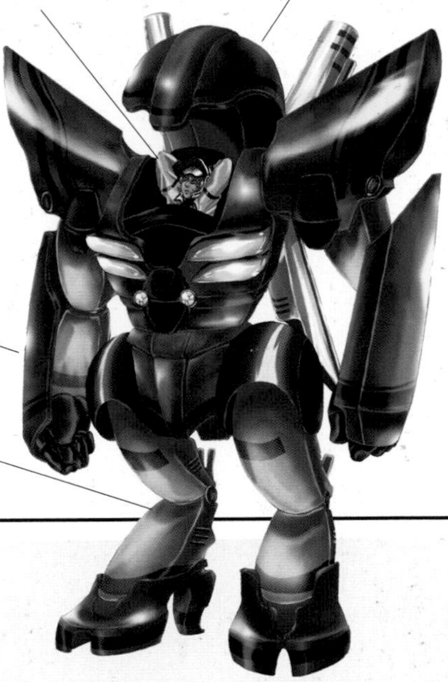
Gigantic size
Robot controller
Mecha robot
Legs and arms to walk, run and fight

Notable Features

- **Skill in controlling, manipulating or piloting robots**
- **Types of controllable robots: super robots (using melee weapons), real robots (using ranged weapons), or humanoid robots**
- **Robot controllers may be humans trained as engineers or pilots, and may have the ability to attack**
- **Attire: heavy armor, including a helmet or military attire**

Outline and Origin

Traces of humanoid robots date back as early as 1070 when the Greek mathematician Heron of Alexandria conceived of a machine that could serve wine to guests during feasts. In 1206, the Islamic scholar and inventor Al-Jazari described robots that could react to music and perform house chores, such as dish washing, offering towels, and filling basins with water.

Mecha robots refer to giant, piloted robots that can walk, run and fight, and are usually controlled by human pilots. A piloted, mechanical elephant powered by steam was described in Jules Verne's novel *The Steam House* in 1880. In H.G. Wells' novel *The War of the Worlds* (1898) tripods appeared as fighting machines. The mecha genre was conceived in the 1956 Japanese anime story *Tetsujin 28-go (Iron Man #28)*, where a young boy controlled a giant robot that could save the Japanese empire during World War II. Since then, these mecha machines have been classified as either super robots (robots who use melee weapons) or real robots (robots who use range weapons). Both usually have two legs, arms and hands that can grab objects from a distance, and are powerful enough to smash buildings, cars, humans and other objects or creatures in their way.

Some mecha robots are trained in martial arts or swordsmanship. Super robots are equipped with high powered weapons and have cockpits where pilots are stationed to have full and direct control of the robots, commanding them using their voices. Real robots are constructed more for military invasions and use human weapons like firearms, cannons, laser beams, shields or swords. Controllers or pilots of such robots must be highly knowledgeable in machinery, mechanical engineering and combat. It is to their benefit if they can use strategy tasks, such as a power drain (the interrupting of a spell), a patriotic power (the fighting of enemies who are already at war), an advance scout move (the tracking of enemies using stealth), or a battle ready move (an attack at first combat). It is also especially helpful if they are able to use explosives and are experts in military warfare.

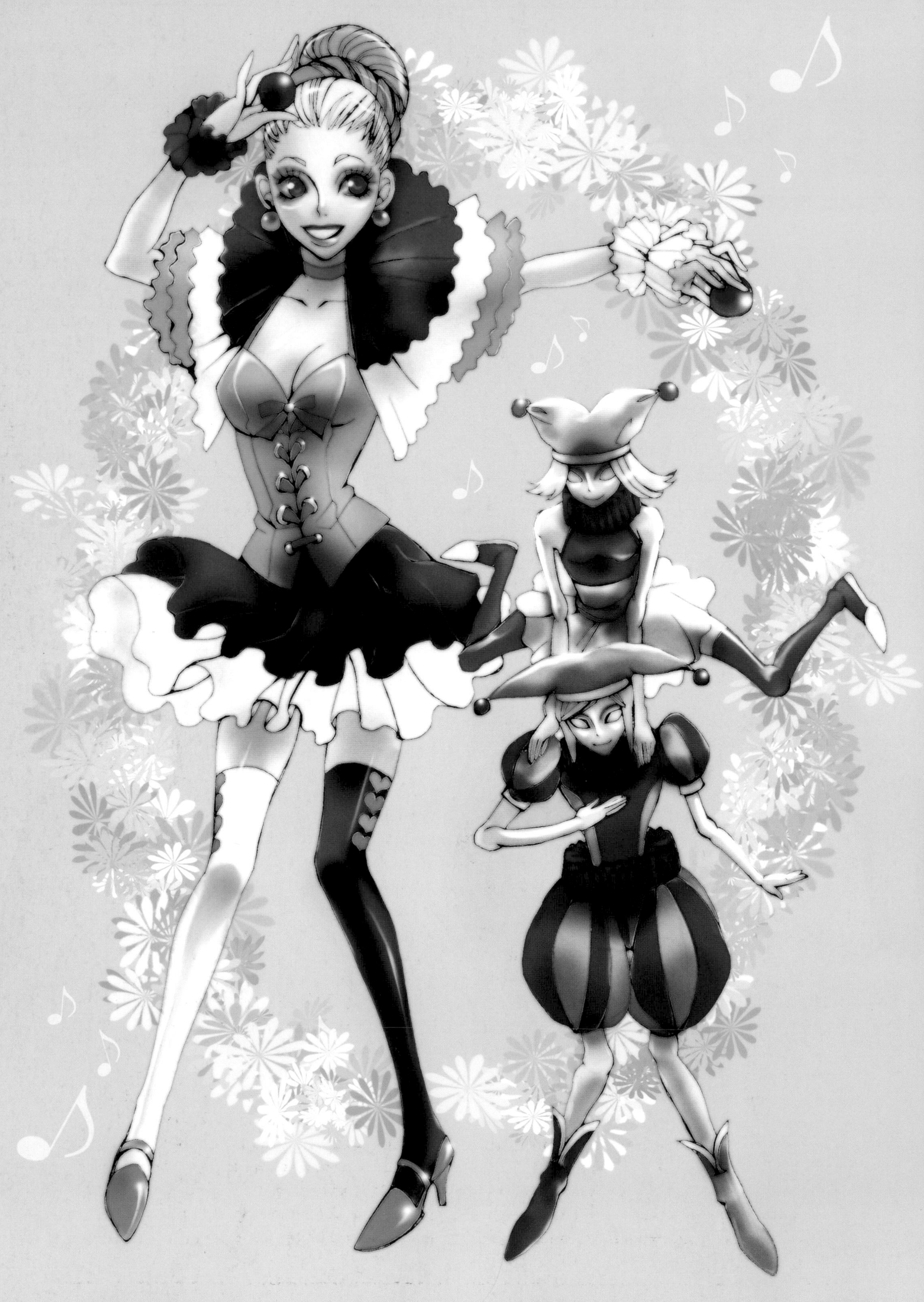

Performing Arts

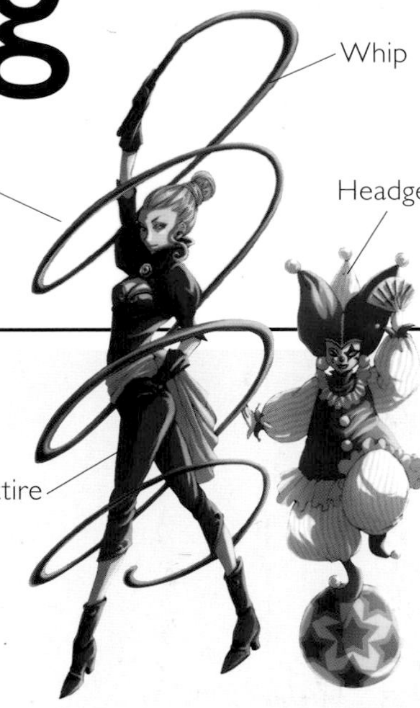
Whip
Dancing and acrobatics
Headgear
Colorful attire

➡ Notable Features

- **Skill in dancing, singing, acting and playing instruments**
- **Types of performing arts skills: acting (comedy, drama, mime); dance (ballet, waltz, jig); musical instruments (harpsichord, piano, fiddle, harp, flute, pipe, drum); singing (ballad, chant, lullaby); oratory (epic, ode, storytelling)**
- **Equipment: headgear, robe, dagger, bow, musical instruments, shield, whip, bow, arrow**
- **Performers can be humans, dwarves, elves, orcs or taurens**

✢ Outline and Origin

The history of performing arts can be traced to Greece around the 6th century B.C. There, poets, dancers and actors performed before kings and queens at royal feasts. Music and drama were crucial for entertainment and peacemaking during times of war and trouble. Performers were peasants, travelers or troubadours who were roughly dressed, or more affluent musician who were hired by the nobles and wore elaborate costumes.

Bards and musicians use performing arts as charisma to receive awards or pets, or to influence the actions of targets by displaying various behaviors during performance, such as: hostility (produces the effects of attack, interference or fleeing); unfriendliness (produces the effect of mislead, suspicion or insult); friendliness (produces the effect of advise or chat); and fanaticism (produces the effect of fighting till death). The bard uses a fascinate ability to distract a target by putting him in a trance with his music. He has a magical voice that can instill fear in enemies or inspire victorious warriors. Bards usually use musical instruments, daggers and bows, while dancers use whips. Some performance skills are: acoustic rhythm (increases resistance against elementals), battle theme (increases attack and defense skills); classical pluck (disables skills); down tempo (reduces defense power); harmonic lock (gives extra armor damage); and lullaby (puts enemy to sleep). Some types of music also have different effects. Metal music is used for transformation and starstruck (heightens the Bard's stage presence) abilities. Punk rock music is used for nonconformity (causes fear and mind control) and mosh pit (increases the movements' speed) abilities. Some of the string instrument skills are valor minuet (enhances attack) and herb pastoral (enhances resistance against poison). Some of the wind instruments are siren flute (flute with power), kingdom horn (horn with power) and fairy magic piccolo. Some of the dancer's skills are dance lessons (increases damage), dazzler (stuns a monster), focus ballet (enhances hit power), hip shaker (drains spell power) and slow grace (decreases attack power).

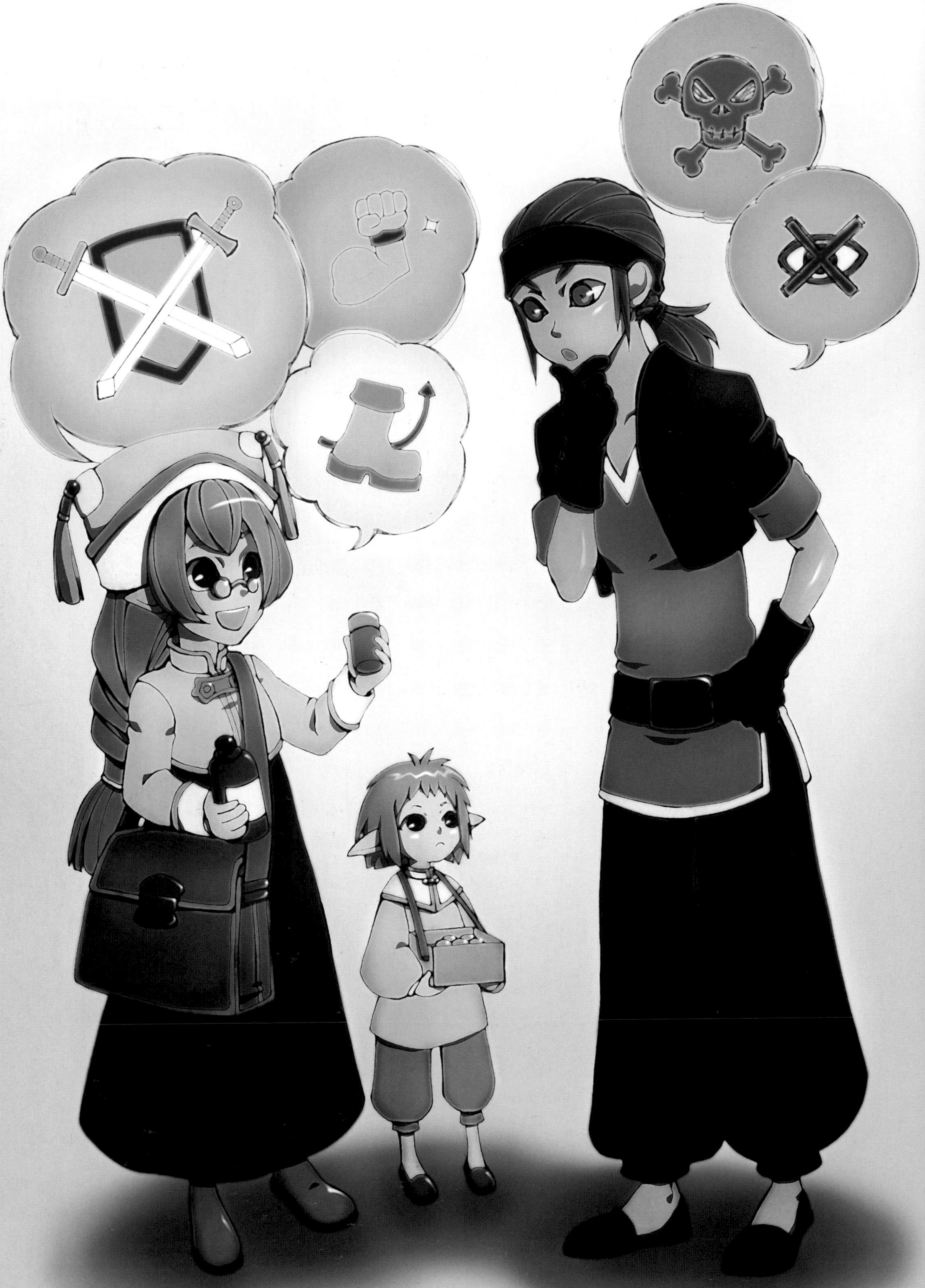

Alchemy

Half-human alchemist

Wand

Can create poisonous smoke

Flask

➡ Notable Features

- Skill of using elements, chemicals or other materials to make potions, herbs or medicines for spells
- Types of alchemy recipes: antidote (cures poison), blinding potion (causes blindness), poison dust, silencing potion (induces silencing), volant serum (turns target into a bat), spore bomb (firework buff), eye drop (cures blindness), endless mana potion (increases mana), flask of the north (increases spell power), paralysis dust (causes paralysis), holy leather (ram skin blessed with holy water to use in armors), deodorizer (neutralizes odors), strength potion (increases strength), antacid (removes bad effects of food) and thunder card (blends with lightning energy)
- Equipment: stone, flask, vial, longbow, dagger, sword, runes
- Alchemists may be male or female humans, half-humans, dwarves or goblins

✚ Outline and Origin

Alchemy traces its roots from ancient Egypt, Roman, Islamic, Indian, Chinese and Western medicine. Around 5000-400 B.C., ancient Egyptians combined metallurgy and mysticism, and produced cosmetics, cement and other chemicals. Throughout the Roman Empire and the Middle Ages, alchemy became a tool for the transmutation of the physical body and to cure diseases.

By mixing chemicals, elements of the earth and other materials, potions, elixirs and medicine are produced for healing, buffing, increasing the strength of users or causing damage to targets. These potions can also be applied to weapons to give weapons holy energies or increased power. Herbs are also used to make potions, such as a peace bloom herb for a minor healing potion, or a silverleaf herb for a minor defense potion. Enchanting is using potions or oils on gears and weapons to give them extra power or energy, such as an enchanted leather or a fiery weapon.

Alchemy expertise is distinguished in levels: apprentice (uses minor healing potion, rage potion and swiftness potion), journeyman (uses holy protection potion, lesser mana potion, and free action potion), expert (uses fire protection potion, frost protection potion and magic resistance potion), artisan (uses invisibility potion, invulnerability potion and dreamless sleep potion), master (uses mad alchemist's potion, sneaking potion and camouflage potion), and the highest level, the grand master (uses icy mana potion, nightmare potion, indestructible potion and transmutation). Learned at the grand master level, transmutation is the highest level of the alchemy skill; it transforms metals into other materials, such as fire to water and air to fire.

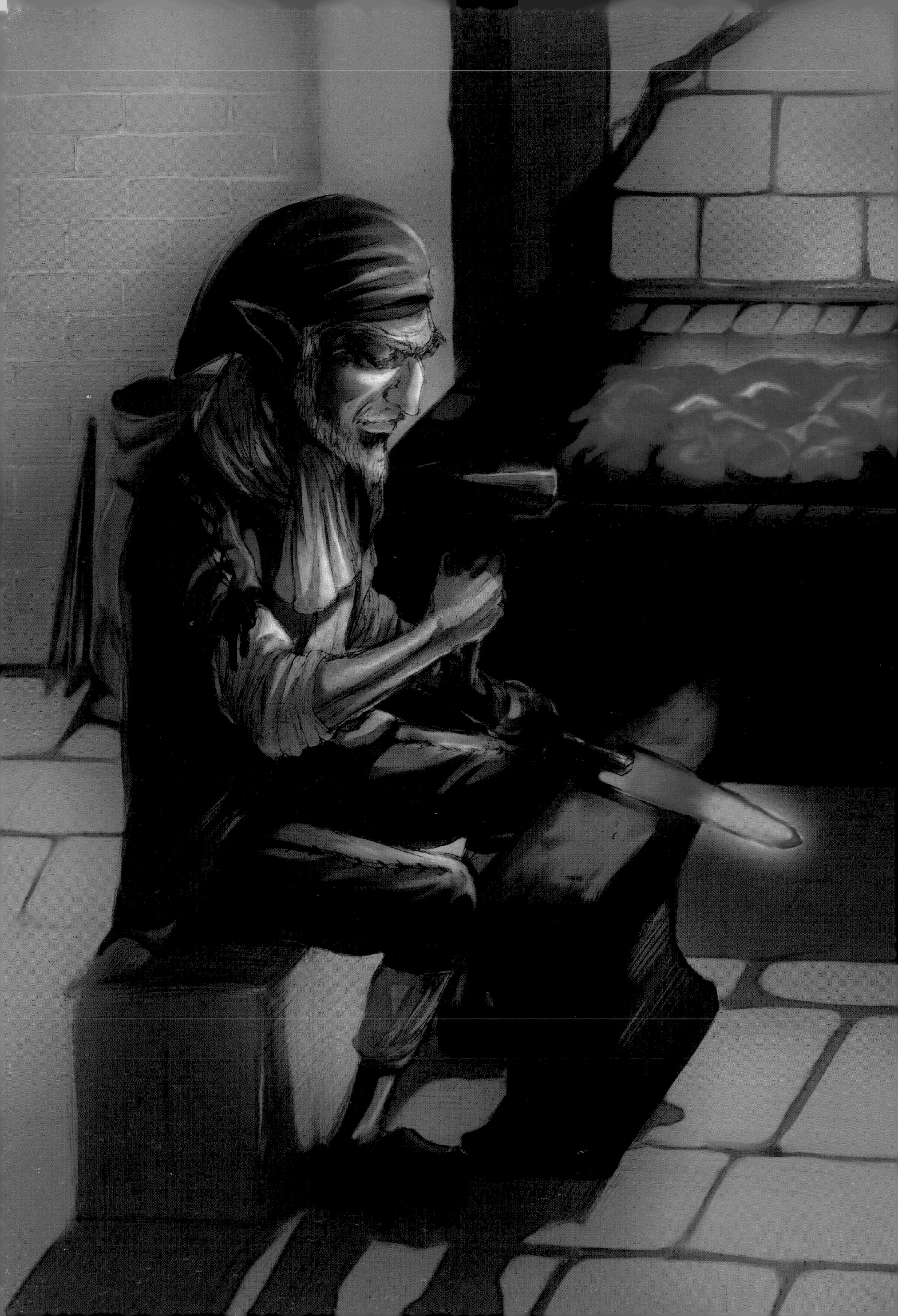

Crafting

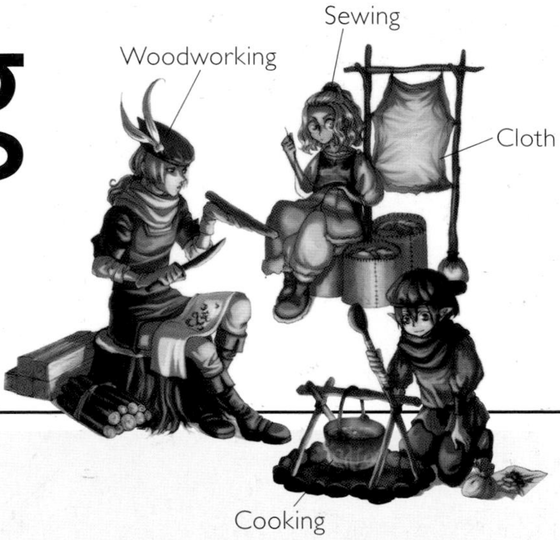
Sewing
Woodworking
Cloth
Cooking

➡ Notable Features

- **Skill in mastering crafts to make or enhance items that can be used in different professions**
- **Types of crafts: bonecraft (uses animal bones to make armor and weapons); clothcraft or tailoring (uses thread and cloth to make capes, robes, armor and other attire); cooking (food preparation and meals for healing players); goldsmithing (uses gems and metals to make jewelry); leathercraft or skinning (uses animal hides to make weapons, armor and other attire); blacksmithing and silversmithing (uses metal and minerals to make weapons, armors and keys); woodworking (uses wood to make weapons, shields and ammunition); inscription or synergy (combines different crafts to make scrolls or inscriptions on weapons); jewel crafting (uses stones, gems and metals to make rings, necklaces and trinkets); pottery (uses clay to make pots and ceramics); glassmaking (uses fire, sand and other materials to make glass objects)**
- **Equipment: bones, cloth, leather, metals, stones, gems, oils, herbs, wood**

✝ Outline and Origin

As early as the year 300, the early Indians created craft associations to distinguish people by their trades. Guilds existed in the 3rd century B.C. in Greece, Egypt and Rome where craftsmen could be trained. The Chinese had craft guilds around 206 B.C., and soon craft organizations spread throughout Europe in Germany, England, France, Spain, and also in Iran. Metalworking, blacksmithing, leather crafting, woodworking and jewelry making were prominent crafts that paved the way for active trading during the Middle Ages and the Renaissance period. Craftsmen normally started as apprentices and learned their craft from master craftsmen who were experts in a particular skill.

In the pottery craft guild, one can make pots, bowls and dishes for cooking or farming. Leathercraft and skinning can produce boots, gloves and armor from snakeskin, dragon hides, scales and other animal skins, and teach skills, such as tanning (soaking animal skin), leather purification (enchanting leather with white magic) and leather ensorcellment (enchanting leather with black magic). Glassmaking can produce beer glasses, oil lamps, vials and candle lanterns. Silversmithing and blacksmithing can produce lightning rods, silver sickles, blacksmith's belts and demonic swords, and can teach skills, such as metal purification (enchanting metal with white magic) and sheeting (shaping ingots). Jewelry crafting can produce gold rings, diamond bracelets and dragon necklaces.

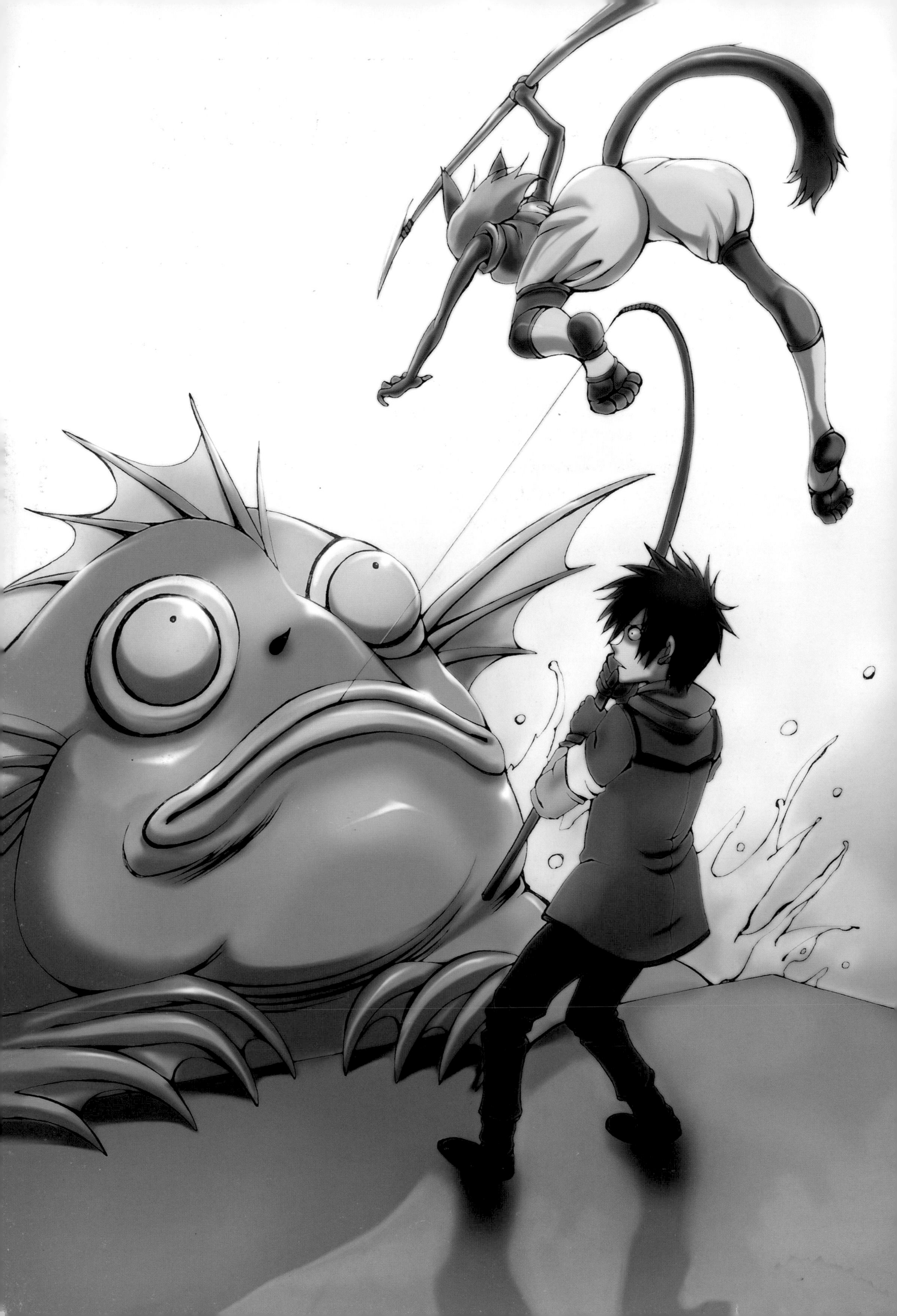

Fishing, Hunting

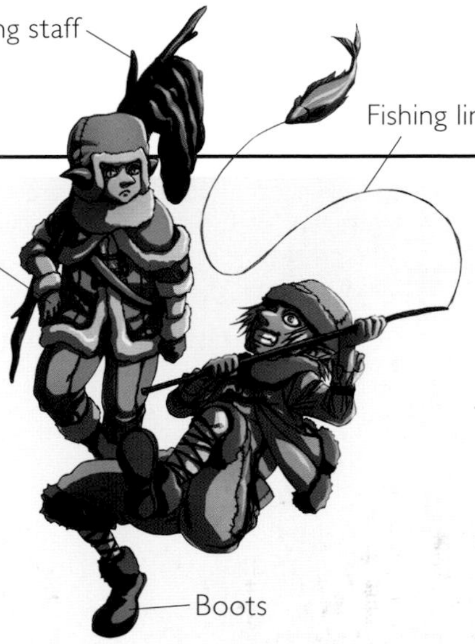
Hunting staff
Fishing line
Gloves
Boots

➨ Notable Features

Fishing

- **Skill in catching fish and other objects under water, which can then be used for casting spells**
- **Types of fish: leaping trout, monkfish, cavefish, rocktail, swordfish and leaping salmon**
- **Types of fishing skills: fly fishing (uses flys on the fish line to catch amphibians), fisherman's belt (uses belt with enchantment), and mooching (uses live fish for bait)**
- **Equipment: bait, fishing pole, gloves, boots, hose, fishing line, fishing hat**

Hunting

- **Skill in catching animals to tame them or eat them, and use the bones and animal skin for weapons and other equipment**
- **Types of animals and targets: beast, monkey, serpent, hawk, eagle, chimera, snake, bear, deer, fox**
- **Types of hunting skills: pitfall trapping (builds a pit as a trap), box trapping (sets a box as a trap) and tracking (uses a special wand to track animals)**
- **Equipment: bow, dagger, pole, staff, mace, shield, armor**

+ Outline and Origin

Since the Paleolithic period, man has practiced fishing as a means of survival. Spear fishing was prominent during this time. The early Egyptians used reed boats, harpoons, fishing baskets and nets. Gillnetting, which attaches stones to the bottom of the nets for weight and wood to the top for floats, became widespread across Europe and Asia around the 19th century.

As a skill, fishing is learned for cooking or for alchemy. Fishing lures enhance the fishing skill with enchantment to make enchanted gloves, flesh eating worm and sharpened fish hooks. Ranks of the fishing skill dictate the type of fish that can be caught, such as recruit (moat carp), initiate (cheval salmon), novice (giant catfish), apprentice (tuna), journeyman (giant freshwater fish), craftsman (marlin), artisan (bladefish), adept (three-eyed fish) and veteran (gigantic squid).

Hunting has also existed since the Paleolithic period. Spear hunting was practiced to hunt caribou or wild reindeer. Animal bones and skin were later used for making clothing, boots and tools. Some of the hunting abilities are: track beasts (locates all beasts), serpent sting (stings the target), and eagle eye (zooms into the hunter's vision). Traps may also be used in hunting, such as crowd control, fire, frost or snake trap.

· WESTERN MAGIC ·

I   Based on Western myths, folklore, monsters, spirits, occultism, and science

2   Influenced by Latin and Ancient Greek chants

3   Classifies magicians into groups, classes, or teams

4   Functions as support power (healing) and assault power (combat)

5   Characterized by references to powers of gods and beasts, mysterious symbols and meanings of magic words or chants

SAMPLE WESTERN MAGICIAN

MERLIN OF THE LEGEND OF KING ARTHUR

1. Born of a human mother and an incubus from whom he acquired his supernatural ability
2. Tall, old, dark, rough-looking, and wise; wears a beard and a pointed hat
3. Known as a madman
4. Lived in a cave
5. Had ability for shapeshifting (disguised as woodcutter, peasant, handsome man, and others), fighting spells, making prophecies, and becoming younger
6. Could talk to animals

JAPANESE MAGIC

I Based on Far Eastern religion, especially Chinese practices

2 Uses chant recitation, charms and amulets

3 Serves magicians as individuals

4 Functions as pleasing the gods or banishing bad spirits

5 Characterized by references to cosmology, calendar science, natural elements, afterlife and numbers

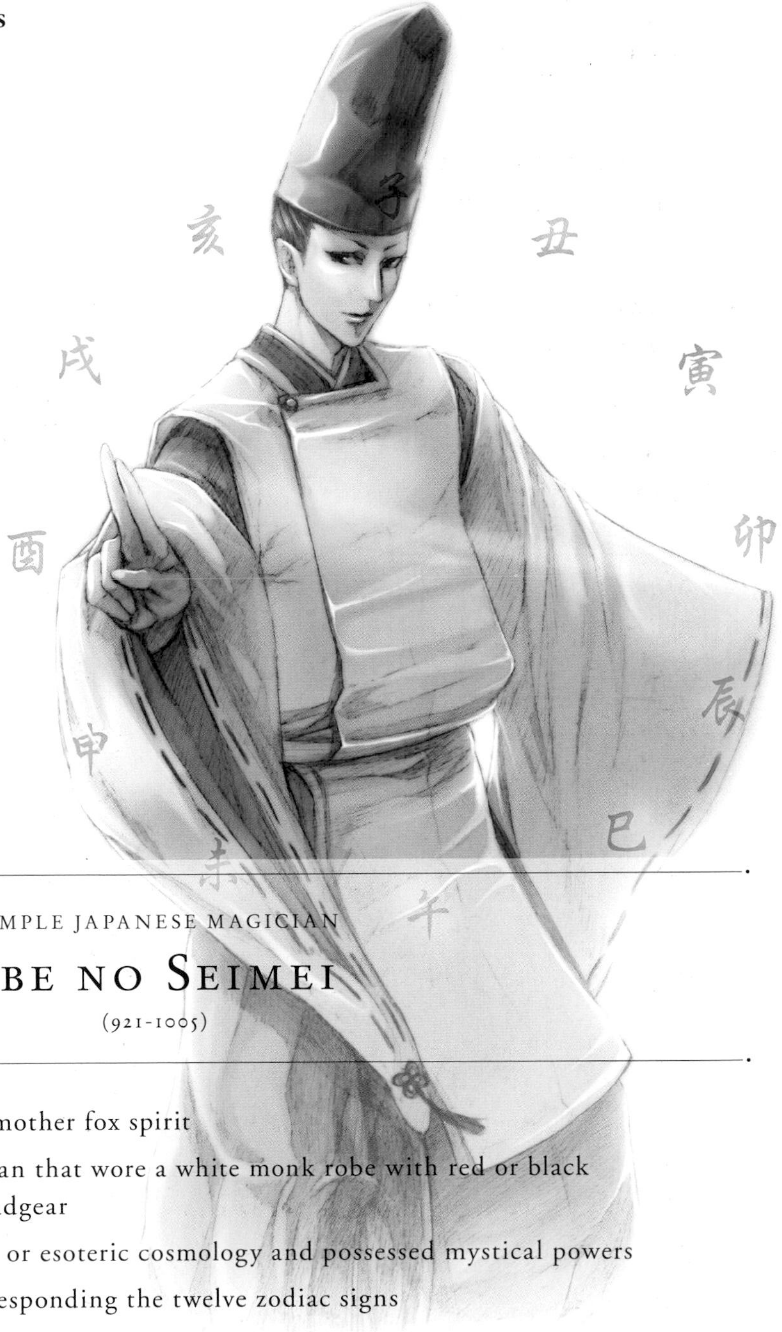
子
亥
丑
戌
寅
酉
卯
辰
申
巳
未
午

SAMPLE JAPANESE MAGICIAN

ABE NO SEIMEI

(921-1005)

1. Born of a human father and a mother fox spirit
2. Beautiful, handsome, young man that wore a white monk robe with red or black trousers, and black pointed headgear
3. Known as a leader of onmyodo or esoteric cosmology and possessed mystical powers
4. Had twelve servant spirits corresponding the twelve zodiac signs
5. Lived a long life without illness
6. Could transform objects into animals, and animals into objects

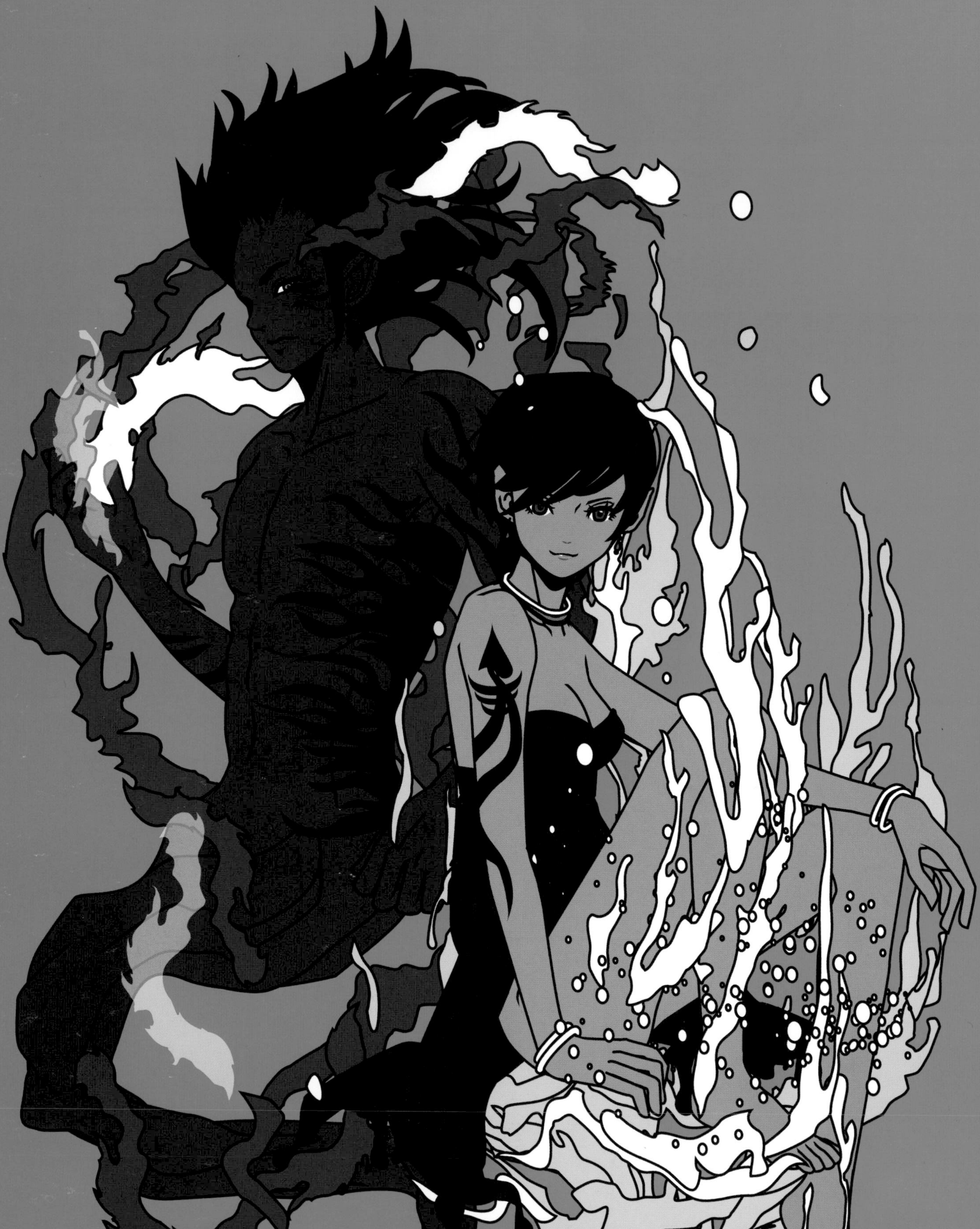

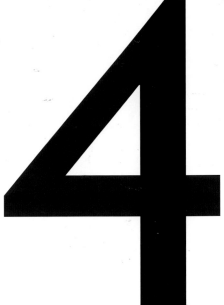

MAMONO

Fighting the Enemy

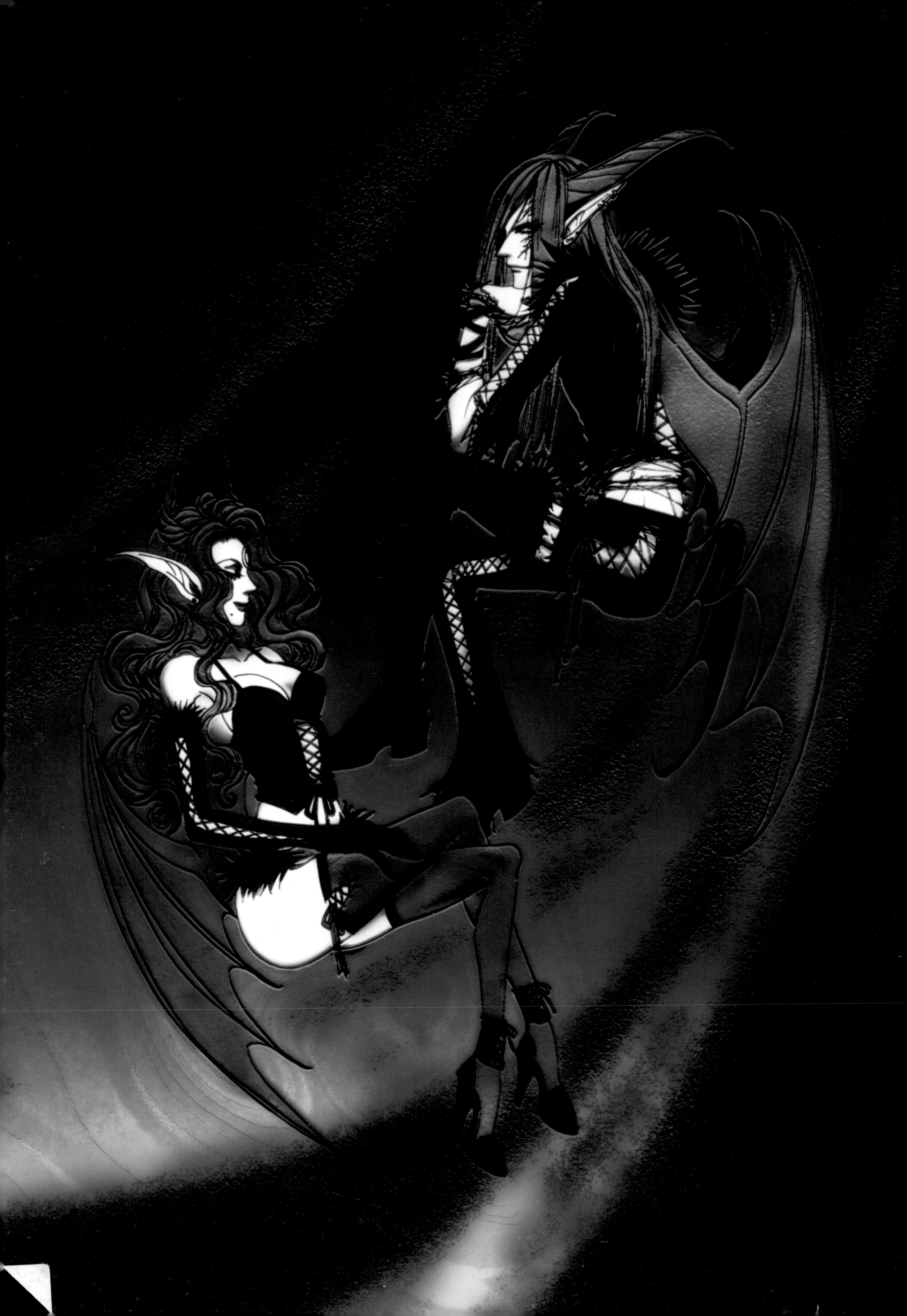

Incubus, Succubus

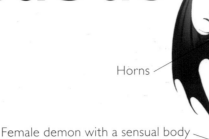

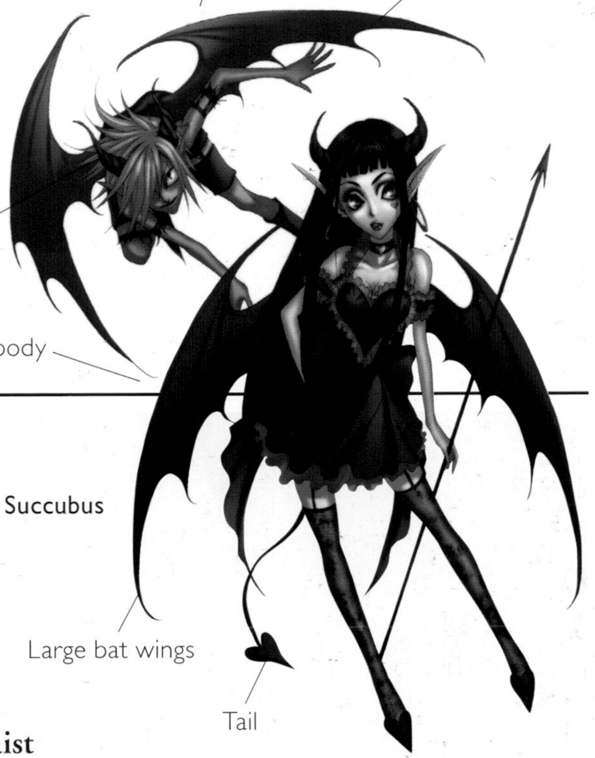

Incubus
Male with a boney structure

Wings

Horns

Female demon with a sensual body

Succubus

Large bat wings

Tail

➡ Notable Features

Incubus

- Male demon summoned by warlocks who attacks humans in their sleep
- Has boney structure; may be naked or clothed around the waist
- Has horns on the head and has wings

Succubus

- Female demon summoned by warlocks who attacks humans in their sleep
- Beautiful with a sensual body; may wear leather body suit
- Has large bat wings, tiny horns on the head and a tail

✚ Outline and Origin

An ancient belief from Mesopotamia recorded that the father of King Gilgamesh of Sumer in 2700 B.C. seduced women who were sleeping. His counterpart was the female demon Lilith who seduced men in their sleep. Ardat-lili and Irdu-lili, female and male demons, respectively, were also known for haunting humans in the same way.

Both incubi and succubi are intelligent creatures who are highly skilled in torturing and tempting humans or other creatures. They are agile, lust for blood and attack ferociously. They also use demonic curses to counterattack a mana used by a spell caster. Some subspecies of the succubus are the snow witch, hell spawn, soul burner, vile temptress, harlot and blood

temptress. Both incubi and succubi are defined by types and levels of resistance, such as damage resist, magic resist, fire resist, cold resist, lightning resist and poison resist. They can attack at melee range and use shadow damage with a whip. By using the lesser invisibility spell, they can decrease their invisibility power by five minutes.

Some abilities of the incubus and succubus are: lash of pain (instant attack with shadow damage), soothing kiss (calms a target while attacking another) and seduction (seduces a target). Siphon life is a talent by which the victim, when attacked by the succubus, releases flowing blood from its eyes, nose and mouth to form a long rope-like stream that is swallowed by a spell caster to strengthen his energy.

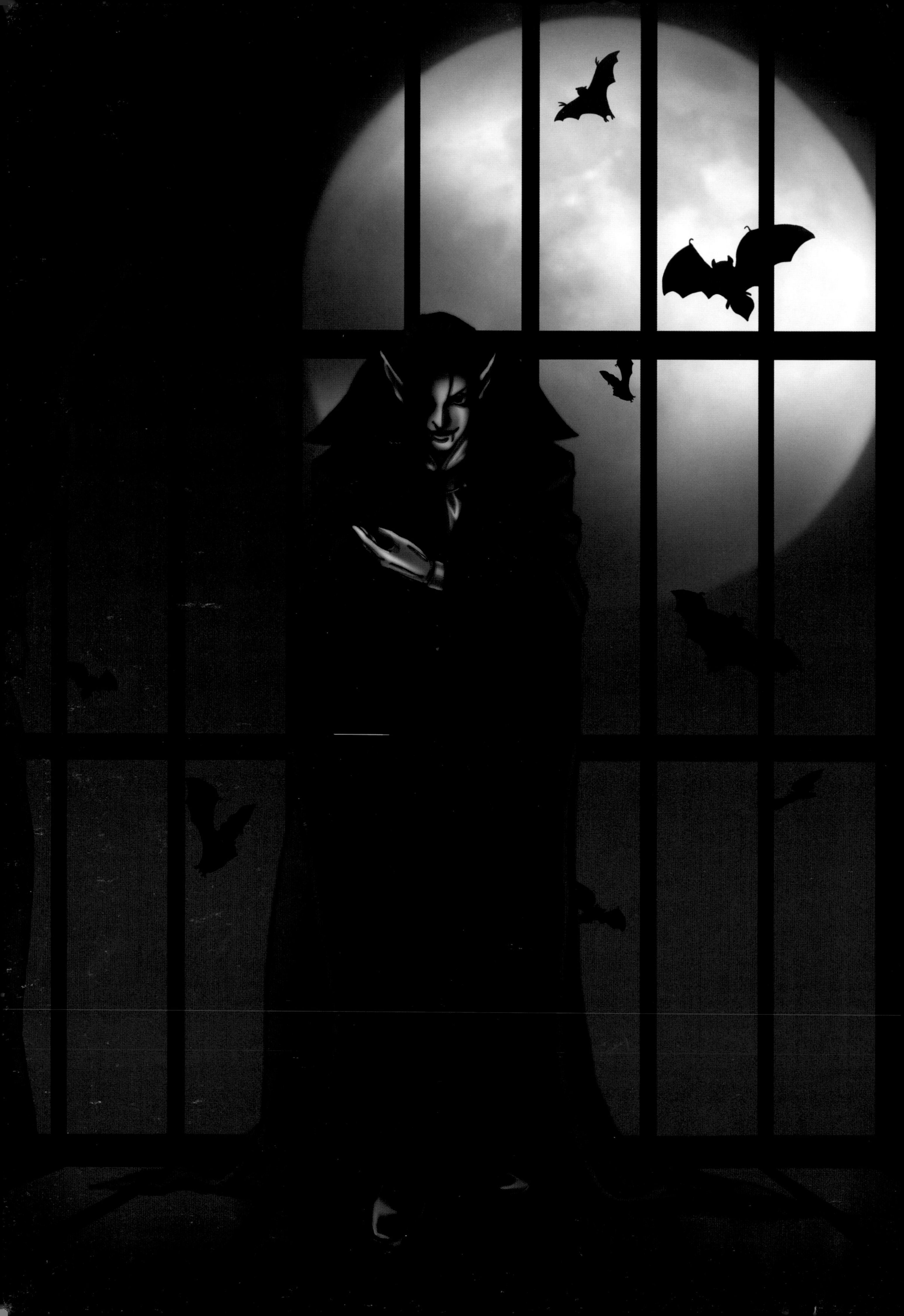

Vampire

Pale, white skin

Fangs

Sensitive to sunlight

Dark clothing

→ Notable Features

- Pale, whitish skin, sensitive to sunlight and has an eye color that changes according to its mood
- Craves blood for food and is easily fatigued
- Highly sensitive, intelligent and may have psychic abilities
- Physically stronger than humans
- May leap for long distances or be able to fly
- May be able to turn itself into a bat
- Sleeps during the day, highly sensitive to light and crosses
- May have sharp fangs
- Immortal

✝ Outline and Origin

Since the 18th century in Europe, vampires have been known as evil creatures possessed by evil souls. Their pale appearances attribute to their lack of blood and reflect that they need to suck blood from humans to revive their power and strength. Slavic and Chinese folklore believe that vampires are the result of humans who were attacked by wild animals, such as wolves. Vampire attacks were said to spread around 1721 in Europe, especially in East Prussia, which created wide panic among villagers. English traditions cite vampire bats as the source of these fearful creatures, which is seen in images of vampires with wide capes that look like bat wings.

In fantasy manga, vampires come in several ranks: banished (undead with green eyes and attack with a fire bolt), ghoul lords, night lords, dark lords and blood lords. They also have different classes, each possessing certain levels of abilities. Vampire acrobats are light-armored and carry bows, daggers and swords. They use skills of illusion, such as invisibility and silence. Vampire battlemages carry shields and staves and use powerful summoning and destruction spells. Vampire monks use alteration skills (such as altering the physical world with fire or frost).

Other vampire abilities are: resist disease, resist paralysis, resist normal weapons, sun damage, destruction, will power, illusion, mysticism (absorbs or dispels magic), sneak, fortify and strength, and sorcerer skills related to elements, such as fireball (explosive ball of fire), fire wall (wall of fire) and meteor (summons meteor to destroy the earth). Vampires use vampire dust to summon vampire bats.

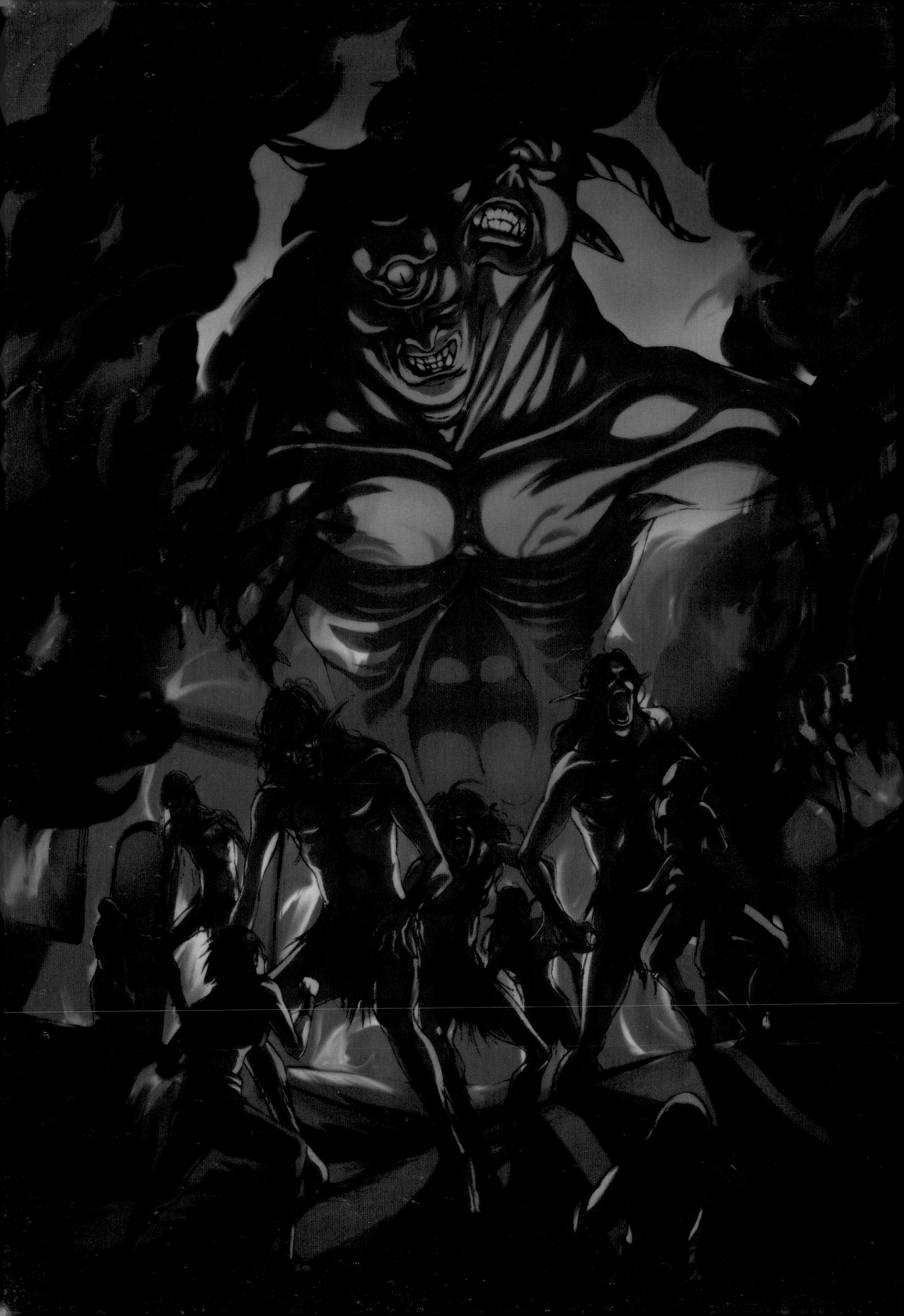

Ogre, Troll

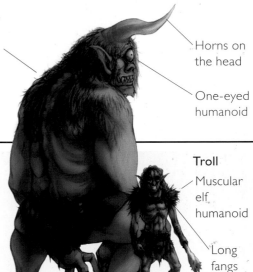

Ogre
Large, bulky and heavy, with dark-colored skin

Horns on the head

One-eyed humanoid

Troll
Muscular elf humanoid

Long fangs

Barefoot and has moss-like skin

➡ Notable Features

Ogre

- Large, bulky, heavy, deformed humanoid with peach, blue or dark-colored skin
- May be two-headed, one-eyed and have horns
- Physically strong, especially in melee combat
- Less intelligent than humans
- May be dressed in rags; carries spear, club or mace

Troll

- Tall, slender, muscular humanoid of the elf race
- Usually has moss-like skin that changes from light green to blue to purple; jungle troll is covered in fur
- Has long hands with two fingers and a thumb on each, strong legs, two toes on each foot, long ears and fangs
- Can grow plants on its body
- Barefoot; may be fully naked or thinly clothed, carries a spear

✚ Outline and Origin

Ogres are humanoid monsters that were first mentioned in late 12th century French verse. They were said to originate from the mythical giants Gog and Magog and the Greek river god, Oiagros. They were known for attacking humans themselves, but also for rescuing them from bandits or evil creatures. Trolls are fearful giants from Norse mythology. In Scandinavian folklore, they possess magical qualities despite their ugly and beastly appearances.

Ogres are very powerful in melee combat, but they are weak in defense attacks and are slow in speed. They are also weak to fire. Among the several ogre classes, there are: barbarian, warrior, mage, bone crusher, hunter, witch doctor, priest, shaman and warlock. Ogre mages are smarter than other ogre types and can perform spells. Ogre lords are one-eyed and grow stones on their bodies. The known enemies of all ogre types are orcs and humans.

Some of the troll classes are: warrior, hunter, mage, priest, rogue, shaman, druid, witch doctor, barbarian, wilderness stalker and healer. There are also forest trolls, mountain trolls, jungle trolls, river trolls, sea trolls, water trolls, undead trolls, ice trolls and dire trolls that are heavier and larger than typical trolls. Darkspear trolls are weak and small, but are highly intelligent. Trolls are weak and prone to physical damage, but they can restore their arms and legs and heal wounds. They mummify their dead and can restore them to life.

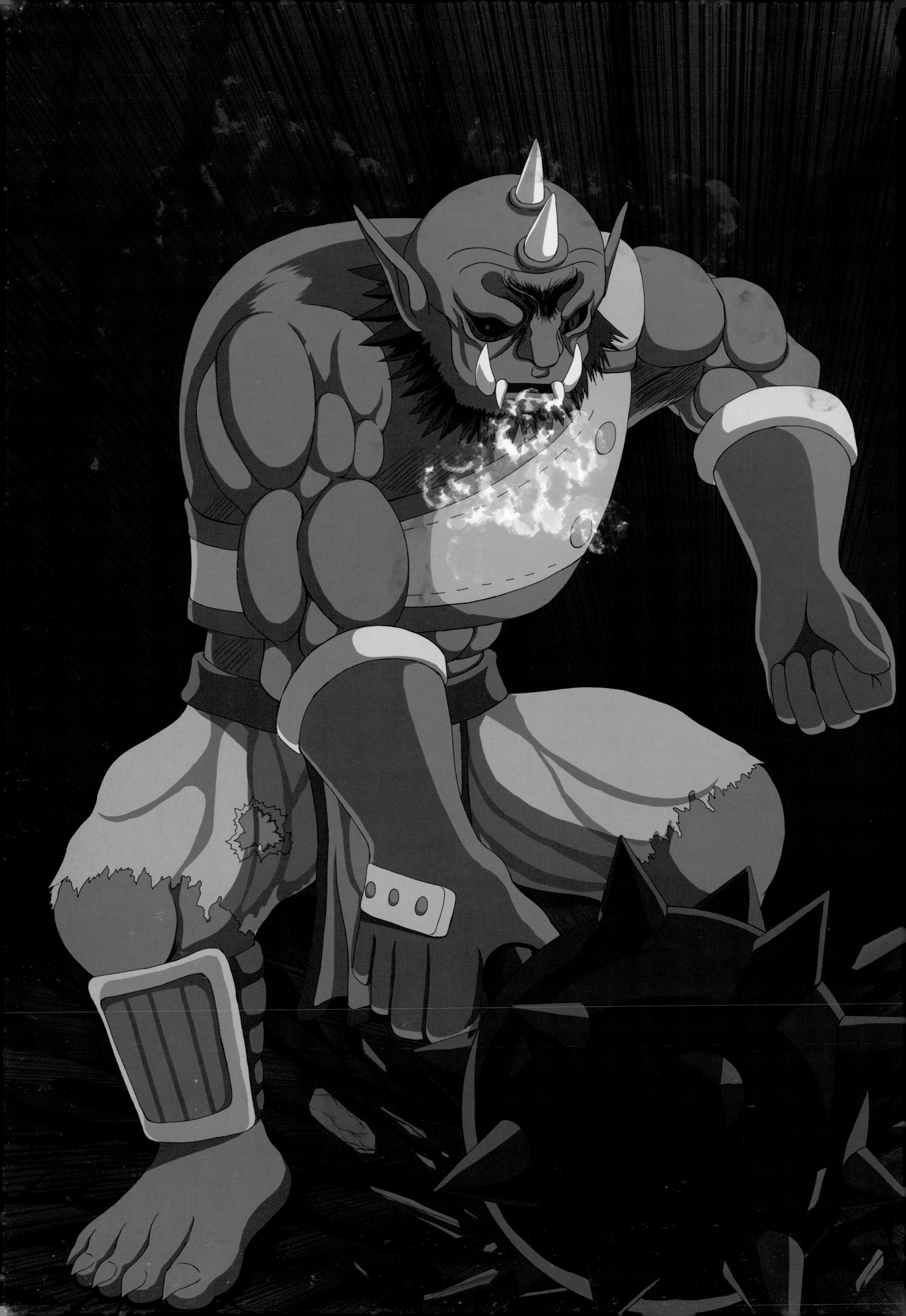

Orc

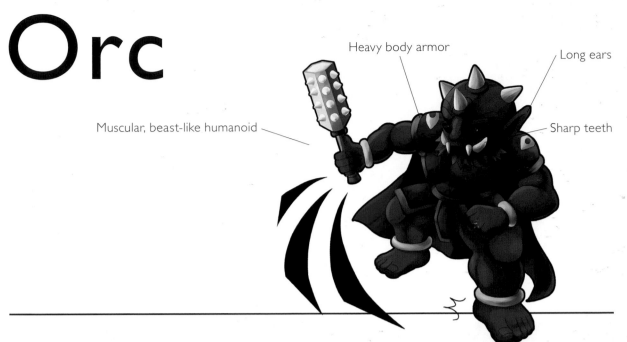

Heavy body armor

Long ears

Muscular, beast-like humanoid

Sharp teeth

➡ Notable Features

- Huge, brutish, muscular, beast-like humanoid with broad shoulders and a strong body weighing at least 200 pounds
- Coarse blue or violet hair and black or grey beard
- Skin color ranging from light green, olive to brown or red
- Flat nose, sharp teeth and long ears
- Eye color ranges can be blue, brown, hazel or red
- Male orc usually slouches; female orc stands erect
- May have tattoos on the body
- Wears fur, animal skin, or heavy armor, and carries a battle axe, dagger or sword

✛ Outline and Origin

Orcs originate from old English folklore when the Normans invaded England in 1066. They were believed to descend from the giant Ymir of Norse mythology. Since then, they have been a part of many English, German and Italian tales that originated in the 18th century. They are portrayed as brutal, sadistic and proud warriors who usually ride boars and wolves.

Orcs are found in the following character classes: hunter, rogue, shaman, beast master, barbarian, assassin and necromancer. They were once part of the noble shaman clan, but were corrupted by their masters, so they rebelled against their masters, regained their powers and honor, and have since fought for their survival. There are different types of orcs, such as the thrall (warrior shaman); frostwolf (known for mercy and compassion); warsong (abides by rigid beliefs); mag'har (orc that escaped corruption); half-orc (combined orc and other species); fel orc (skilled in chaos damage) and revenant orc (undead orc). Orcs have good relations with taurens because taurens provide them shelter and aid them with their needs. Orcs are also close to the elements of nature, and harming them is gravely forbidden among their clans.

Some of the orc abilities are: threatening essence (buff that increases level of threat), focus slash (severe physical damage), sneaky raid (causes blinding effect), body slam (stuns the target), sharp vision (increases accuracy) and triple slash (attack target with two attacks). Orcs can use a bronze dagger, iron dart, bronze battle-axe, steel dagger and other weapons.

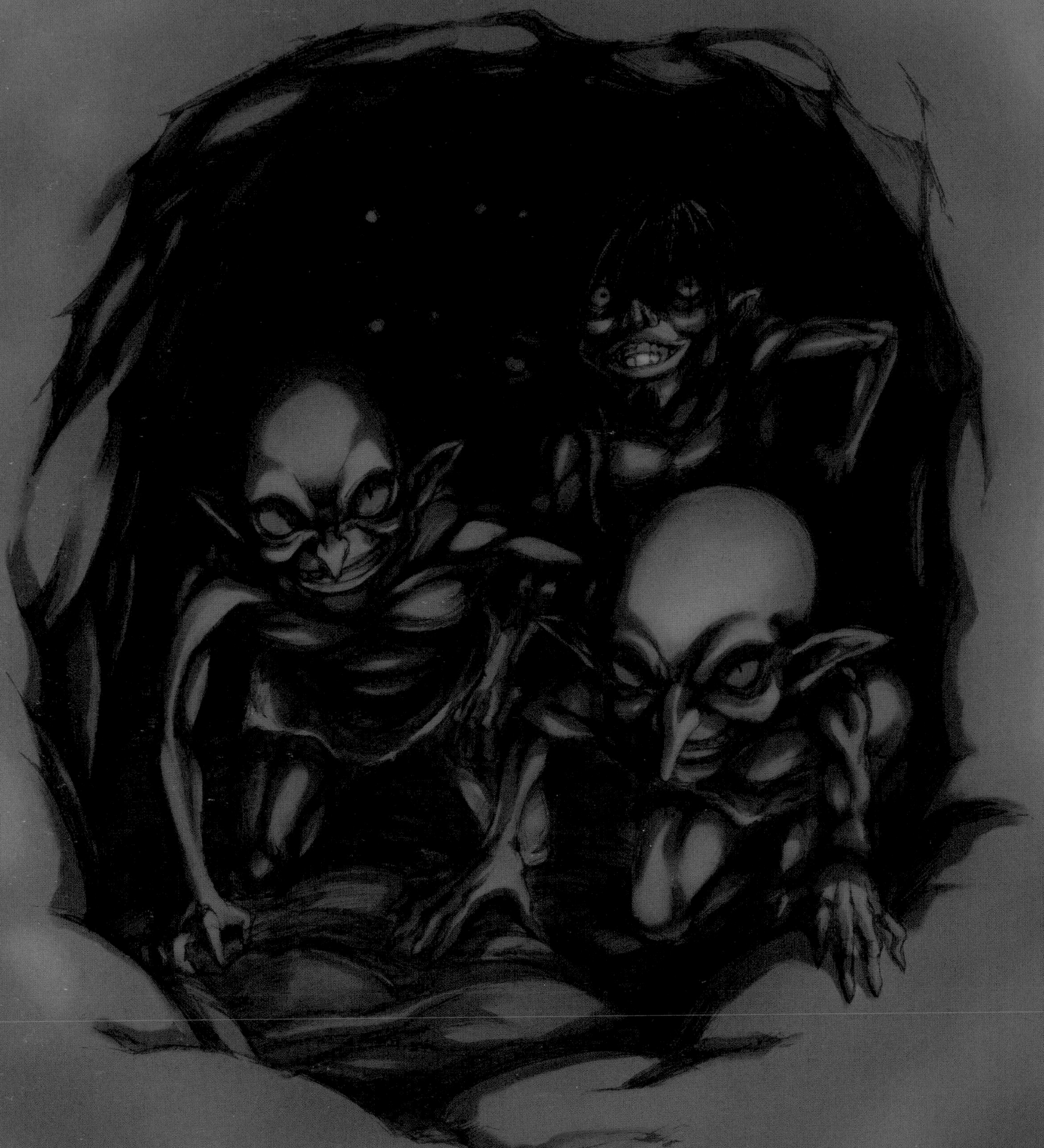

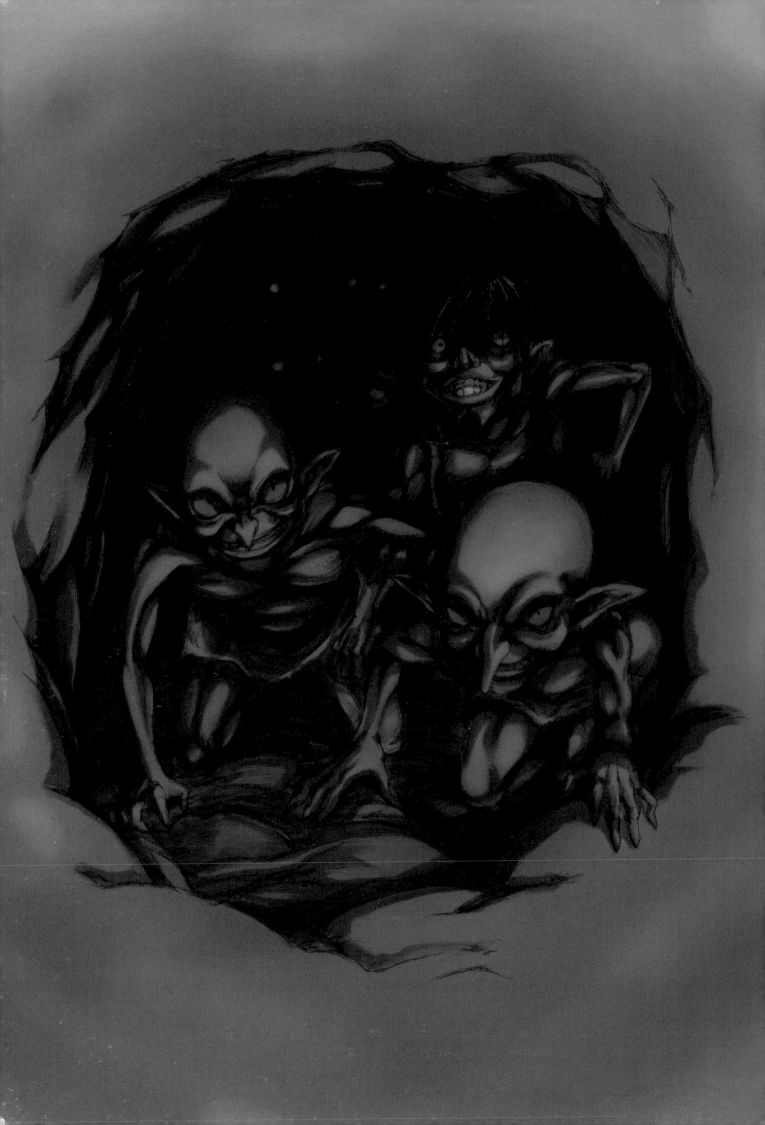

Goblin, Kobloid

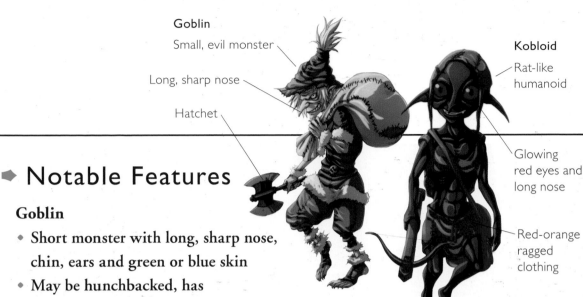

Goblin
- Small, evil monster
- Long, sharp nose
- Hatchet

Kobloid
- Rat-like humanoid
- Glowing red eyes and long nose
- Red-orange ragged clothing

➤ Notable Features

Goblin

- Short monster with long, sharp nose, chin, ears and green or blue skin
- May be hunchbacked, has long arms and quick fingers
- Hair in ponytail, spiky or mohawk style
- Wears apron-like leather attire and carries an arrow, hatchet, javelin, spear and dagger

Kobold

- Short rat-like humanoid with large, glowing red eyes and a long nose
- Scaly skin with brown or red hides, reptilian head and tail, and clean horns, claws and teeth
- Wears red or orange ragged leather or silk clothes
- Carries candle, darts, shovel, mace, blade and a crossbow

✚ Outline and Origin

Goblins are small, evil monsters that originate from Germanic and English folklore. They are evil spirits in pagan belief, and have existed in Latin tales since the 13th century, as the German legendary Erlking in 18th century tales, and in Chinese folklore since the early 1900s. They live in dark caves, and engage in commerce and trade, inventing machineries and tools.

The goblin character classes are tinker (invents tools), sapper (creates explosive items), steam warrior (builds gas-powered armor suits), techno mage (combines magic and technology), ace (expert of wheeled vehicles), shaman and death knight.

Some goblin abilities are: goblin punch (uses weapon attack and blue magic), counter (follows up an enemy attack) and weapon defense (increases weapon defense).

Kobolds originate from Germanic mythology. Their character classes are rogue, healer, warrior, geomancer and sorcerer. Kobolds are afraid of light and live in tunnels. Though ferocious, they are weak in one-on-one combat, thus, attack in groups. They are skilled in mining, and use polearms, slings, bows and staves to perform spell casting, enchantments, summons, transmutations, and fire, ice, air and poison magic.

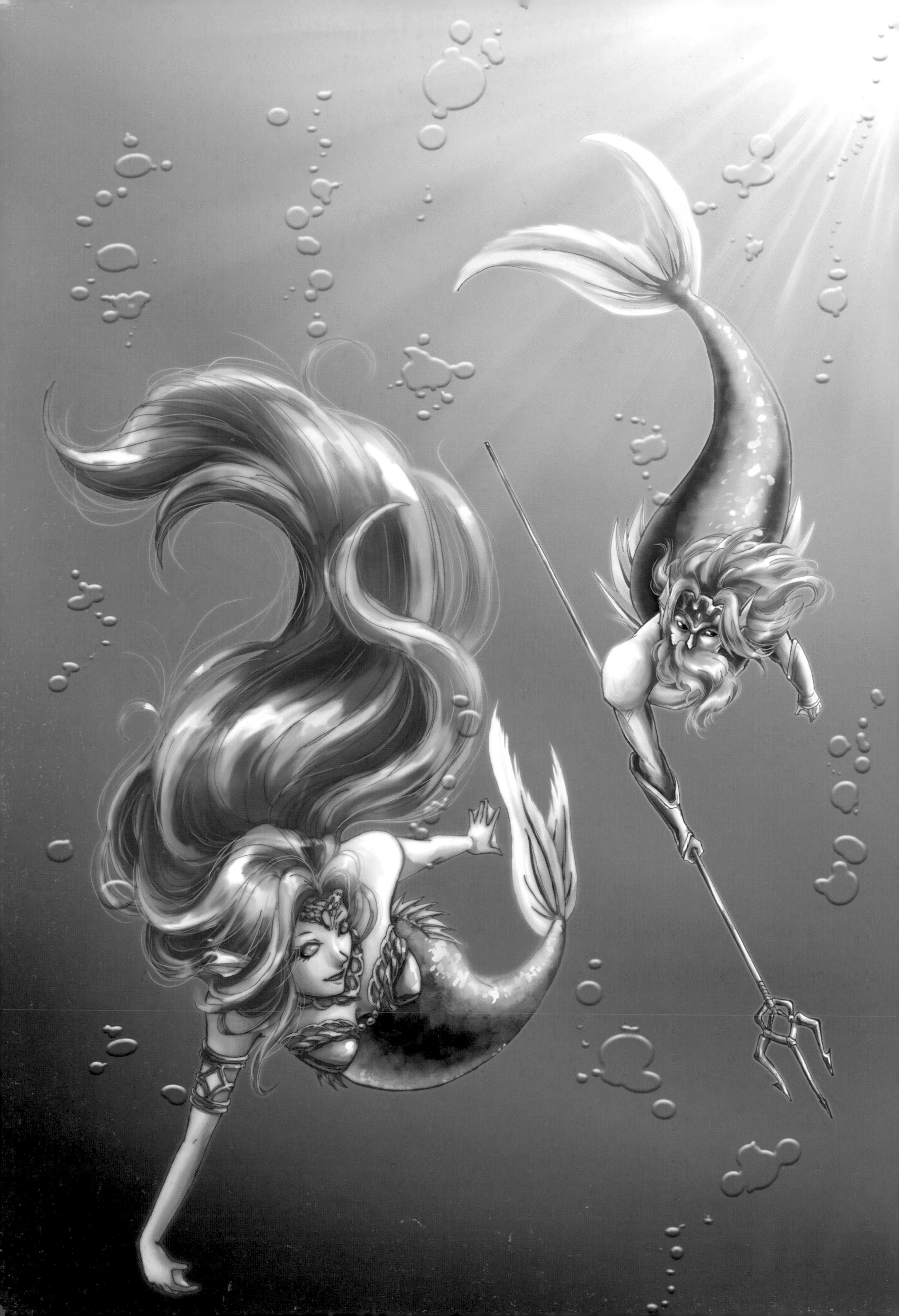

Merman, Mermaid

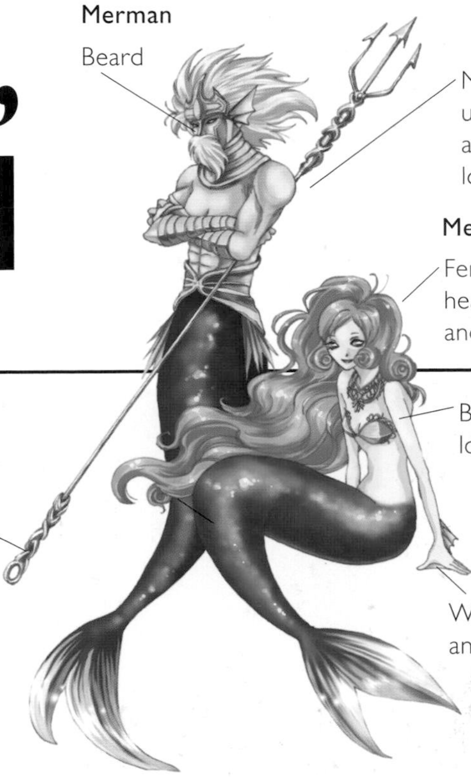

Merman
Beard
Male human upper torso and fish-like lower body
Mermaid
Female human head and body and tail of a fish
Beautiful, with long silky hair
Trident
Webbed hands and scaly skin

Notable Features

Merman

- **Aquatic humanoid with a male upper body and fish-like lower body**
- **Beard, pointed green teeth, pig's eyes, green hair and red nose**
- **Fins behind the ears, clawed and webbed fingers and thick fish scales**
- **Usually carries a trident**

Mermaid

- **Aquatic humanoid with a female upper body and fish-like lower body**
- **Beautiful with long silky hair, fair skin, scales and a short fin on the back of the tail**
- **Has a beautiful singing voice**
- **Does not usually carry a weapon**

Outline and Origin

A mermaid was known to appear in 1000 B.C. in Assyria when the goddess Atargatis accidentally killed a human whom she fell in love with. She jumped into the waters and took the form of a fish to punish herself, but instead became a mermaid.

Mermen appeared in Greek, Irish, Finnish and Asian mythologies as green, bearded, and powerful sea creatures that had magical abilities to heal. Both the mermaid and the merman play and sing with other sea creatures, but mermen hide more deeply in the ocean to escape the traps of enemies. They are more serious than mermaids and hold tridents.

Both mermen and mermaids can take on a human form when their bodies are completely dry. They also swim in great speed. Their tails are extremely strong they can smash objects. Some of their magical powers are: hydrokinesis (moves water with the power of the mind), hydro-cryokinesis (freezes water to create an ice ball) and hydro-thermokinesis (heats and boils water, and creates fire to summon lightning).

Mermaids and mermen use their aura to lure enemies and then slowly draw the life out of them. Mermen use their clawed, webbed hands to attack enemies, and may throw a fireball at an enemy. A fish-head merman uses his fish mouth to shoot water at its target. A triton merman is god-like, holds a trident and a horn, and sits on a throne. A giant merman summons fishermen to attack the enemy.

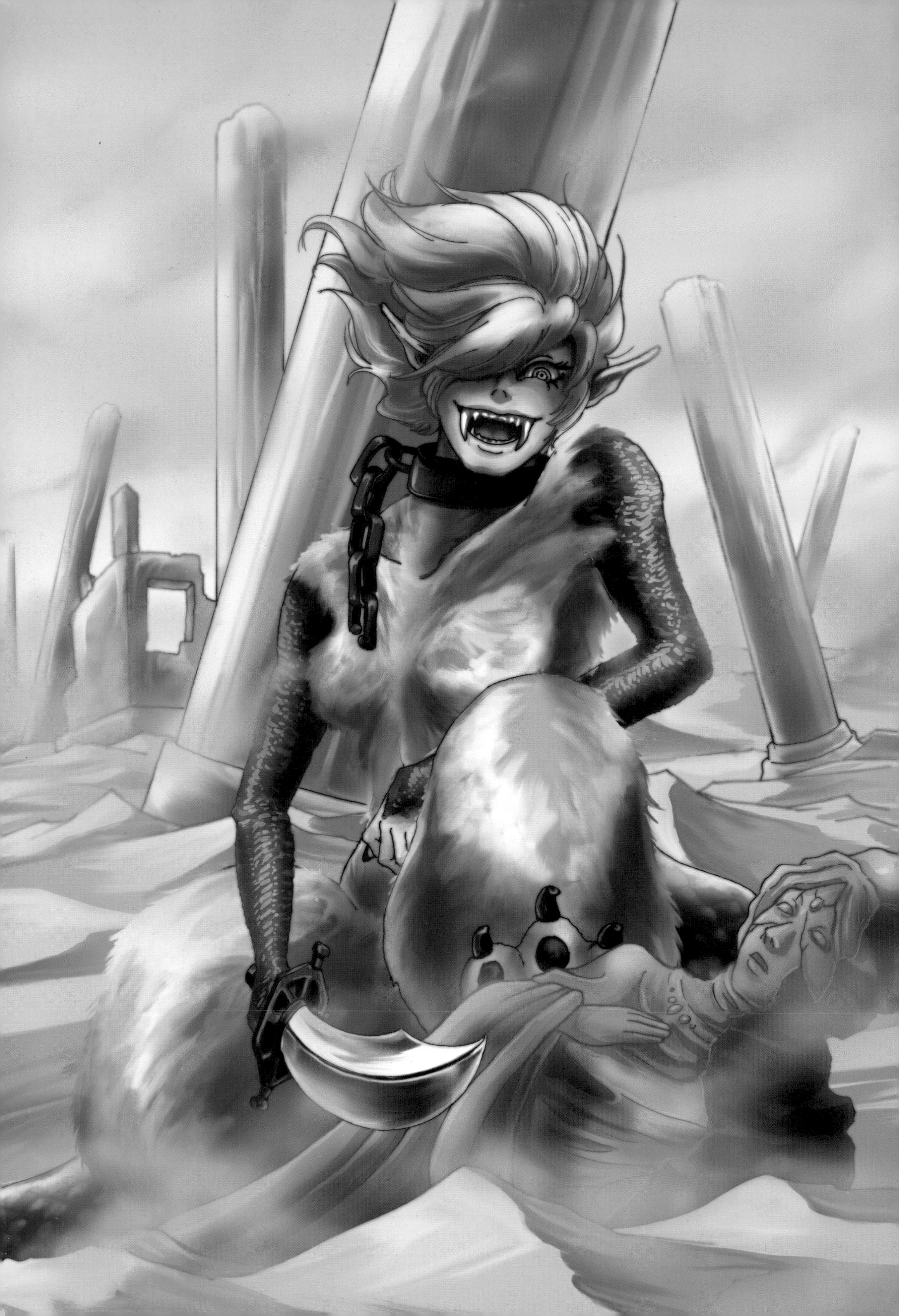

Lamia

Serpent's tail

Scaly, snake-like skin

Female human upper body and a beast's lower body

Seductive and sucks blood

➡ Notable Features

- **Magic beast with a female human upper body, head and arms, a beast's (goat, lion or deer) lower body, and a serpent's tail**
- **Has scaly, snake-like skin**
- **Lives in deserts, caves and abandoned cities**
- **Carnivorous**
- **Seductive and stalks children to suck their blood**
- **Possesses magical abilities**
- **May carry a dagger or bow**

✛ Outline and Origin

In Greek mythology, Lamia was the granddaughter of Poseidon who became the queen of Libya, and was accused of bearing Zeus' children. Zeus's wife, Hera, killed the children out of anger, driving Lamia insane, and causing her to eat other children. In her enraged state, her body became distorted. Zeus gave her the ability to remove her eyes to help her erase visions of her murdered children, but she continued to obsess over children. Throughout classical Europe, the symbol of Lamia threatened children and marriages.

The lamia character is known to live in dark caves or remote towers, waiting to eat human flesh. She haunts ghosts who give her powers of illusion to seduce men. She moves with great speed and uses her spells to capture targets. Sometimes, she is seen with a dagger that she uses to attack her prey and scrape out their flesh. Some of her spells are charm person, mirror image, suggestion and illusion, which all aim to lure or seduce victims. She also uses a wisdom spell that tricks the target to do whatever she says, such as attack other victims.

Some illusions the lamia can take on are: a beautiful maiden, female ranger, elf maiden and distressed child. The lamia noble is a subspecies of the lamia, with a lower body of a serpent and an upper body of either a male or female human. It is not armed with physical weapons, but attacks with magic, usually using a human disguise.

Other attack skills used by the lamia are: gusting gouge (causes wind damage), arrow deluge (threefold ranged attack), pole swing (focuses on a single target), tidal slash (causes water damage), grim reaper (causes doom effect), hysteric barrage (fivefold attack), tail slap (causes stun effect), hypnotic sway (causes amnesia), belly dance (charms the target) and gorgon dance (causes petrifying effect).

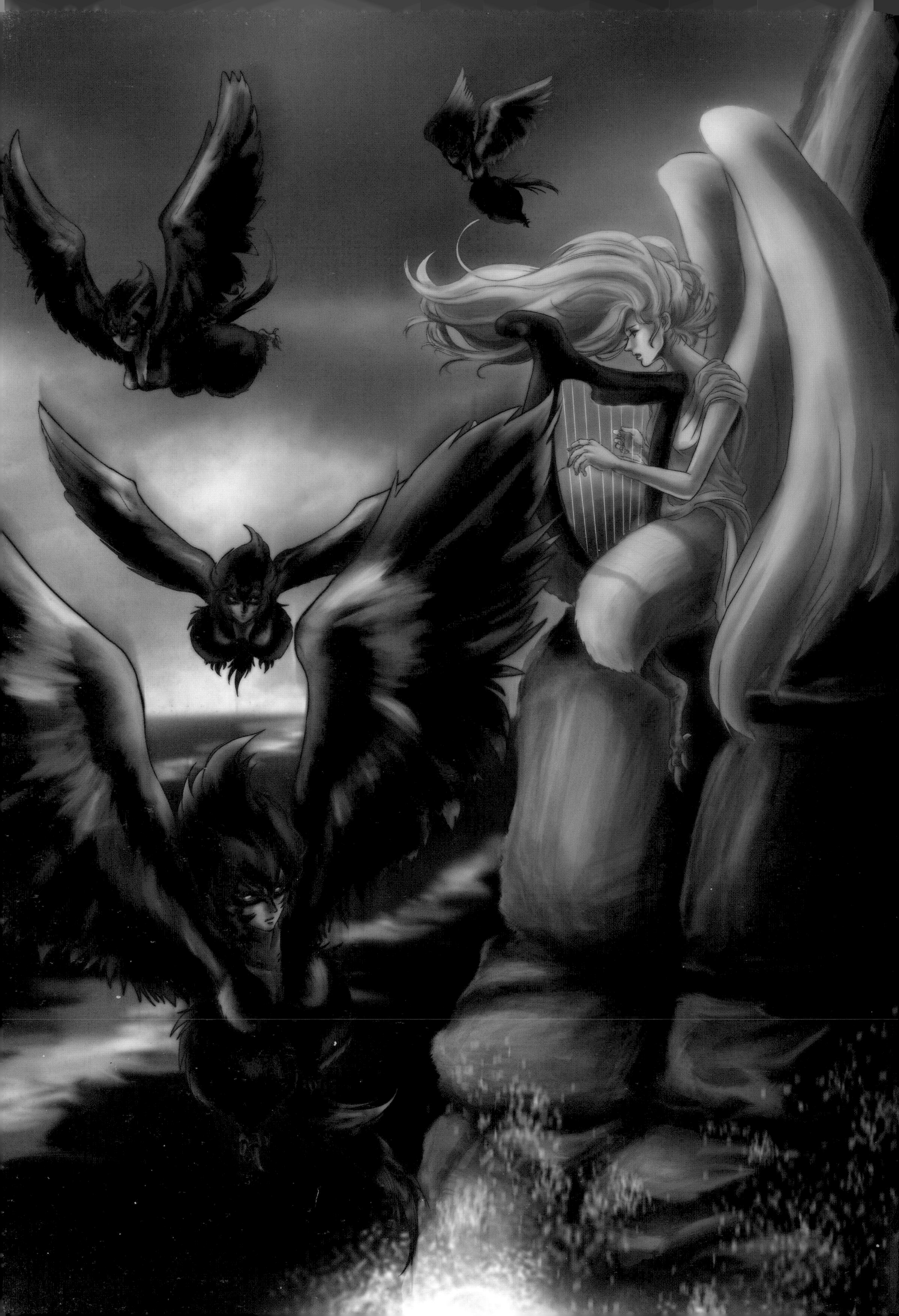

Harpy, Siren

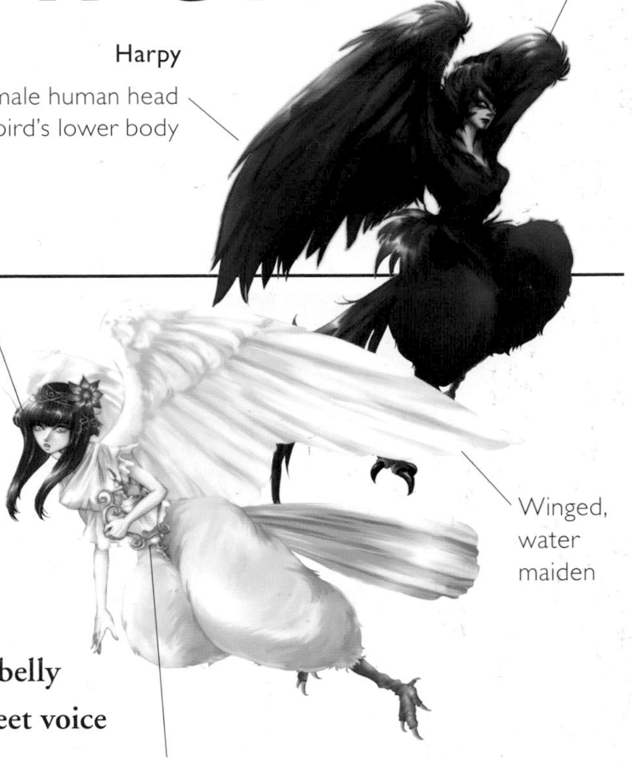
Huge, broad wings
Harpy
Female human head
and bird's lower body
Siren
Long black hair and blue eyes
Winged,
water
maiden
Musical instrument, such as a lyre

Notable Features

Harpy

- **Winged creature with a female human head and a bird's lower body and legs**
- **May have eagle or vulture parts, clawed feet and a swollen, feathered belly**
- **Dirty, evil and solitary, but has a sweet voice**
- **Flies at great speed**
- **Lives in warm hills and mountains**

Siren

- **Winged, water maiden creature with a bird's body and a female human head**
- **Has blonde or black hair, grey or blue eyes, and dark skin**
- **Has a beautiful and seductive voice**
- **Plays a musical instrument, such as a lyre**
- **Dwells along the coast**

Outline and Origin

In Greek mythology, the harpies were the daughters of the sea god Thaumas and the oceanid Electra who were summoned by Zeus to steal food from Phineas, King of Thrace. They abducted children and weak or wounded people.

Harpy monsters are close to kobolds, and are like female night elves and hunting birds with huge, elegant wings. They invade taurens, viciously attack any intruder, and can resist disease. They are also intelligent and communicate with other races. The types of harpies are: coldwind (colored black and keeps goblins away); dustwind (colored blue and red and assaults caravans); screeching (colored blue, and lives in caves); and snowblind (lives in the ice region). Harpies possess enchanting singing skills for luring targets.

The sirens were daughters of the river god Achelous. They seduced seamen with their music, putting them to sleep or leading them to danger. As naga (night elves mutated into humanoid sea serpents) spell casters, they make whirlpools and cyclones to trap enemies. Like monstrous mermaids, they have sharp claws and teeth, and vicious eyes, and attack by slithering, slashing, piercing and bludgeoning. They cause blood drains when they bite victims, or poison on a target.

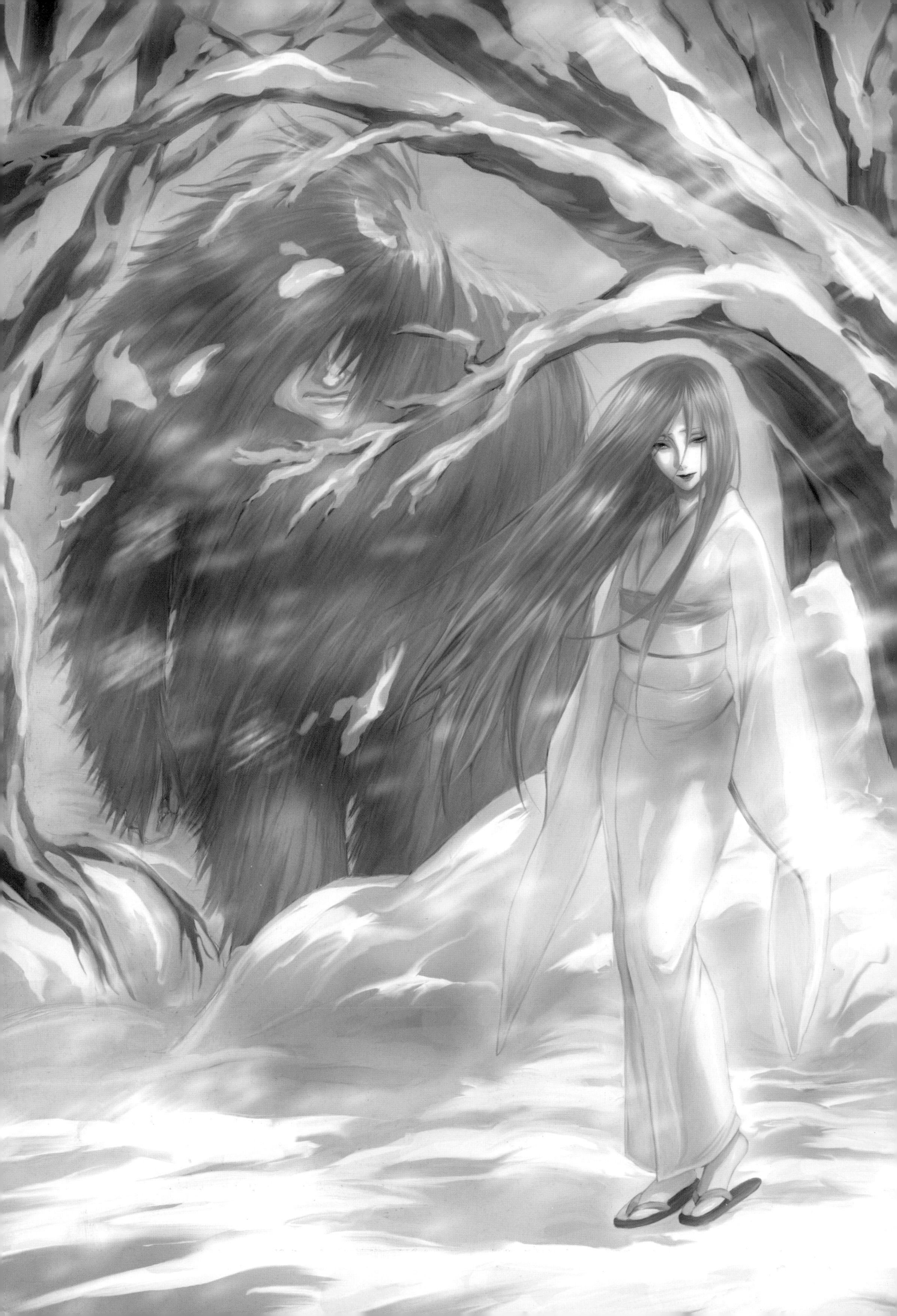

Yeti, Yuki-onna

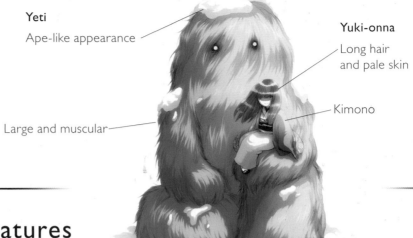

Yeti
Ape-like appearance
Large and muscular
Yuki-onna
Long hair and pale skin
Kimono

Notable Features

Yeti (abominable snowman)

- **Huge, furry ape-like humanoid that lives in cold climates near caves**
- **Has reddish hair, yellowish skin, a large muscular build and cone-shaped head**
- **Usually comes out at night**
- **Has great physical strength**

Yuki-onna (Japanese snow woman)

- **Japanese female snow spirit**
- **Tall and beautiful with long black hair, red lips and very pale skin**
- **May be kind or cruel**
- **Wears a kimono**

Outline and Origin

In the 19th century, mountain trekkers in Nepal saw tall and hairy creatures, leaving giant ape-like footprints in the snow. Reports concluded that they had seen three types of yetis: the rimi, which stands up to eight feet tall; the nvalmot, which stands up to fifteen feet and is carnivorous; and the rakshi-bompo, which stands up to five feet tall and is vegetarian.

Yetis dwell in cold climates and are aggressive and territorial, attacking humans and animals. They use their ice-cold and melee combat skills as weapons. Some yeti skills are: focus blow (causes severe physical damage), sneaky raid (causes blindness) and body slam (charges and stuns the enemy).

Like the yeti, the yuki-onna lives in the cold. One legend of the Yuki-onna, the Japanese snow woman, depicts her as a moon princess who descended to the earth, and could not return to the skies. Another legend comes from Lafcadio Hearn, a Greek-Irish author of many Japanese stories, about a beautiful snow lady who helped a lost man in the snowy mountain. When her disguise as a snow lady was revealed, she melted away and began to appear in the snowy mountains, either as an evil spirit that breathes ice on humans to freeze them, or as a gentle maiden who guides lost people in the snow. Yuki-onna can turn targets into ice blocks, transform into a cloud of snow, and use skills such as ice claw (freezes the hands of an enemy), ice shards (frost spells that shoot a target) and cold subtype (inflicts cold on an enemy).

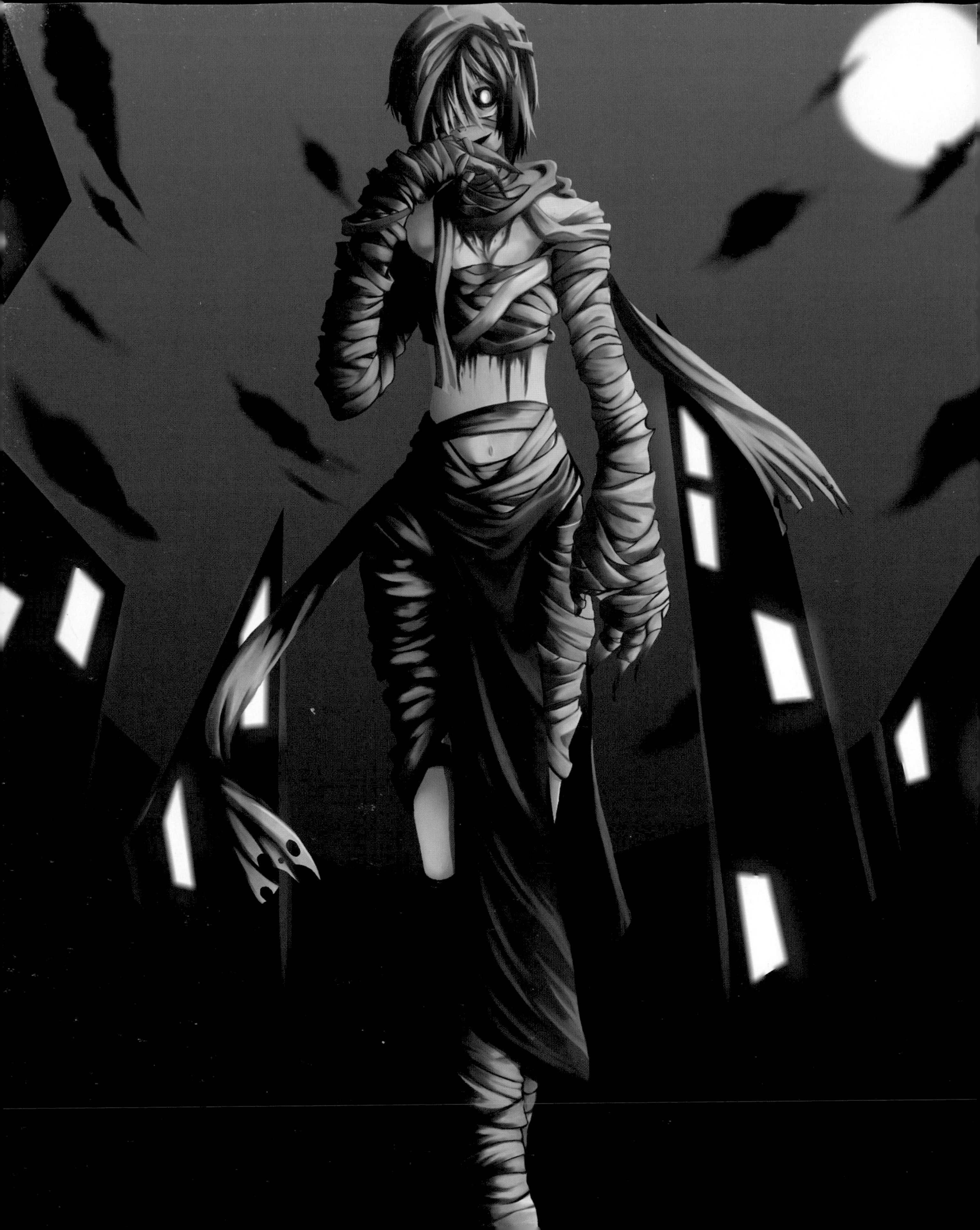

Undead Monster

Immune to poison and sickness

Skeletal body or spirit

Evil-looking

Human or animal

➡ Notable Features

- Regains physical life as a spirit or supernatural being after death
- May have the body of a skeleton, spirit, human, animal or other creature
- Types of undead creatures: ghoul (monster that eats humans), vampire, zombie, ghost, phantom, poltergeist, death knight, bone golem (inanimate monster made of bones), gargoyle, mummy, skeleton and corpse gatherer (giant made of earth and stone)
- Immune to poison and sickness, fear, sleep, mind control spells
- Hostile, bloodthirsty, evil, destructive

✚ Outline and Origin

The Greek keres female death-spirits, dark and vengeful Roman lemure spirits, draugar (dead viking bodies from Norse mythology), ghouls (from Arab tradition), hopping corpses (from Chinese tales) and medieval revenants (ghosts from medieval ages) are restless spirits that are controlled by necromancers and transposed to dead corpses or skeletons. Undead monsters may be: corporeal or skeletal, which have a physical body and attack with their legs, but have no brain; the skeleton warrior, which is intelligent and casts spells; the corpse, which is trapped in a physical body, such as that of a ghoul, zombie or mummy; the construct, which consists of bones and dead flesh; the incorporeal, which has no physical form; phantom; the poltergeist; or the higher undead, which is a resurrected slave of a

master, such as a vampire or lich (spell caster).

Ghouls, zombies, mummies and lichs are the most well known undead monsters. Ghouls run fast, jump in multiple directions and use swords. A grave-touched ghoul is very powerful and blessed by the King of Ghouls. A lacedon ghoul is aquatic. Zombies are restless spirits trapped in bodies and rise from the grave. There are zombie dragons, minotaur zombies, ogre zombies, and centaur zombies. Mummies are created from dead kings or rulers, and spread sickness. There are ice mummies, clay mummies, salt mummies and mummy lords. The lich has a skeletal structure, and is formed by using a magic potion. The lich has high intellectual powers, can paralyze humans, summon other undead monsters and fight poison, sickness or fatigue.

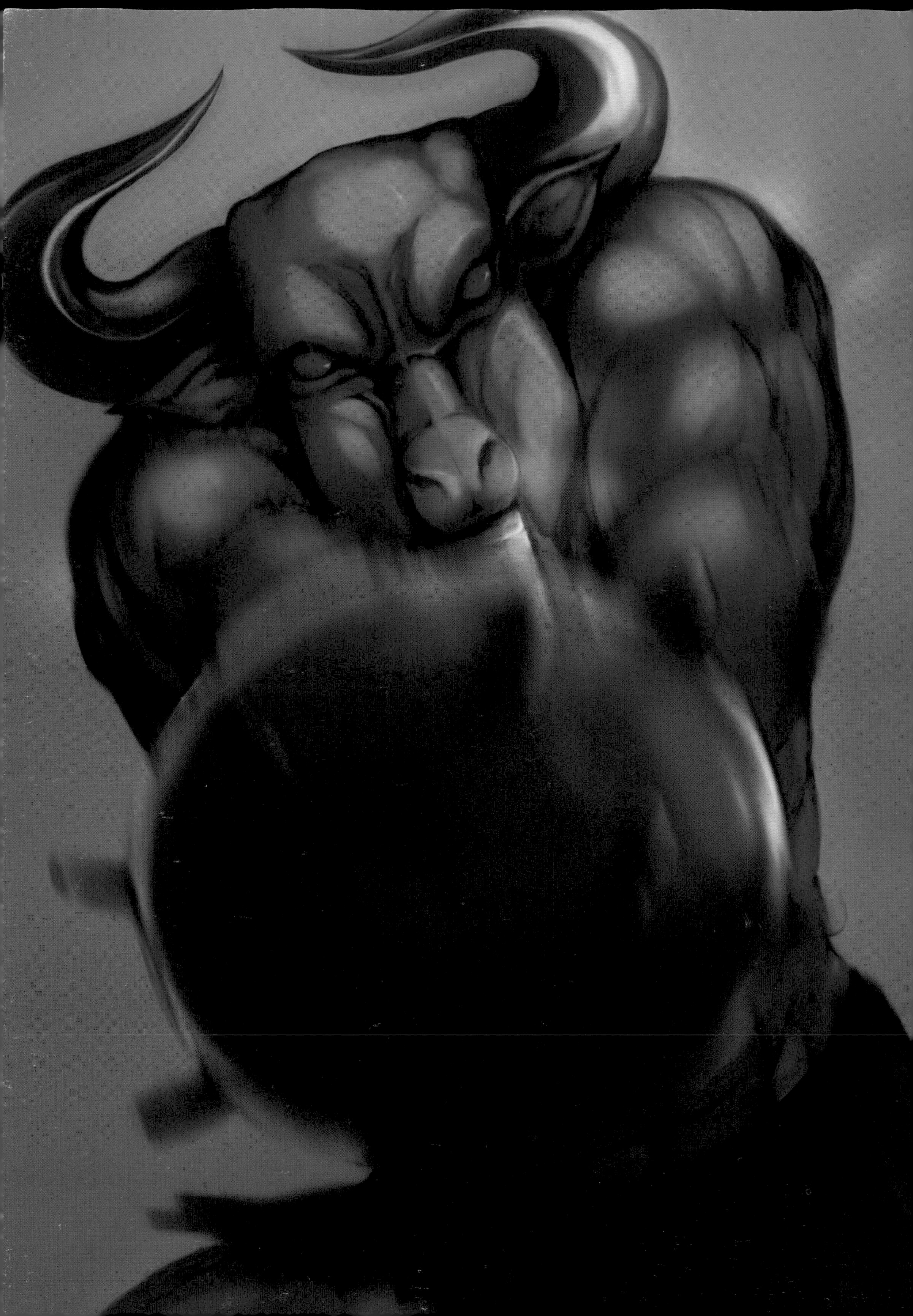

Minotaur

Head of a bull

Huge and tall monster

Bull's tail

Walks on hind legs

➡ Notable Features

- Huge monster (horizontally and vertically) with the head and tail of the bull and body of a human
- Carnivorous and walks on hind legs
- Weak in water
- Fights with different kinds of axes and other weapons

✢ Outline and Origin

Minotaur was the offspring of King Minos of Crete in Greek mythology. When Minos became king, he prayed to Poseidon for a snow-white bull and intended to offer the bull as a sacrifice, but kept it instead because of its beauty. As punishment, Aphrodite made Minos' wife fall in love with a sea bull, and they bore a child with a bull's head and a human body, that child was Minotaur. Minotaur grew up wild and fierce. He was locked in a labyrinth to prevent him from attacking, and was eventually killed by the Greek hero Theseus.

There are several classes of minotaur creatures, such as the minotaur grunt that fight in pairs with a battle axe; minotaur warrior that is larger than the grunt and fights with a war hammer; minotaur tormentor, one of the largest and most dangerous kinds and wears spiked armor and carries a giant spiked battle axe; titan minotaur, made of volcanic rock and lava; minotaur sword, the type that fights with giant swords; hades minotaur, the type covered in flames; and erebus minotaur, the type that is covered in ice. Some of the minotaur ranks are: wisenkin or bull demon, a type that is green, lives in the mountains and fights with a battle axe; minitaurus, a type that fights with a coral sword; and sacred, a type that fights at long range with a holy lance.

Minotaur abilities are: pick axe (attack the target with a pick axe); feral spin (swings the pick axe); beef up (absorbs the earth's energy); earth splitter (stomps the earth to send shockwaves); and breath fire (exhales fire). It also uses attack skills, such as draw in (pulls the enemy forward); and mortal ray (stuns the enemy causes it to fall on the ground).

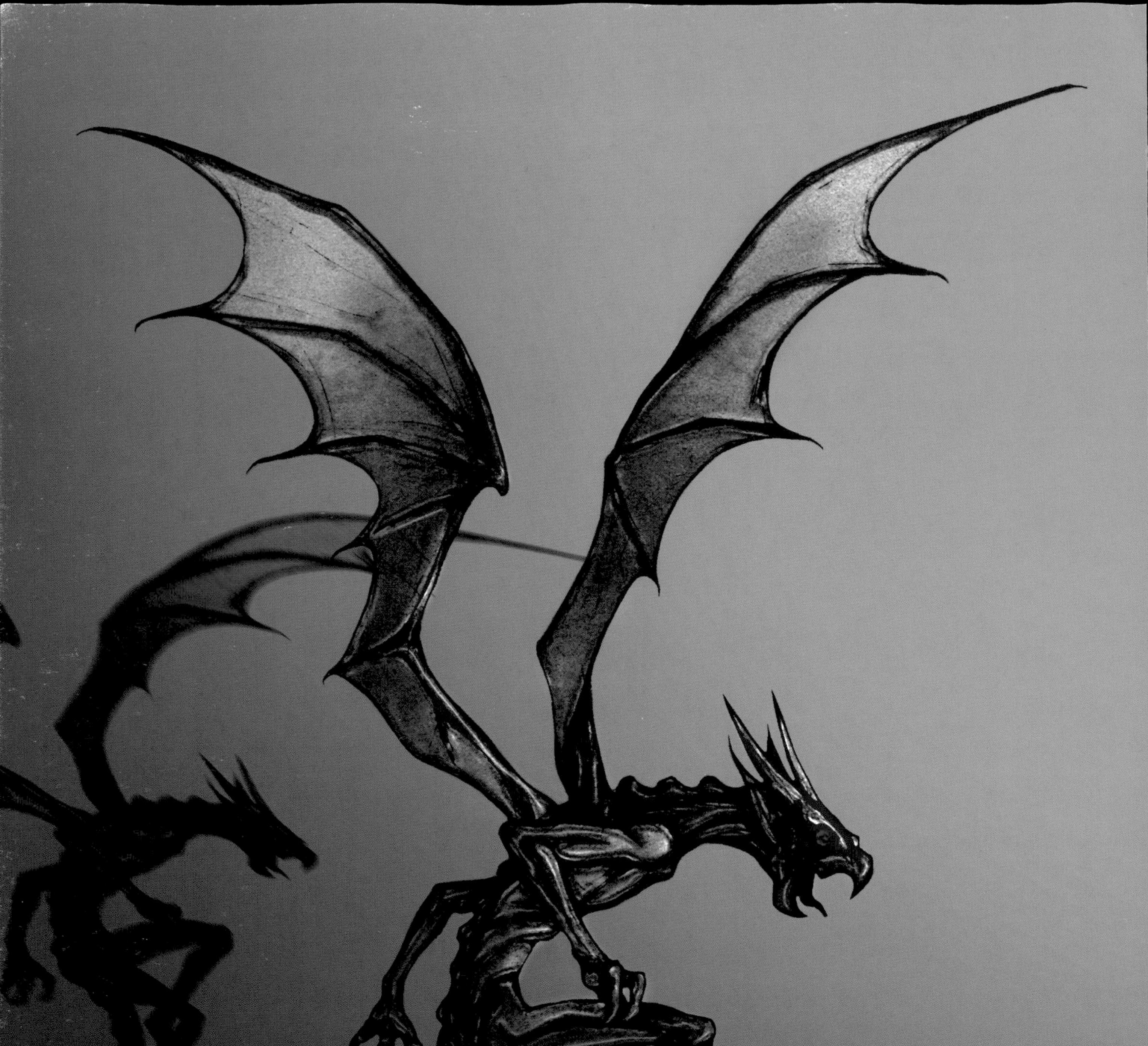

Gargoyle

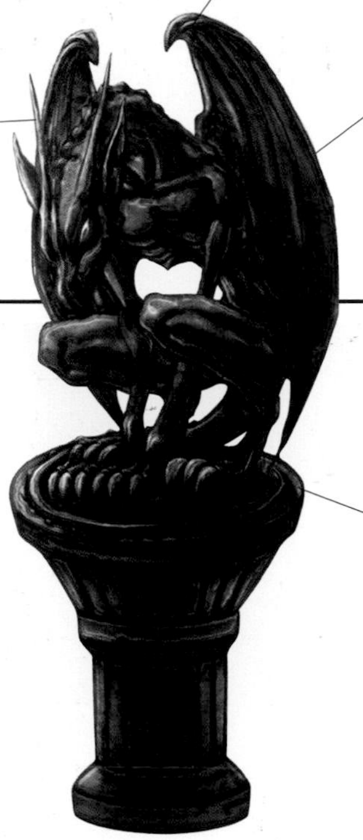
Bat-like wings
Dragon-like demon
Long horns
Can change
to stone structure

Notable Features

- Flying dragon-like demonic monster
- Has rough, crystalline skin that can change to stone
- Sleeps in a stone form
- Has bat-like wings, horns, long neck, long tail and talons
- Fires guts from its mouth
- Weak against wind
- Types of animals animated as gargoyles: lion, dog, wolf, eagle, snake, goat, monkey and chimera
- Weapons: dragon spear, steel battleaxe, steel hatchet

Outline and Origin

The gargoyle comes from a French legend from around 631-641 A.D., about St. Romanus, then bishop of Rouen, France, who saved the country from the monster Gargouille, a dragon beast that gushed fire from its mouth. The monster lived in the wild swamps and attacked the villagers until St. Romanus condemned it to death. It was then brought to Rouen for burning, but due to the beast's strong fiery breath, its neck and head could not be burned, thus the head was mounted above the Rouen Cathedral to scare away bad spirits and to protect the town. Created in the image of Gargouille, the gargoyle has become a common stone architectural ornament in temples, palaces, and churches. It frequently has water sprouting out from its mouth, and is said to protect against evil. Ancient Egyptian, Greek, Roman and Etruscan temples depicted it using a lion's physical form.

As a monster, the gargoyle slays humans and wild beasts. It can transform its skin to a stone texture as a defense tactic while regenerating its powers. Gargoyle types include: the dire gargoyle (ice-skinned), rockwing gargoyle (female gargoyle that deals with melee damage), putruid gargoyle (drops smooth stone chips and winged claws), plagued gargoyle (drops cloth and chain straps), stoneskin gargoyle (shoots acids at enemies), stone spine gargoyle (grey-skinned and uses blood damage), four-armed gargoyle, green gargoyle and rock gargoyle (uses magic defense). Rock gargoyles sit like statues and wait to be activated. Once hit, they fly and attack the enemy.

Rogues and mages can easily attack gargoyles using their ranged abilities. Gargoyles are weak in duels, especially against fire, thunder and wind elementalists, but are fast in flight. They can be killed by a gravity spell, which will take away their power to fly and therefore allow the gargoyle to be crushed, or by rock hammers.

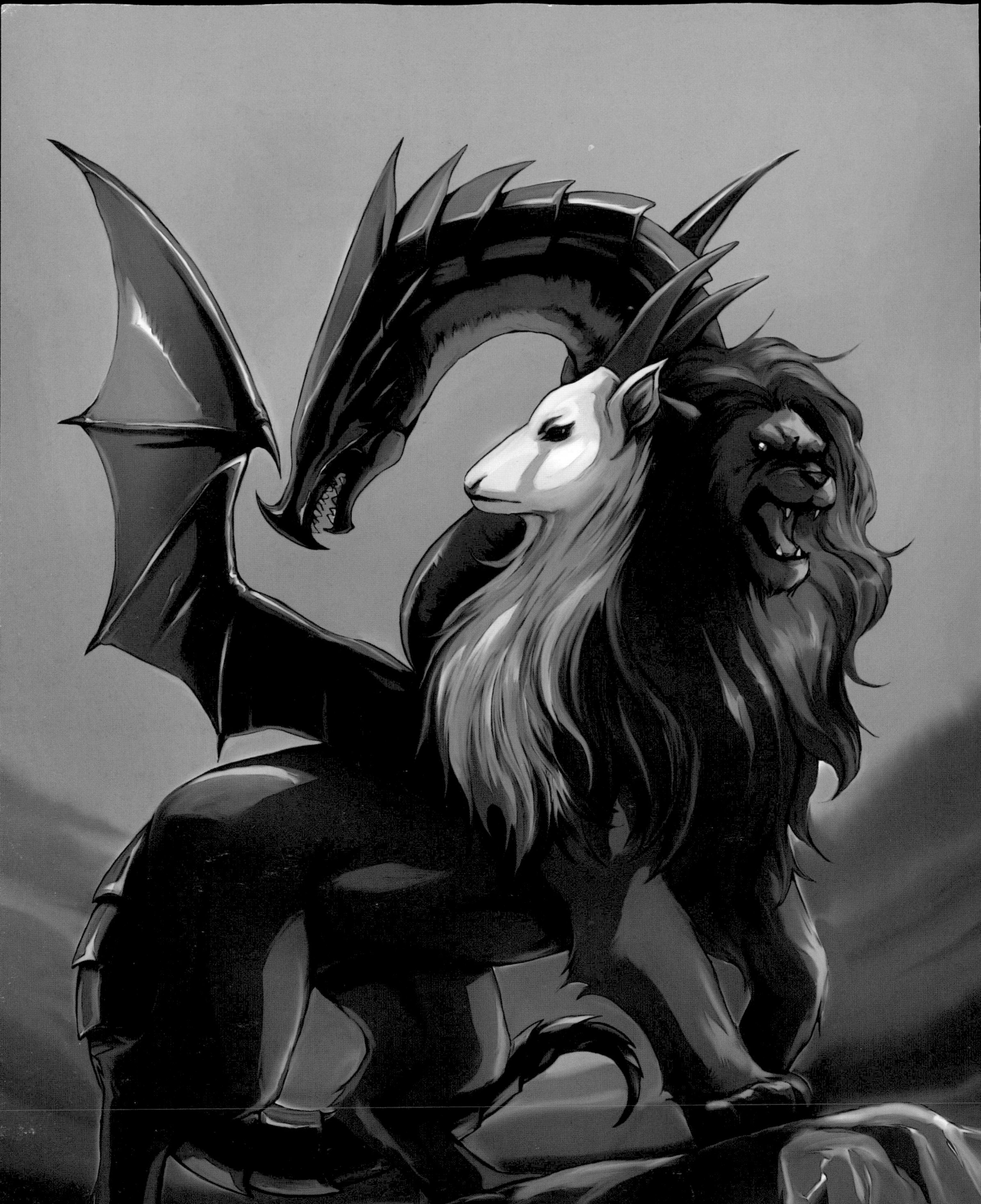

Chimera

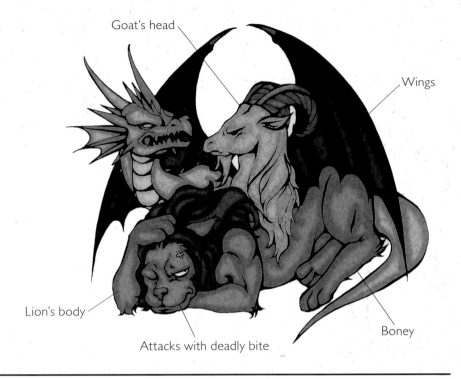

Goat's head

Wings

Lion's body

Attacks with deadly bite

Boney

➥ Notable Features

- Fire-breathing, winged monster with a lion's body in front, snake's body behind, goat's head on top and a lion's head at the bottom
- Gushes fire from its mouth
- May have smooth, shiny skin and boney structure
- Strong in physical attack and can cast spells
- Symbol of storms, shipwrecks and natural disasters

✚ Outline and Origin

The chimera originates from a Greek mythological fire-breathing monster with body parts of a lion, goat, and snake. It was the daughter of the Greek monster Typhon who attempted to destroy Zeus, and was eventually killed by the Greek hero Bellerophon who struck a spear into its stomach while riding on Pegasus.

The chimera is a deadly beast, but a friendly ally of the night elves. It attacks other creatures, especially those who come to invade the forests or harm nature, using its bite and its breath, which it can use as a fire storm or a frost storm (so that it breathes out frost and lightning).

Some of its other skills are dive (rush forward), bullhead (removes effects that impair movement), carrion feed (eat a corpse to revive energy), roar of recovery (use a roaring effect), wolverine bite (deadly bite attack), aqua breath (uses water and wind elemental damage) and fireball (release ball of fire).

There are several types of chimera. The mage chimera has grey fur and uses blaze and lightning attacks. The sphinx chimera uses a bad breath or sour mouth attack. The brain chimera is colored green and uses fire, ice and lightning attacks. The dhorme chimera fights in the desert.

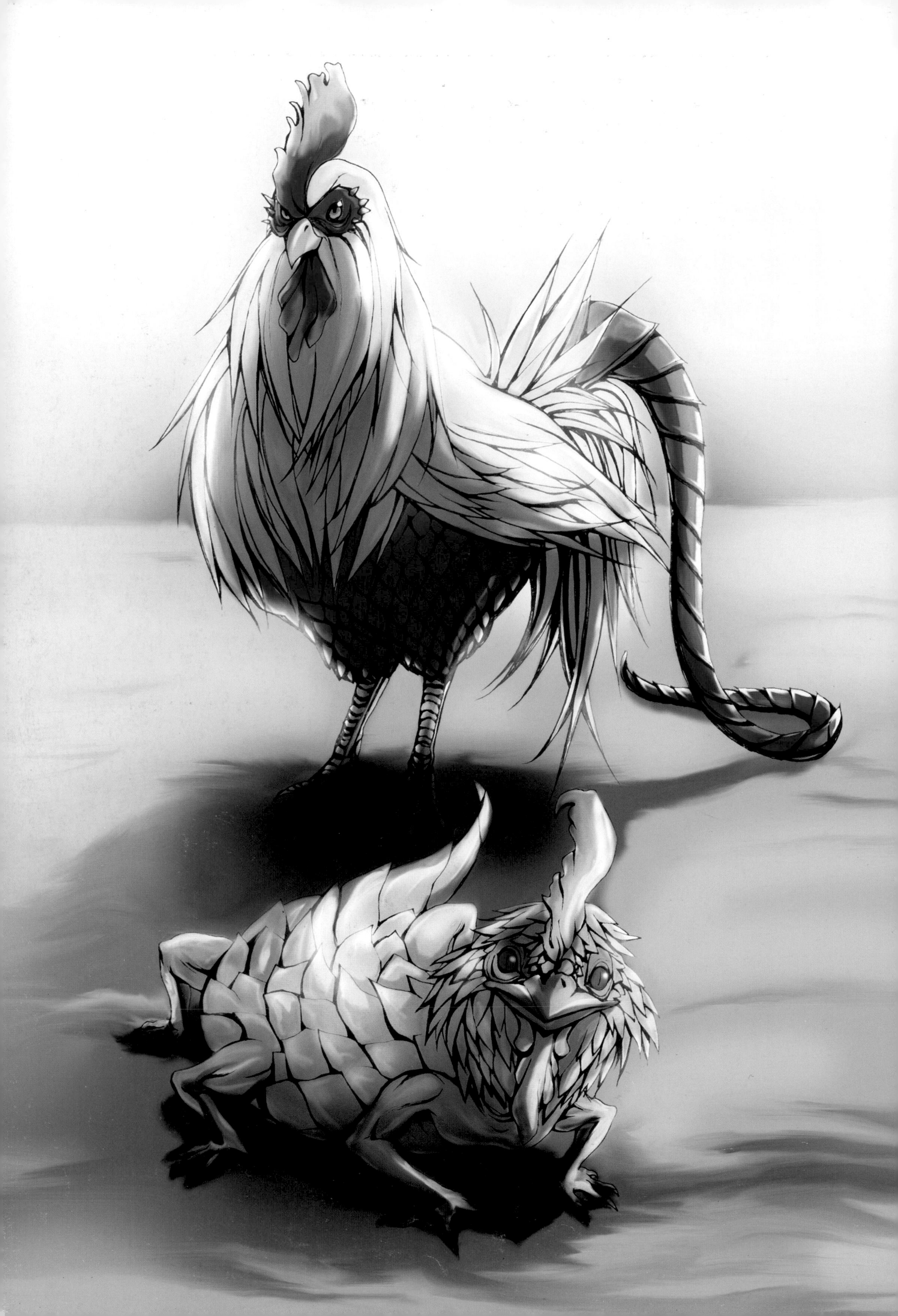

Cockatrice, Basilisk

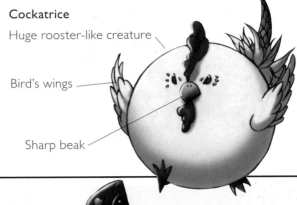

Cockatrice
Huge rooster-like creature
Bird's wings
Sharp beak

Notable Features

Basilisk
Small snake or lizard creature
Legs of a cock or bird
Reptilian tail

Cockatrice

- **Huge rooster-like creature with a lizard-like tail, sharp beak and wings**
- **Has large, dark eyes, reptilian scales and bones made of rock minerals**
- **Gentle, but breathes poison; weak against earth and wind attacks**
- **Lives in deserts, walks rather than flies**

Basilisk

- **Small, deadly snake or six-legged lizard with a crown-shaped crest on the head**
- **Has a cock's head, body and legs, and a snake-like tail**
- **Green-black or yellow with a white spot and three spikes on the head**
- **Has scaly, crystalline skin; eats crystals and rocks**

Outline and Origin

Based on 12th century legends, the cockatrice was a remake of the basilisk. Its egg was born from a cock but incubated by a snake, while the basilisk was born from a snake or toad egg and hatched by a cock. In English literature, the cockatrice invaded a village near Hampshire and was locked up in the dungeon. A man by the name of Green made the cockatrice look at itself in a mirror and fight itself, then he killed it.

The basilisk, known as king of the serpents, was found around 79 A.D. and comes from the Ethiopian creature Catoblepas who had a buffalo's body and a hog's head, and killed people with its stare and breath. It also has origins from a hooded Indian cobra with a golden crown.

Both the cockatrice and the basilisk have poisonous breath and use the petrify ability that kills or turns creatures (except the weasel) into stones by looking at a mirror shield. A rooster's crow can also kill the cockatrice and the basilisk.

In battle, the cockatrice summons a character who will stone its enemy. The basilisk dissolves rocks and crystals in its stomach and uses its powerful crystalline skin to kill enemies. When a basilisk is killed by a spear, its poison can infect the spear, the horse and the horseman who used the spear. The evil eye of the basilisk is found in the third eye on its crown, which destroys humans, creatures, rocks and objects. Its breath can also kill vegetation and crops.

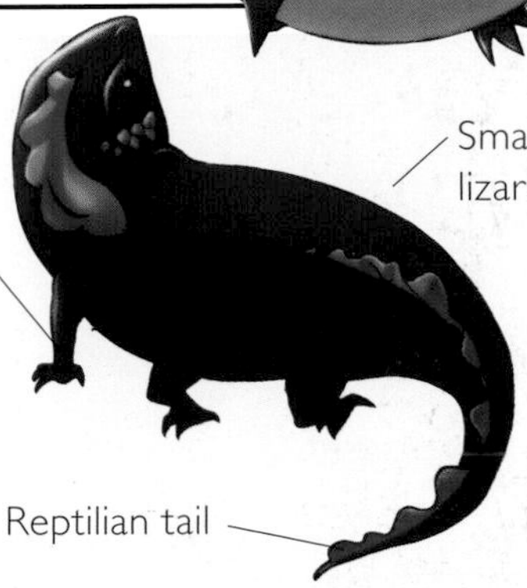

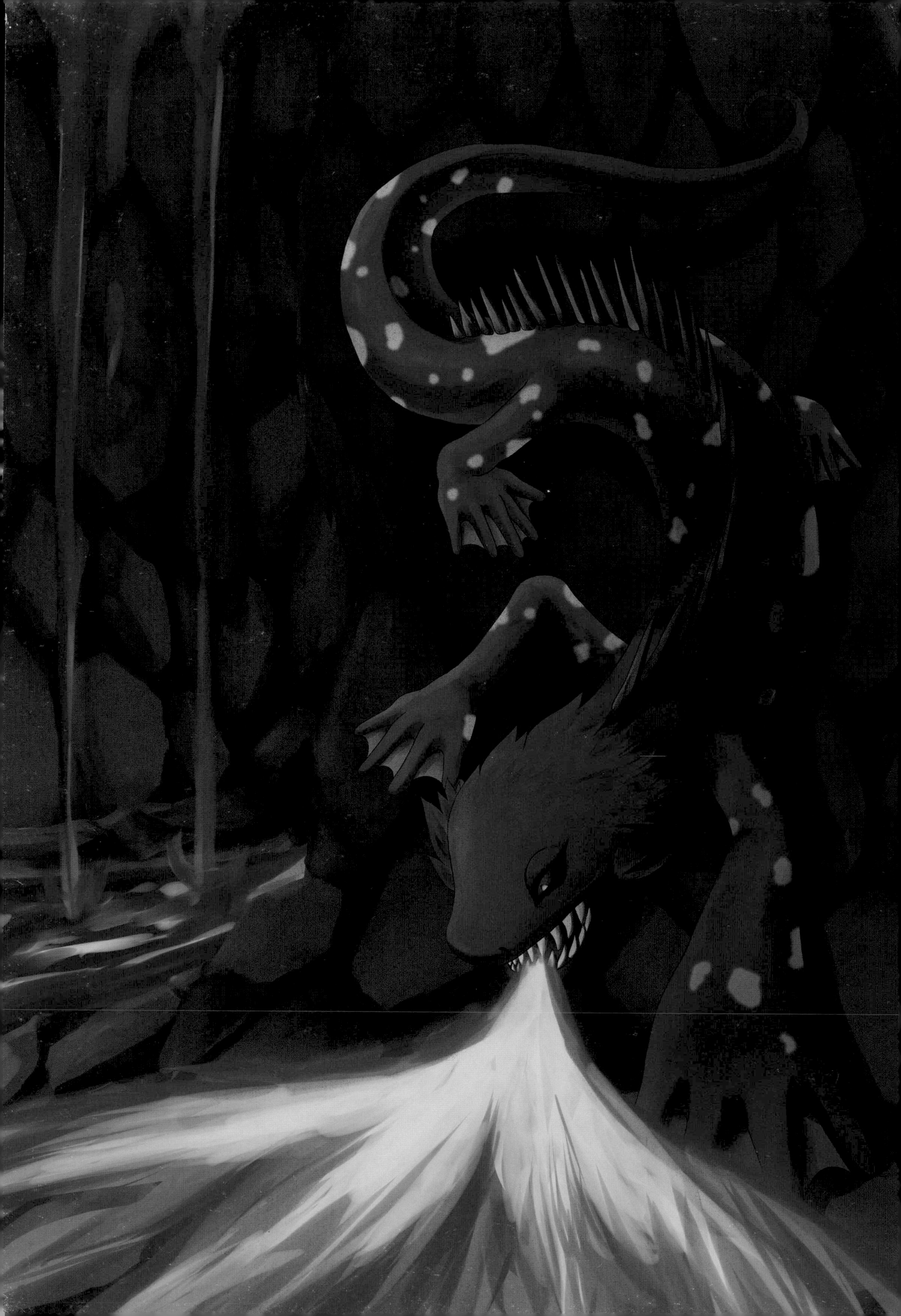

Salamander

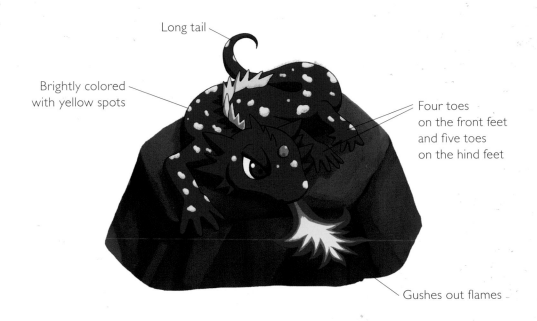

Long tail

Brightly colored
with yellow spots

Four toes
on the front feet
and five toes
on the hind feet

Gushes out flames

➡ Notable Features

- Has a slender body, short nose, long tail, moist and slimy skin, four toes on the front feet and five toes on the rear feet
- May be aquatic or terrestrial
- Can regenerate its body parts
- Brightly colored, frequently with yellow spots, except for terrestrial species, which are pink or white
- Gushes flames and poisonous fluid

✛ Outline and Origin

The salamander appears in many classical, medieval, and renaissance legends. Around the 8th century, it was described as a half-human and half-beast tailed creature; in the 12th century as a fire-breathing worm; and in the 13th century as a bird in flames. It is closely related to the golden alpine salamander with gold spots on its back and the fire salamander from Europe.

The salamander's fiery breath is its greatest weapon against enemies. It is a merciless predator that eats anything it catches. It uses fireball and blaze skills to cause fire damage. Due to its physical connection with fire, it is weak against ice. Mages and priests can summon salamanders. Some types of salamanders carry steel spears, which give off heat, and some use their poisonous tails to slash enemies and cast spells on them. A unique type of salamander is the frost salamander that lives in frosty areas. It has six clawed feet and a blue hue.

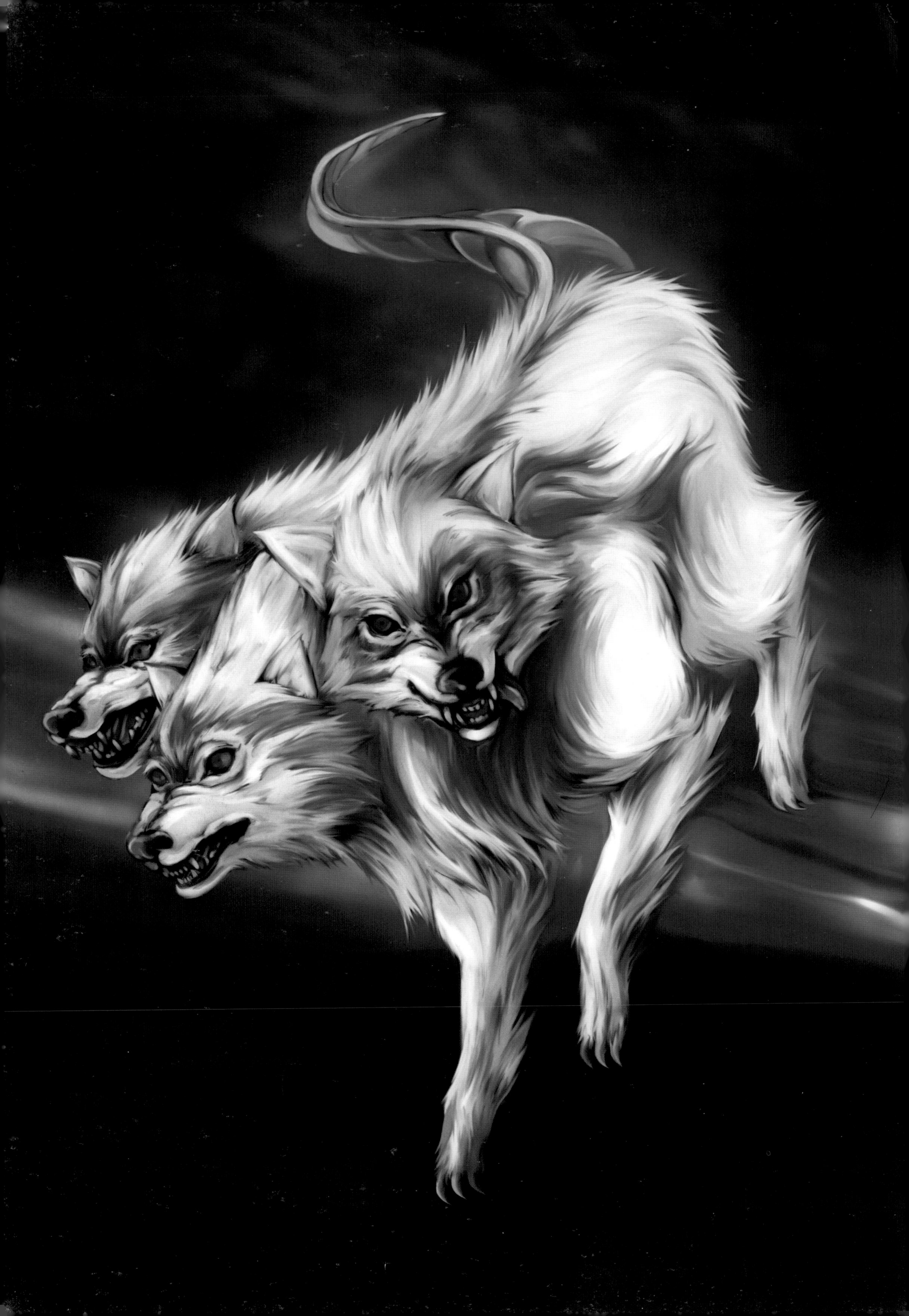

Cerberus

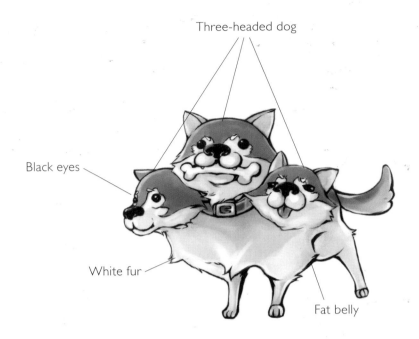

Three-headed dog

Black eyes

White fur

Fat belly

➡ Notable Features

- **Three-headed dog (heads are in the shapes of a lion's, a dog's and a wolf's) with a serpent's hair and a snake or dragon tail**
- **Lives in the underworld and guards the gates of hell**
- **Has red eyes, black and greasy beard, large belly, sharp claws, and a poisonous spittle**
- **Has excellent jumping ability**

✛ Outline and Origin

Cerberus originates from Greek mythology as one of the offsprings of Echidna, a half-serpent/half-woman, and Typhon, a deadly monster. Hydra and Chimera are two of its brothers. It was the guardian of the gates of hell and was always seen beside Hades, the god of the underworld. Its duty was to prevent mortals from entering and spirits from escaping the underworld.

One story tells that Hercules captured Cerberus by finding a way into the underworld and brought him before the king of Eurystheus, but returned him to the underworld when the king was frightened by him. Other stories relate that Orpheus' (the greatest musician and poet in Greek mythology) music and Hermes' and Psyche's use of water put Cerberus to sleep.

Cerberus is weak against ice, but resistant to elemental magic, such as the paralyze skill. Some of its attack skills are: lava split (causes fire damage), sulfurous breath (causes fire within a restricted area), ululation (paralyze attack), magma hoplon (covers the enemy with fiery spikes), scorching lash (attacks from behind), gates of Hades (causes fire and burn), blaze spikes (covers enemy with magical fire spikes) and stoneskin (absorbs physical and magical attack).

In some fantasy manga, Cerberus is sometimes depicted as having more than three heads, and sometimes as having only two. He also is sometimes depicted as being covered in white fur with the ability to control ice and summon icebergs.

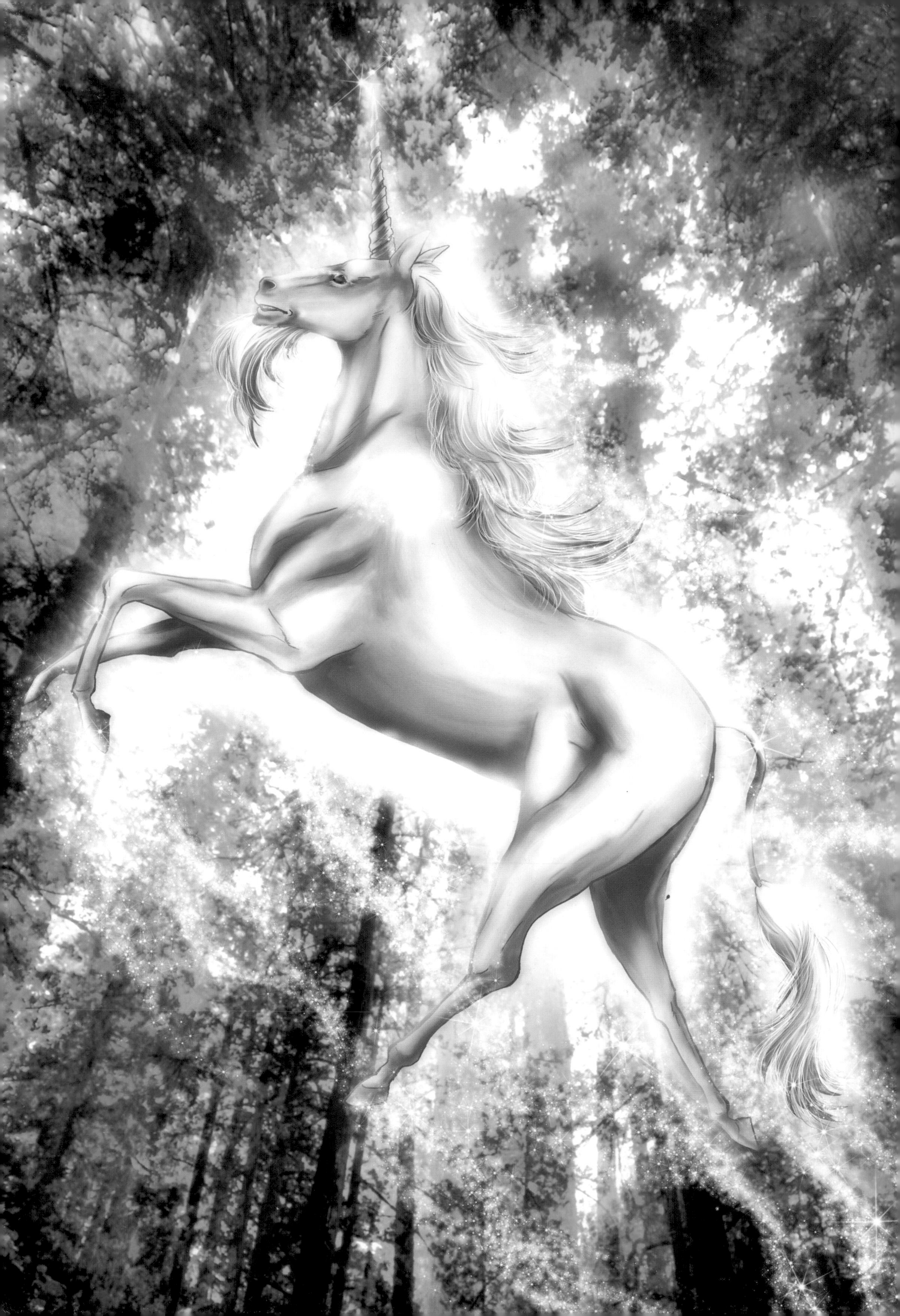

Unicorn

Shell-shaped horn on the head

White, horse-like creature

Goat's beard

Lion's tail

➡ Notable Features

- White, horse-like creature with a shell-shaped horn on its forehead, a goat's beard, a lion's tail and cloven hooves
- Has shiny eyes and a silky mane and tail
- Strong, wild and can only be tamed by a maiden
- Horn has medicinal and poisonous powers
- May wear a broken chain collar
- Lives in woodlands
- Symbol of chastity and purity

✛ Outline and Origin

Records of one-horned animals existed during the Indus Valley Civilization (3300-1300 B.C.). Other accounts are from Hebrew scriptures and describe a wild, strong, agile animal with horns. In medieval accounts of the beast, the unicorn is protected by an angelic maiden who resembles the Virgin Mary. When it sees her, it stays calm, laying its head on her lap. This attributed to the notion that maidens have the ability to tame the unicorn. In the 17th century, the unicorn's horn was believed to carry medicinal powers; hence, people drank from unicorn-made goblets to avoid being poisoned.

Some subspecies of the unicorn are: zhevra (zebra-hybrid beast with a horn on the head), celestial charger unicorn (powerful unicorn that can be summoned by druids), hornsaw unicorn (savage unicorn), black unicorn (aggressive, dangerous unicorn), unicorn stallion (healing unicorn), starlight (bodyguard that uses melee attack) and alicorn (winged unicorn that heals).

Being a creature of the woodlands, the unicorn is protective of the forest and attacks any creature that comes to harm its elements. It uses its magical horn to cause poison damage or to cure illness. It can detect evil enemies from afar, and uses a teleport skill to move from one part of the forest to another. The unicorn drops unicorn bones, unicorn horns and unicorn hides, which can be used to make ointments and amulets to protect against poison. When angered, the unicorn is quick to kill, unless calmed by the presence of a maiden.

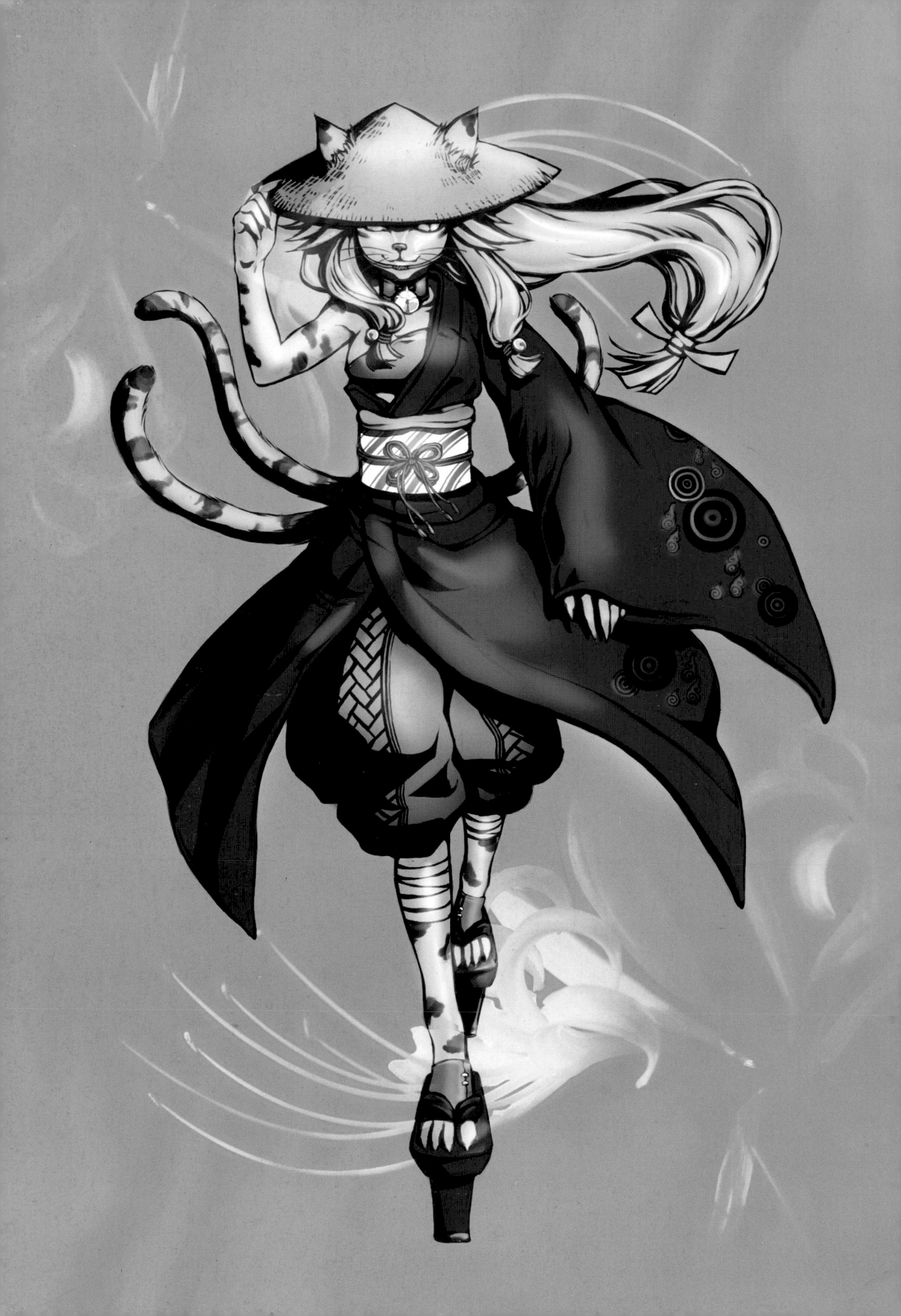

Nekomata

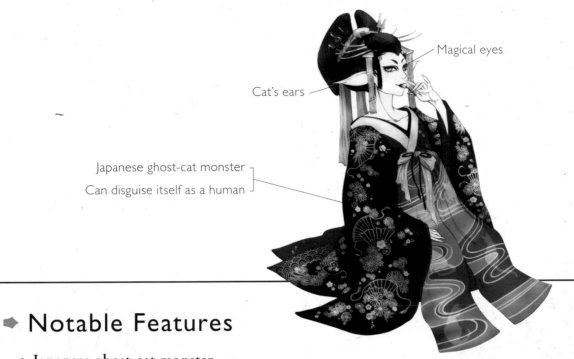

Magical eyes

Cat's ears

Japanese ghost-cat monster
Can disguise itself as a human

Notable Features

- **Japanese ghost-cat monster**
- **Has a forked tail and walks on its two legs**
- **Can change its form or disguise itself as a human**
- **Can reanimate bodies**
- **Mischievous, evil and haunts humans and other creatures**
- **May be capable of martial arts**

Outline and Origin

One legend of the nekomata tells of a cat that burned its tail while keeping warm next to a fire. It fled all around the city, burning households and buildings, so the emperor ordered all cats' tails to be cut off. Another legend tells of a woman who became deranged when her cat went missing. She was found in her room as a cat-like monster, dressed in her own clothes, but eating dead animals' bodies, then she turned into the missing cat the next day.

Around the 17th century, cats in Japan were used to frighten away mice that harmed silkworms. People were not allowed to buy or sell cats, thus, they remained as stray cats roaming the streets. Their ambiguous nature led to many beliefs about their supernatural powers, such as that they walk on two legs, fly, and are capable of transforming their bodies or animating dead bodies. If a cat reaches age thirteen and retains its long tail, it is said to possess attributes of a nekomata.

The nekomata is a fearful monster that haunts households and preys on humans while they are asleep. It makes fireballs, can disguise itself into a human or other type of creature, and can increase its size, especially for combat. It is often seen licking the oil of a lamp, since lamp oil is associated with fish oil. Some of its skills are: beast claw (sudden attack using beast-like claws), iron claw (claws with iron), charm bite (bite that charms an enemy), eternal sleep (puts an enemy into a permanent sleep), lullaby (sings a song to distract an enemy) and silent eyes (stares with magic-filled eyes that enchant and distract an enemy).

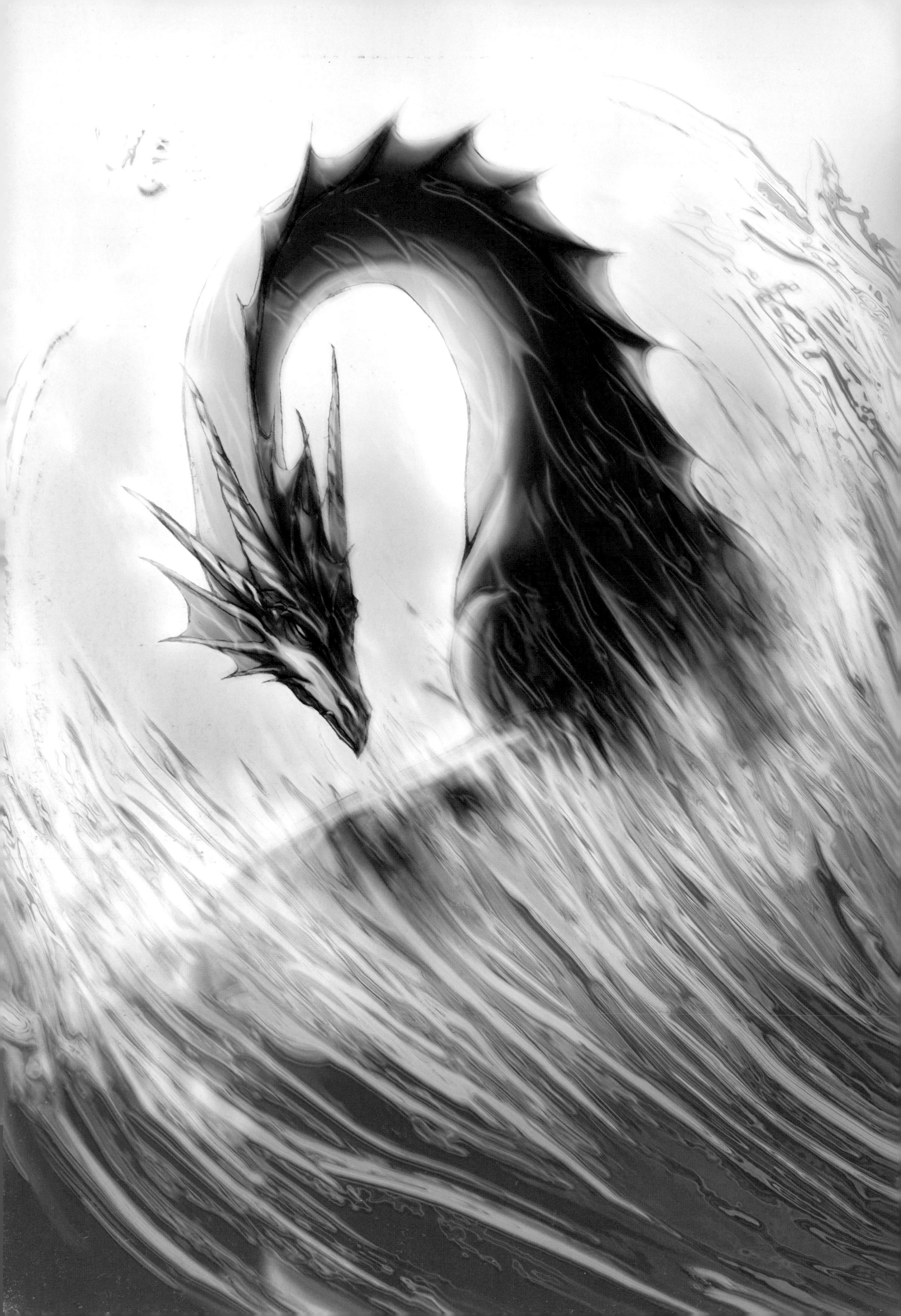

Dragon

Bat-like wings

Breathes fire from the mouth

Large, lizard-like body with reptilian scales

Clawed feet

➡ Notable Features

- **Large, lizard-like body and legs with reptilian scales, large eyes, clawed feet, and bat-like wings; may be colored gold, bronze, green, red, black, or blue**
- **Breathes fire**
- **Strong and wise, but also vicious**
- **Moves fast**
- **Has a long lifespan and magical powers**

✛ Outline and Origin

The dragon is one of the most popular creatures of European, Asian, African and American legends. In 600 B.C., symbols of dragons were traced in Assyria, and in 300 B.C. similar symbols were found in China. The ancient Greek dragon was depicted in the Iliad as a blue, three-headed creature. In ancient China, the dragon was depicted as a very large, very long serpent without wings, but with four claws on each foot. It was a great symbol of power, especially over weather and water. The Japanese dragon has three claws and is also a benevolent creature of water, like Chinese and Korean dragons. The European dragon may be winged or wingless, depending on the region it comes from, usually has two legs, and is considered malevolent. The American dragon is traced from its Messo-American roots and is regarded as a symbol of death and reincarnation.

There are many types of dragons, differing in age, color and physical attributes. The black dragon has a huge body with hard, black scales, shiny red fangs, orange or brown wings and horns. It lives 100-500 years, is carnivorous, and attacks prisoners and animals. The blue dragon rises from the water and is muscular, with shiny scales and cobalt patterns on its neck. It is wise and can change its form. The bronze dragon is small and slim with metallic scales. It uses spells to buff enemies. The green dragon has crystalline scales and glowing eyes, and is not as strong as the other dragons. The red dragon has a long neck, ruby-like skin and golden eyes. Its fire tortures enemies, but also gives new life. There is also the iron dragon (causes fire and electric damage), revenant dragon (two-headed slain dragon's ghost), frost dragon (attacks using water spells), infinite dragon (prevents events from happening), nether dragon (semi-transparent and can become humanoid), proto-dragon (ancient dragon) and twilight dragon (vampire dragon).

Dragons can release many kinds of breaths as their combat weapon, such as breaths of fire, sand, acid, gas, ice, razor thorns, sonic energy, lightning, poisonous vapors, howling sound, blinding light and rustic liquid.

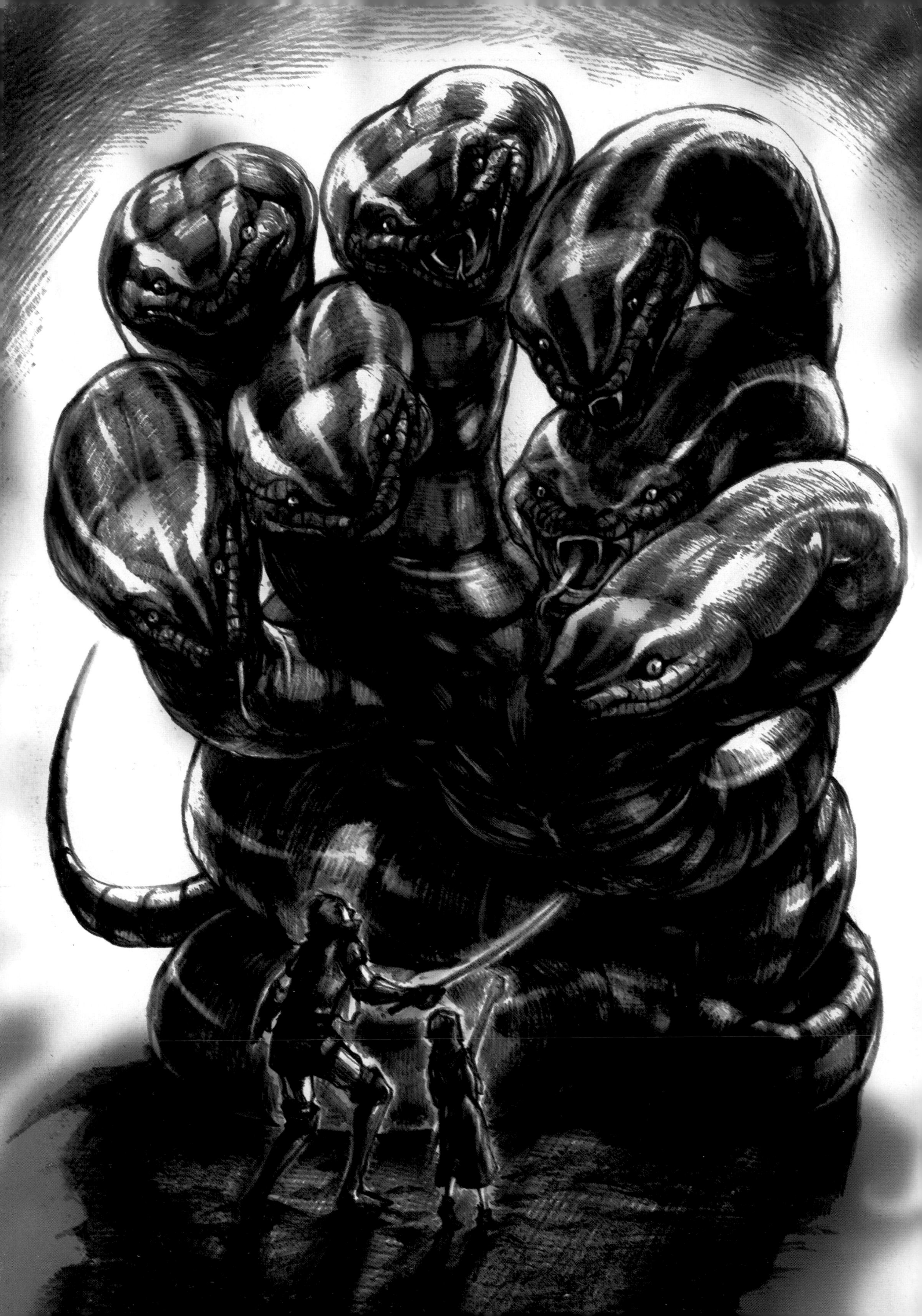

Hydra

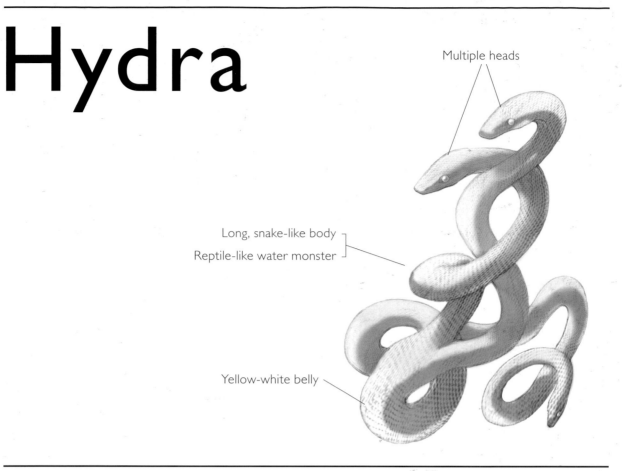

Multiple heads

Long, snake-like body

Reptile-like water monster

Yellow-white belly

➡ Notable Features

- Reptile-like water monster with five to twelve heads, a yellow belly, dark red eyes, and yellow-white teeth
- Body is grey or brown, usually twenty feet long, and weighs around 4,000 pounds
- May have horns and multiple eyes
- Has a poisonous breath
- Can regenerate its parts
- Lives in marshes and swamps

✛ Outline and Origin

In Greek mythology, the hydra was one of Typhon and Echidna's offsprings. Hercules tried to kill it with a sickle, but found that two of its heads regenerated. Hercules' nephew, Iolaus, helped him by using burning wood to burn the hydra's neck after Hercules cut off every head, and placed the immortal head under a holy rock. Hercules then used the hydra's poisonous blood to kill the centaur Nessus.

The hydra monster attacks with its multiple heads, and cannot die unless all its heads are cut off. Before the other heads grow back, its enemy can use fire or acid damage to burn the head stumps. The hydra uses powerful ranged and melee attacks, with high combat reflexes, and has a fast healing skill. When it is wounded, it can split up into small hydras.

The pyrohydra is a large, red magical hydra that gushes out more than ten feet of fire. The cryohydra is a magical purple hydra that breathes out frost as its weapon. The five- to eight-headed hydras use dark vision skills and scent buffs, while the nine- to twelve-headed hydras use blind fighting.

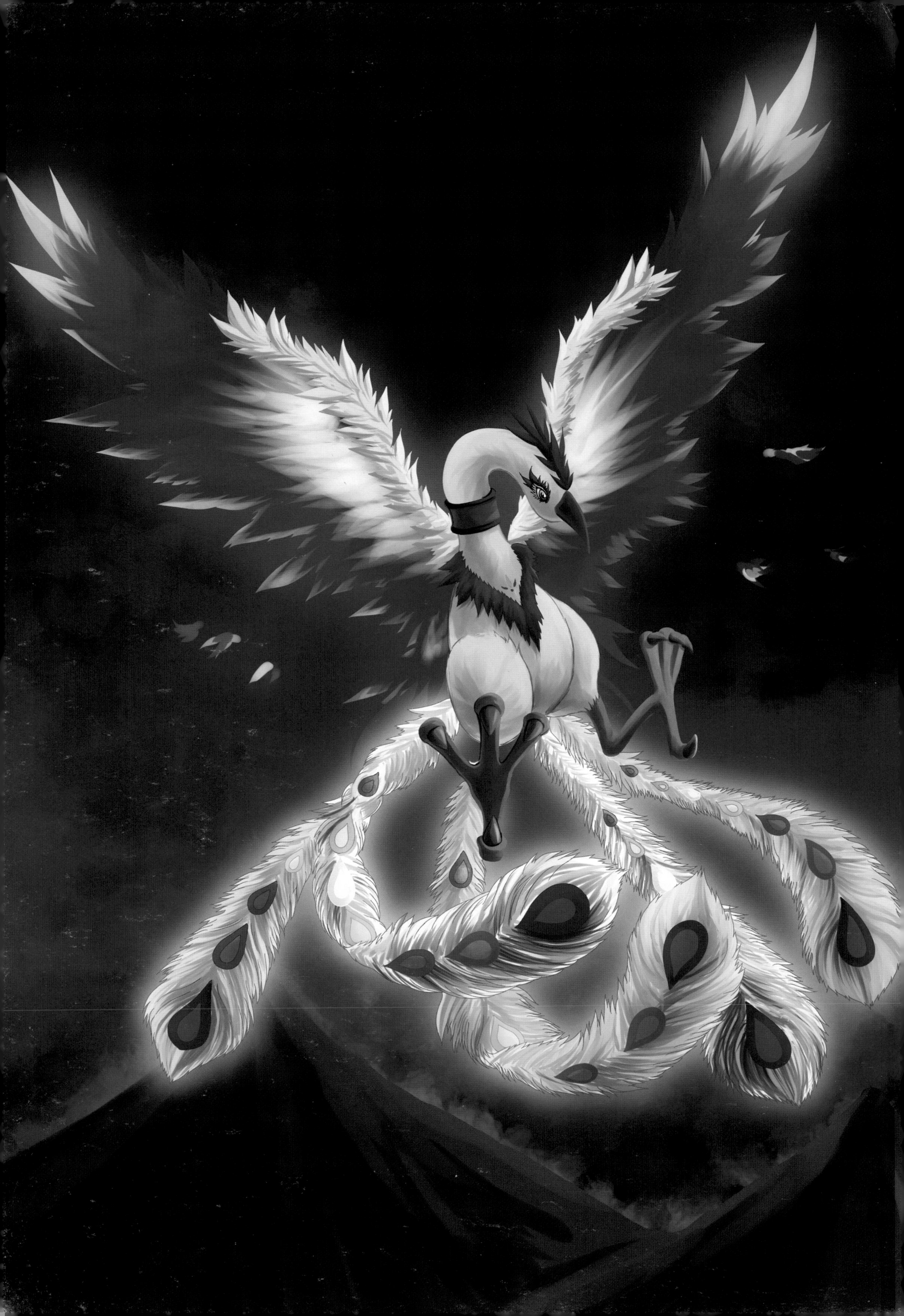

Phoenix

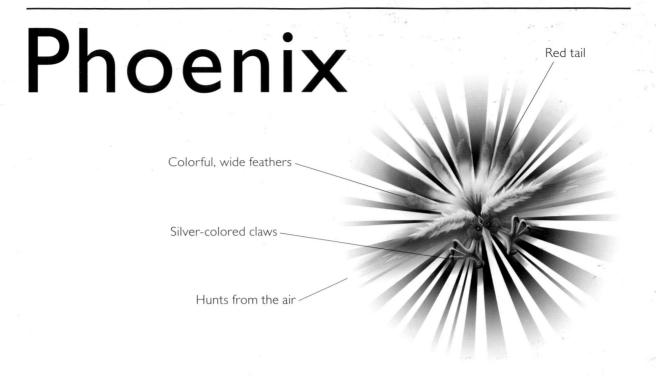

Red tail

Colorful, wide feathers

Silver-colored claws

Hunts from the air

➡ Notable Features

- Fire-bird monster with a red beak; spiky-feathered crest on its back, purple and silver feet; colorful feathers; purple, blue, green, gold and red tail; and wings stretching more than thirty feet
- Cross between an eagle and a heron, with wings that give off flames when flapped
- Fearless, aggressive and has a long lifespan
- Can regenerate into small phoenixes when it dies or transform into a human
- Attacks using magic
- Hunts prey from the air

✛ Outline and Origin

The phoenix originates from mythologies of Persia, Phoenicia, China, Egypt, Greece and Rome. In Egyptian myths, it lived in the sanctuary of Heliopolis and was worshipped as a symbol of gold and rebirth. Ancient Greeks referred to it as a singing bird that attracted the sun god. When it dies, it builds a nest and sets fire to it, then, and new birds are born. A Chinese myth called it a feng-huang that had a swallow's face, a cock's beak, a duck's forehead, a snake's neck, a goose's breast, a turtle's back, a stag's rear and a fish's tail. It symbolized the sun, moon, sky, wind, earth and planets, and was a symbol of virtue and harmony.

As a monster, the phoenix is a predator that hunts from the skies. It attacks with its aggressive bite and flames that cause fire damage and burn targets to the ground. The summon phoenix spell is used by blood mages, and allows the phoenix to rise from its ashes or regenerate other monsters. It has powerful abilities in using fire, such as fire beam and fire wave. Its other skills are: regen dance (revives another slain monster with holographic feathers), fire daze (shoots feathers of fire at a target), supernova (fire energy explosion), inferno (shoots fire balls at a target), fiery blast (huge fire explosion) and flee (escape from battle).

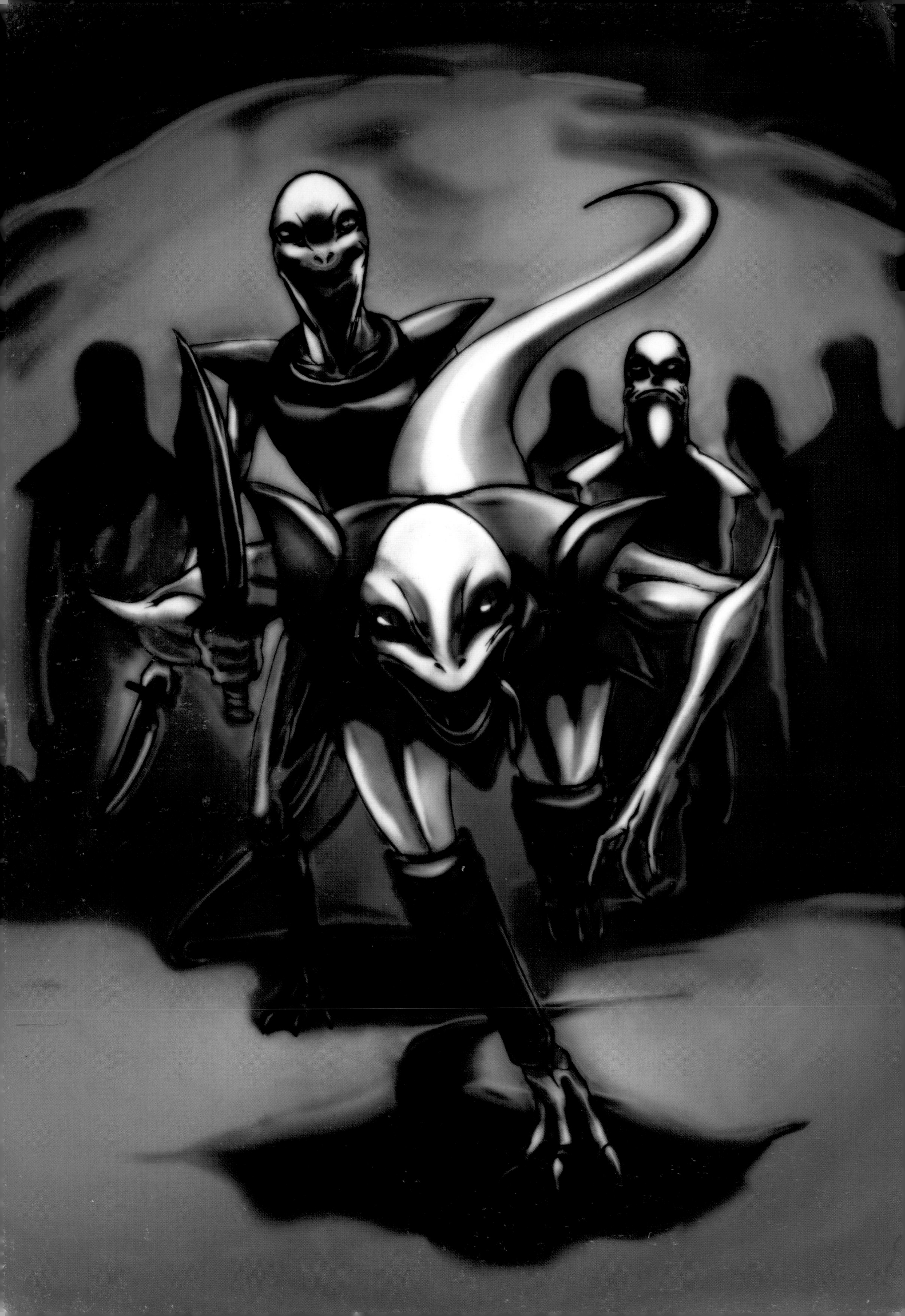

Lizard Man

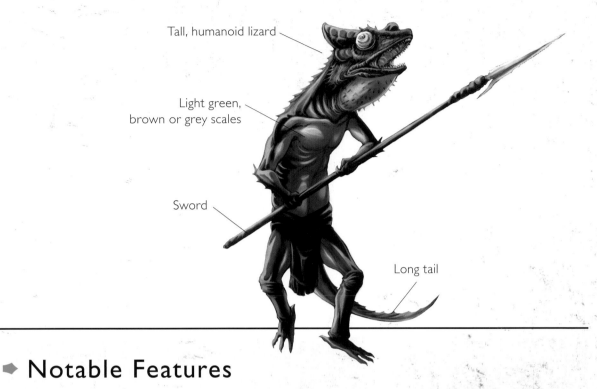

Tall, humanoid lizard

Light green, brown or grey scales

Sword

Long tail

➡ Notable Features

- Tall, aquatic or terrestrial humanoid lizard about 6-7 feet tall, with light green, brown or grey scales, vicious claws and a tail measuring about 3-4 feet long
- Carnivorous and eats human flesh
- Lives in marshes, swamps and underwater caves
- Skilled in wind magic
- May carry a sword, ax, arrow or shield

✝ Outline and Origin

Lizard men can be traced from myths about reptilian humanoids. Ancient Mayan beliefs describe them as descendants from the sky that came to earth to control civilization. Indian scriptures record similar creatures that lived underground and formed a cannibalistic culture. More popular beliefs describe the lizard man as a humanoid cryptid measuring more than seven feet, with a large and muscular build, and has green scales, orange eyes, three fingers on each hand and three toes on each foot.

Lizard men are known to feed on humans. Some species are: blackscale (huge, dark-scaled, barbaric and uses acid); dark talon (murderous

and uses black dragon blood); lizard king (demon-blooded and rules tribes); poison dusk (small, chameleon-like and uses poisoned arrows); quanak (uses paranormal abilities); shazak (formerly slaves); and viletooth (similar to black dragons). There are also lizard men that are powerful mages and priests who use wind magic.

Some lizard men are warriors with very thick scales, while others are small, aquatic and attack during war. There are also lizard men that are not very intelligent, but have huge bodies and can crush legs. The lizard man moves by spinning on his side, attacking a target with an axe or shield, then jumping and spinning in the air again.

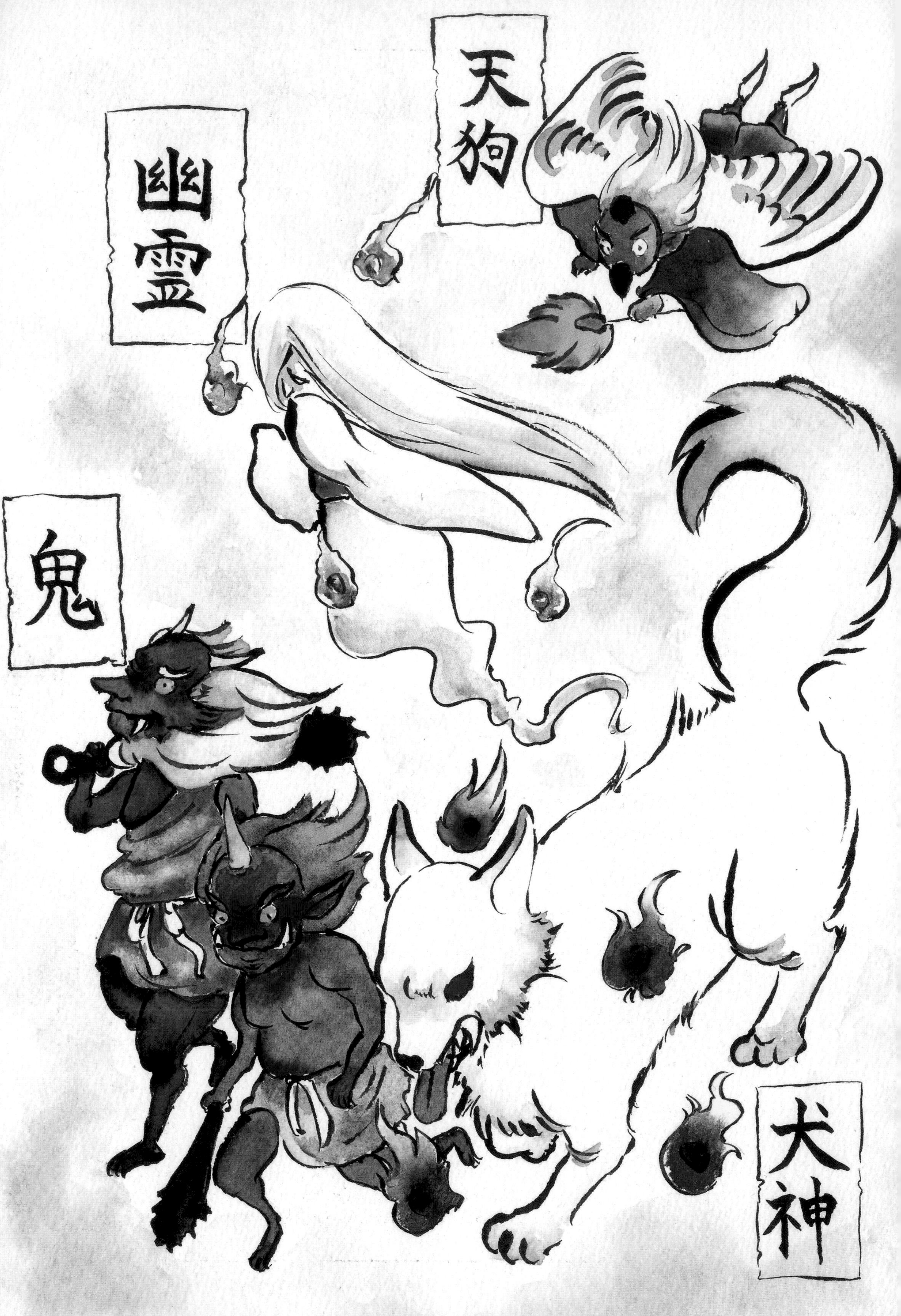
天狗
幽霊
鬼
犬神

Tengu, Oni, Yokai

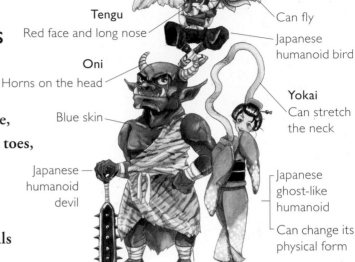

Tengu
Red face and long nose
Can fly
Japanese humanoid bird
Oni
Horns on the head
Blue skin
Japanese humanoid devil
Yokai
Can stretch the neck
Japanese ghost-like humanoid
Can change its physical form

Notable Features

Tengu

- **Japanese supernatural humanoid bird with a red face, long nose, clawed fingers and toes, and a bird's head and beak**
- **Can fly**
- **May carry a feathered fan and wear Japanese geta sandals**

Oni

- **Japanese humanoid devil with sharp claws and horns on the head; may have an irregular number of eyes, fingers and toes, and red or blue skin**
- **May be invisible or take multiple forms**
- **May wear a tiger-skinned loincloth and carry an iron club**

Yokai

- **Japanese supernatural ghost or humanoid**
- **Has shape shifting and transformation abilities and spiritual or supernatural powers**
- **Physical features and clothing vary by type**

Outline and Origin

The popular Japanese monster spirit tengu originates from the Chinese dog-like devil Tiangou, a dog with avian features. Japanese classical records from the 7th century also tell of a dog with these features; in their version it comes from the Hindu eagle Garuda. The tengu is mischievous and can become a woman to allure holy priests and steal from them. It is arrogant, vain and abducts children. It flies, uses martial arts, has telepathic powers and possesses people in their dreams. In some modern manga, the tengu is an avian humanoid from a war tribe and fights with weapons.

The Japanese demonic oni has invisible powers. Its horns, fangs, claws and tiger-skinned loincloth come from the Japanese and Chinese esoteric cosmological belief in a demon gate, a kimon. It can cause storms, earthquakes, volcanic eruptions and floods. The oni can shape shift itself to move or fly far distances. It uses shadow arts and its horns and fangs to attack targets.

Yokai is a Japanese supernatural creature from the Edo period. It can shape shift into humans, such as the tanuki (raccoon dog) that can stretch its body; kitsune (fox) that releases fire from its tail; inugami (dog spirit) that possesses humans; tsuchigumo (giant spider) that steals; futakuchi-onna (woman with a mouth on the back of her head); and rokuro-kubi (human that has super ability to stretch its neck).

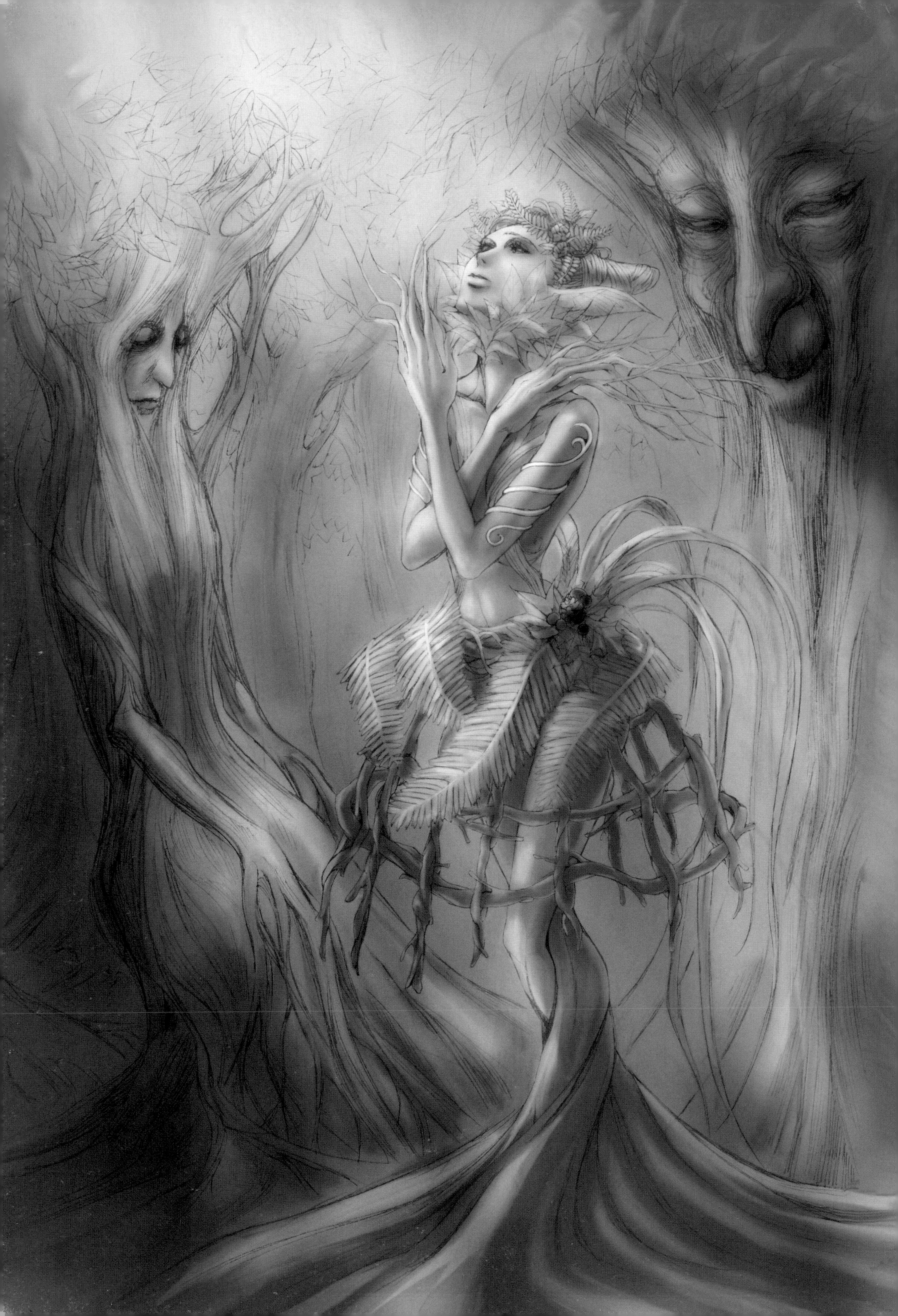

Ent, Dryad

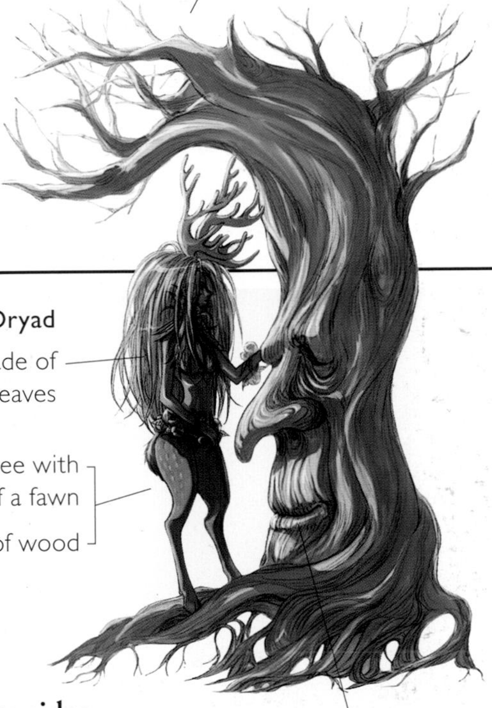

Ent
Giant tree humanoid
Rough, hard, brown skin and twigs as arms
Dryad
Hair made of grass and leaves
Female elf tree with lower body of a fawn
Body made of wood
Can talk and move

Notable Features

Ent

- **Giant tree-like humanoid that can talk, run, walk and move**
- **Has a long head but no neck, and numerous toes**
- **Has grey or green beard and deep eyes**
- **Has rough, hard, brown skin and twigs on its sides**
- **Capable of erosion and destruction of rocks**

Dryad

- **Tree nymph with a female night elf's head, arms, and upper body, and a fawn's lower body**
- **Body is made of greenish-brown wood; hair is made of grass and leaves**
- **Gentle, playful and adventurous**
- **Can destroy or prevent magic**
- **Carries a spear**

Outline and Origin

Ents originate from talking trees in many different myths. An Indian tree visited by Alexander the Great and Marco Polo was said to be able to tell the future. In J. R. R. Tolkien's description of the Middle-earth in *The Lord of the Rings*, the ents were created by the Queen of the Earth and Giver of Fruits, Yavanna, to protect trees against dwarves and other misfortunes. Ents are very powerful and resist harm due to their hard and tough skin, but they can be easily burned, become weak and die at old age.

Some ents are known as treants. Treants are shorter than Tolkien's ents, have three claws on their fingers and are covered with green leaves except in fall when they change to yellow, red and orange. Treants attack violently with their wooden claws, and run over their targets to move quickly. They also have low-light vision, which makes them see clearly in moonlight.

Dryads were originally nymphs of oak trees in Greek mythology. They are peaceful and protect the forest, but easily become violent, attacking intruders with their spears at close range. They apply poison magic to their weapons and use charms to control their enemies. Some of their abilities are entangle (wraps enemies with twisted branches and leaves), sleep slumber (causes deep sleep) and tree stride (enters trees).

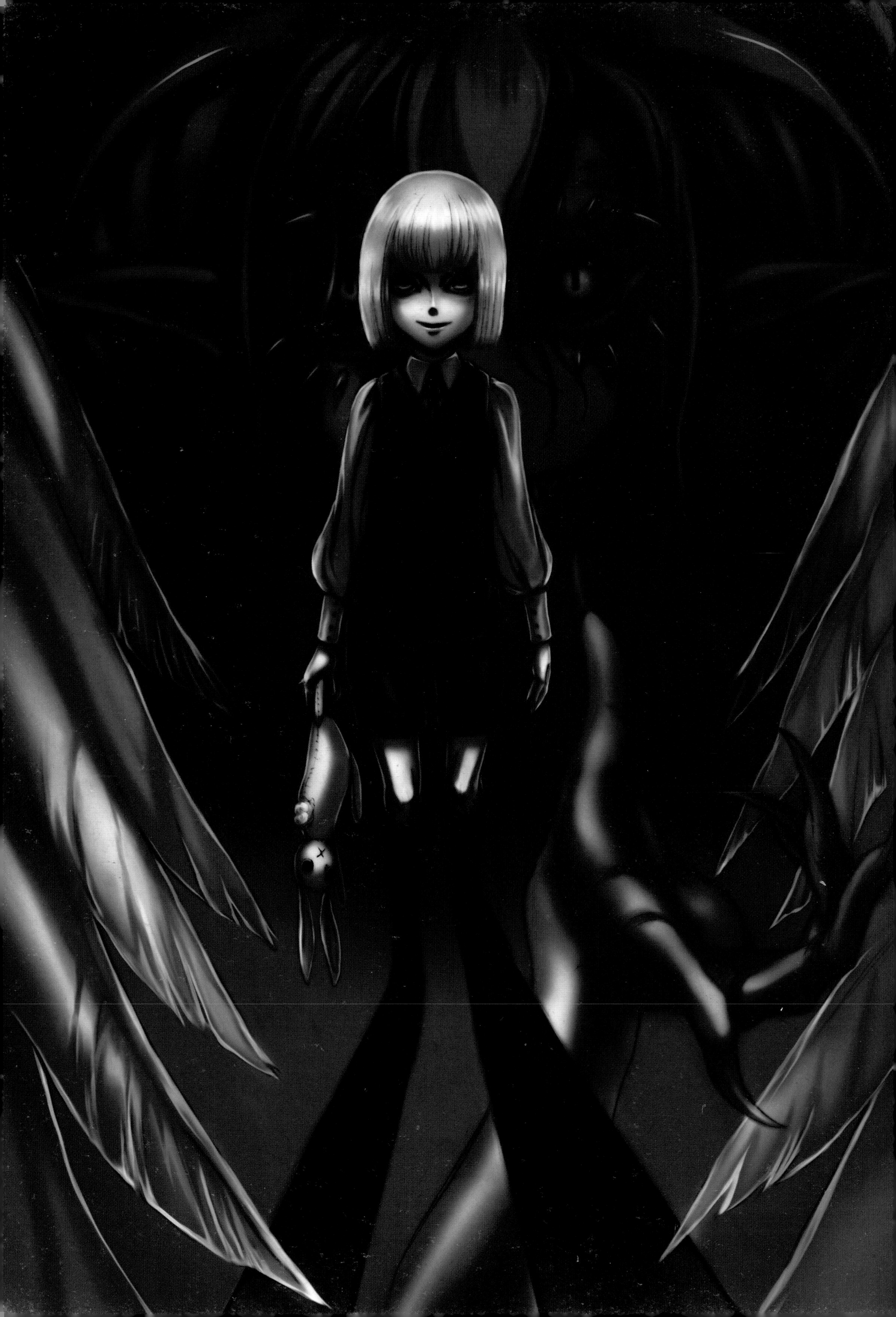

Underworld Monsters

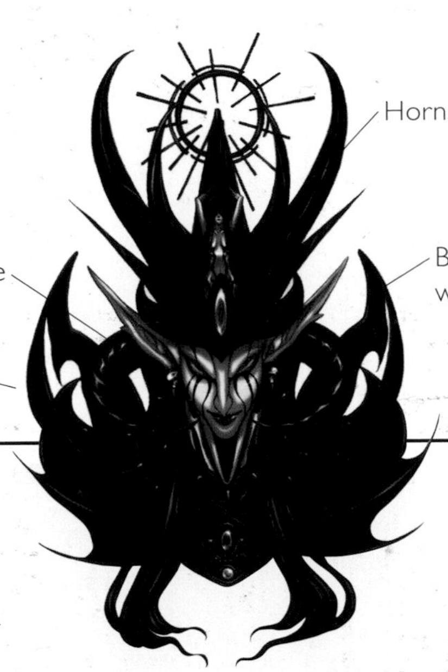
Horns
Beast-like wings
Demonic appearance
Wears black

Notable Features

- **Live in a deep realm below heaven and earth**
- **Corrupt, treacherous and evil**
- **Types of underworld monsters: balrog, diablo, goat man, lightning demon, magma demon, overlord, butcher, viper, scavenger, skeleton, winged fiend**
- **May be winged, horned, distorted, animalistic or beast-like**

Outline and Origin

The underworld is a mystical realm of the afterlife that serves as a dungeon for demonic monsters, beasts and dead souls that were corrupt in life. This concept exists in almost all mythologies of every culture, including the Aztec, Babylonian, Buddhist, Egyptian, Greek, Hindu, Roman, Slavic, Norse and Persian.

In Greek mythology, Tartarus is an underworld kingdom. It is considered worse than hell, and it is where unworthy creatures, such as the one-eyed giant Cyclopes, the deceitful Sisyphus (king of Corinth) and the notorious Ixion (king of the Lapiths), were sent to after being punished by the gods. In Egyptian mythology, Duat was the underworld where dead souls were judged.

Some of the gods and goddesses who lived in Duat and passed judgment, were Osiris (god of the afterlife), Isi (goddess of motherhood and magic) and Nepththys (goddess of the night and lamentation).

One of the most powerful underworld monsters is the balrog, a huge, winged, horned and steel-clawed creature that controls shadows and fire with its fiery whip. It uses melee and inferno attacks, and moves at great speed. The goat man, a demon with goat legs and head, and a human upper body and arms, fights with a bow or a mace, and uses a spinning backhand strike. The lightning demon has long arms, walks on two legs and uses grave melee attack with lightning. It can be fought with fireballs. The diablo corrupts anyone to make him a demon. It is one of the most powerful underworld beasts that uses spells, such as bone prison (prevents one from escaping), fire nova, red lightning, cold touch and firestorm. The scavenger is a four-legged beast that transforms itself into another creature, becoming stronger and bigger after eating meat. The ragnar is a giant wolf with ferocious fangs that became corrupt as pets of the dark elves. The overlord is a ruthless demon that descended from corrupt angels. It is a bloated, distorted and bloodthirsty warrior that fights using hand-to-hand combat.

Most underworld monsters use spells and magic and can fight using hand-to-hand combat or use weapons, such as swords, clubs, axes, bows and staves.

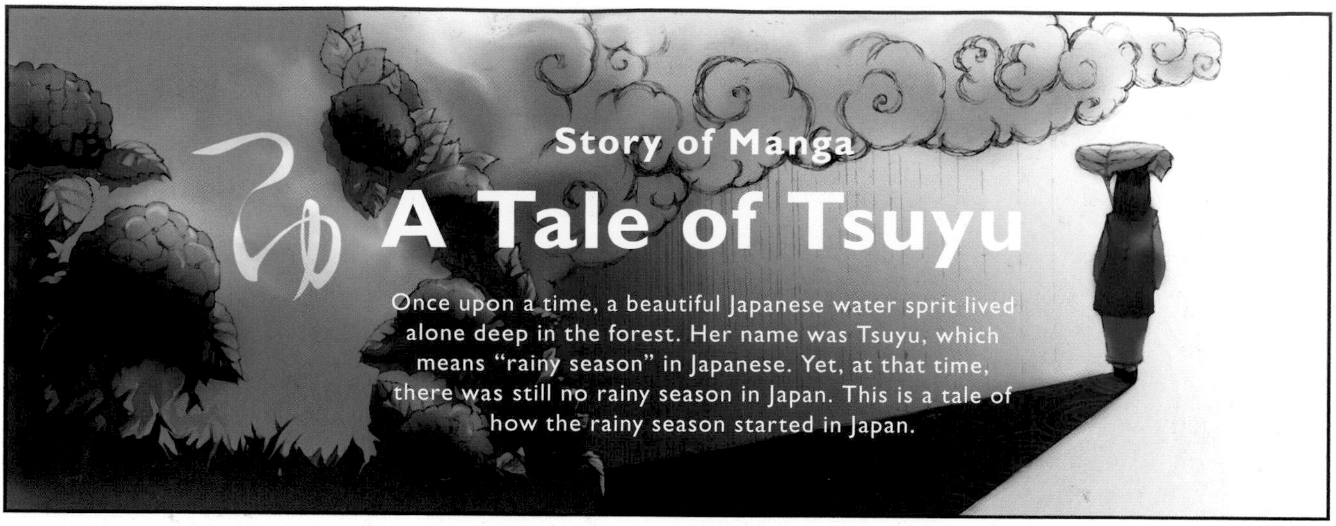
つゆ
Story of Manga
A Tale of Tsuyu
Once upon a time, a beautiful Japanese water sprit lived alone deep in the forest. Her name was Tsuyu, which means "rainy season" in Japanese. Yet, at that time, there was still no rainy season in Japan. This is a tale of how the rainy season started in Japan.

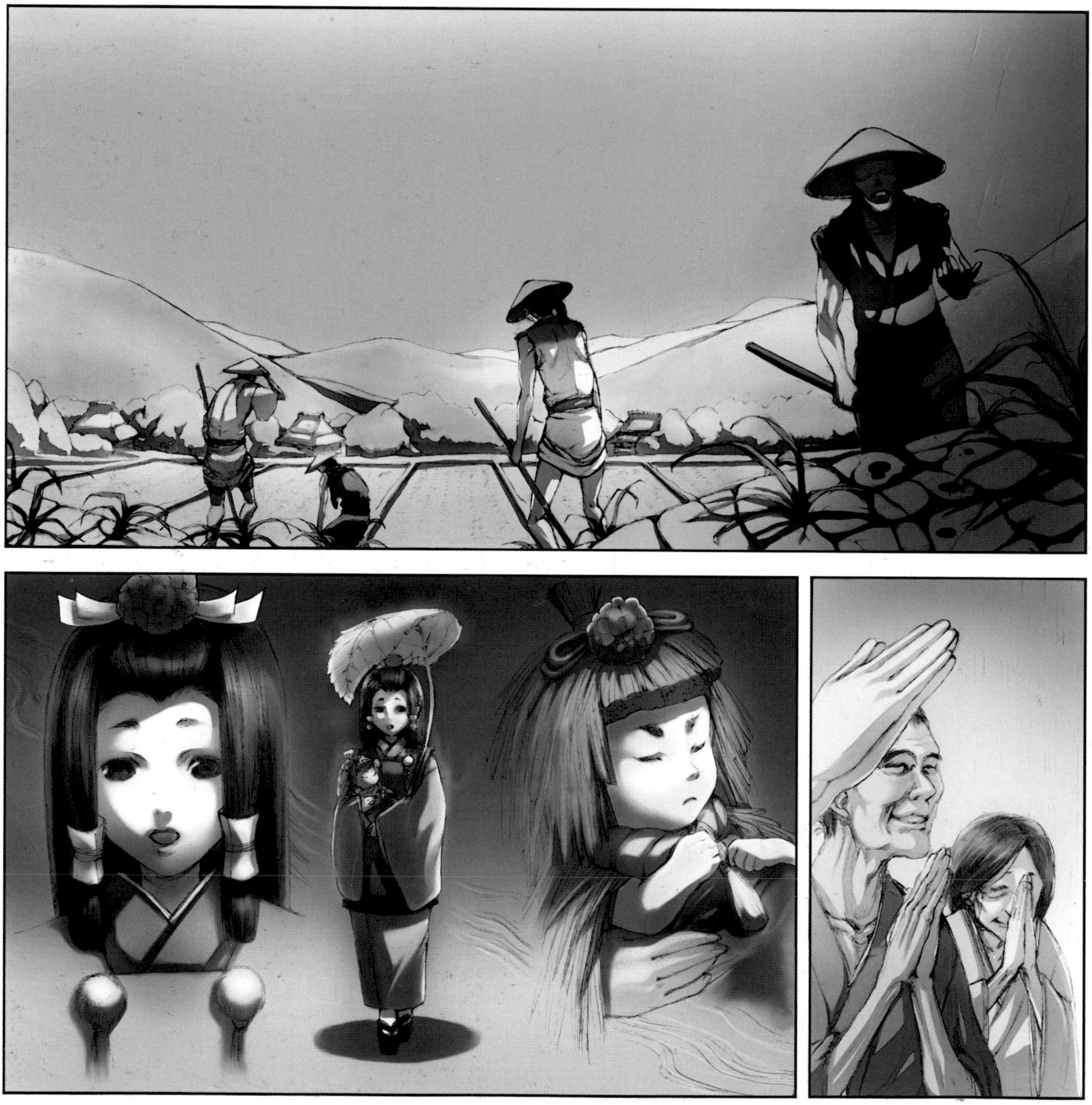

Heavy drought spread all over old Japan, and the fields and rivers around a village in a certain ravine dried up. Then, it began to rain mysteriously when Tsuyu, the water spirit, transformed into a woman holding a baby who was called, Amebou, which means rain child. The villagers were overjoyed with the rainfall, and so welcomed Tsuyu and Amebou to celebrate with them.

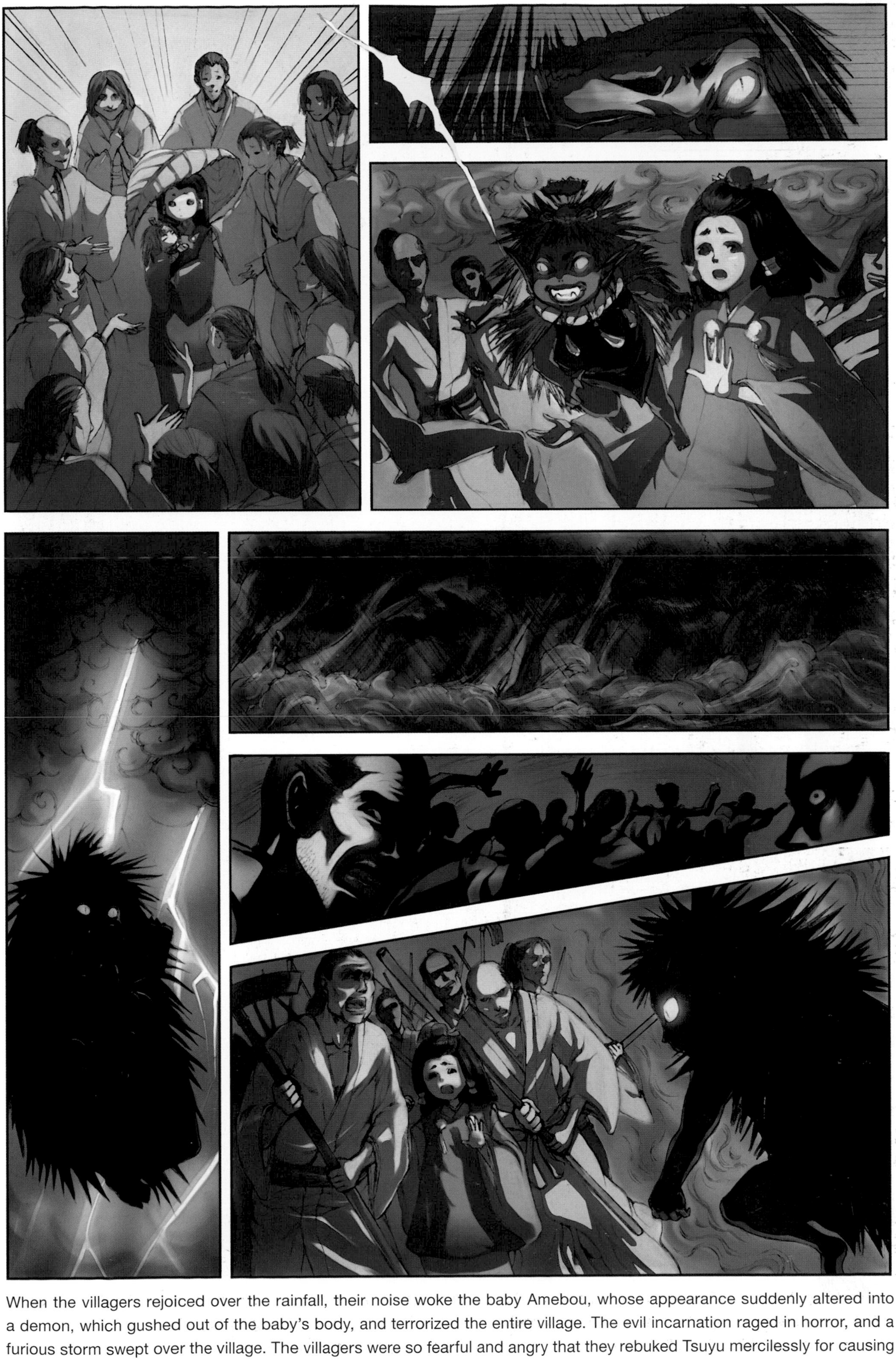

When the villagers rejoiced over the rainfall, their noise woke the baby Amebou, whose appearance suddenly altered into a demon, which gushed out of the baby's body, and terrorized the entire village. The evil incarnation raged in horror, and a furious storm swept over the village. The villagers were so fearful and angry that they rebuked Tsuyu mercilessly for causing the horrible condition that had befallen on them.

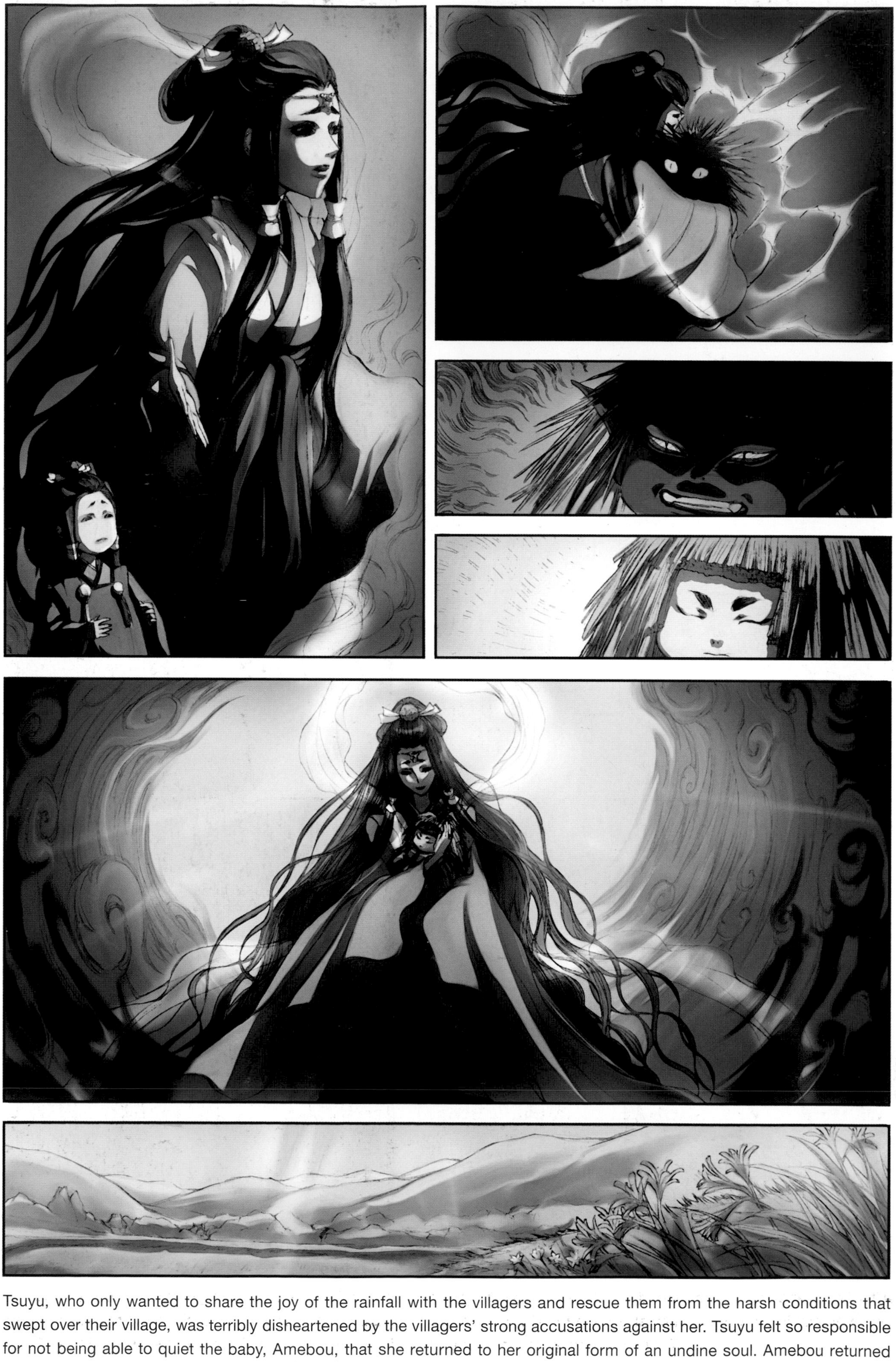

Tsuyu, who only wanted to share the joy of the rainfall with the villagers and rescue them from the harsh conditions that swept over their village, was terribly disheartened by the villagers' strong accusations against her. Tsuyu felt so responsible for not being able to quiet the baby, Amebou, that she returned to her original form of an undine soul. Amebou returned to the form of the baby when Tsuyu embraced the storm demon, and so the storm quieted down. However, Tsuyu still felt unwelcome and so left the village with the baby Amebou.

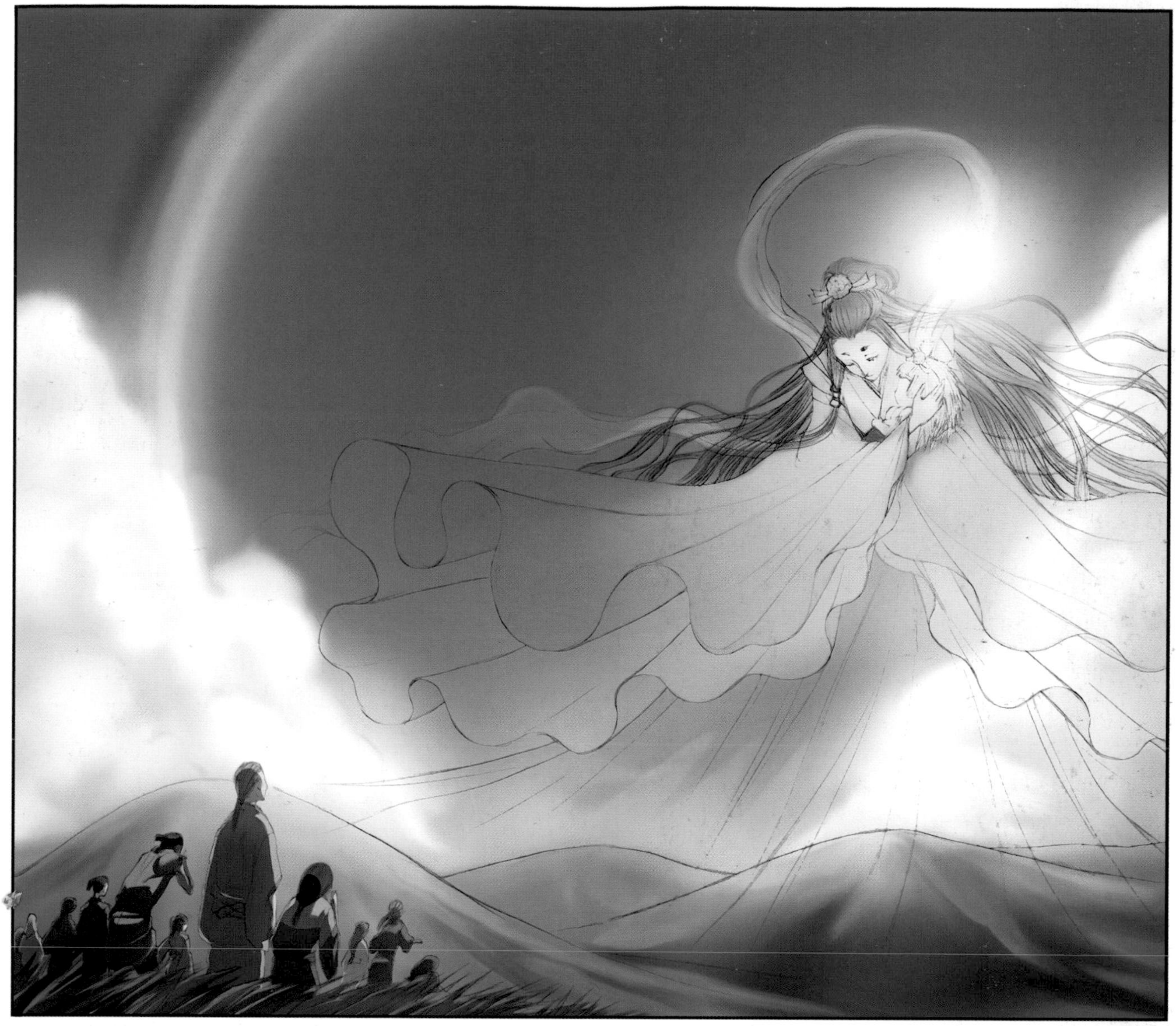

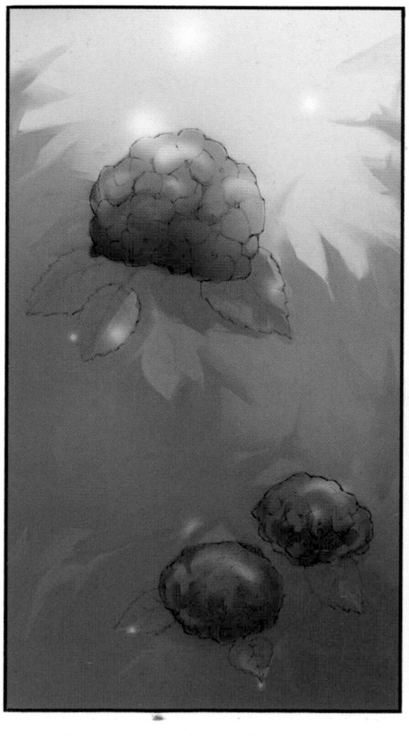

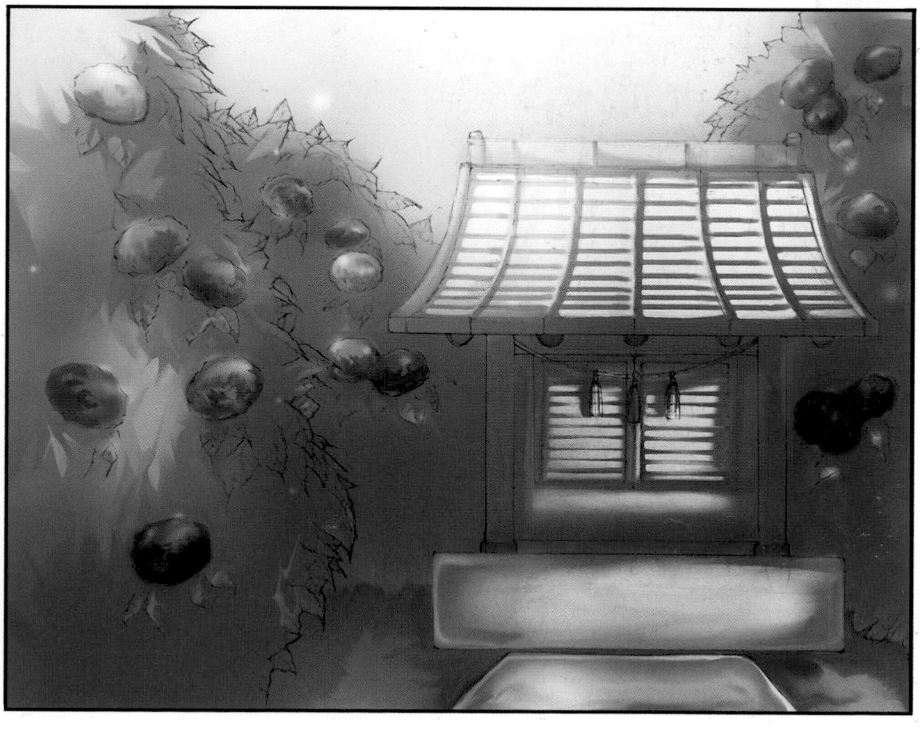

After Tsuyu and the baby departed the village, the earth was enriched, the fields overflowed with crops, and the trees and flowering plants grew abundantly all around the village. The villagers realized the true reason for the transformation of their blessed land, and thought of Tsuyu with both gratitude and apology in their hearts, and dedicated a shrine to Tsuyu. Since then, the rainy season in Japan has come once a year for a period of one and a half months, and people have came to call it "tsuyu" to commemorate the water spirit.

Index

NOTE: BOLD ENTRIES REFER TO CHAPTER TITLES.

Acknowledgments

In thanking all those who have made the production of this book possible, I would like to mention primarily Marta Schooler, the publisher of Harper Design, who gave me this chance to present my very first project to her, and who commissioned me to write and edit this book. She placed her tremendous trust in me to complete this project. Many thanks, likewise, to her colleagues at Harper Design, namely, Julia Abramoff and Iris Shih, for their constant support and encouragement in helping me launch this difficult challenge.

Special appreciation must be given to all the contributing artists who drew all the excellent illustrations in this book, and extended their time and effort, despite their extremely busy schedules. In particular, I would like to thank Shinn Komamori, who possesses a wealth of knowledge about the story, history, and background of the fantasy world, and who offered me many ideas for this book. Thank you Eri Kamijo for drawing all the illustrations in the chapter opening pages. I respect you, not only as a good and long-time friend, but also as a professional illustrator who continues to create fascinating artwork.

My gratitude also goes to Alma Reyes for her excellent text contribution. She is one of the most capable editors and writers I have ever known.

Lastly, I would like to give special credit to the core members of the production team who have given everything they can to the production of this book upon my request: Rico Komanoya and Atsushi Takeda. Rico, my teacher as editor and producer, has made an enormous contribution by leading, advising, and watching me throughout the entire production stage, from beginning to end. As an art director, Atsushi offered innovative ideas throughout the pages of the book. Without his passion, good eyes, and patience, this book would not have been completed. I thank you both for giving birth to another one of ricorico's "baby" products.

Watching my lovely cats Mikiko and Calcifer enjoy the sunshine through the window, Tokyo, 2010.

Aki Ueda
ricorico